THE PURITY WAR

Jim Levy

www.puritywar.com

THE PURITY WAR

A Biblical Guide to Living in an Immoral World

With Study Guide
and
Personal Accountability Program

James M. Cecy

To order this book please visit www.condeopress.com

ISBN 978-0-9829199-7-2 PAPERBACK
ISBN 978-0-9829199-8-9 eBOOK

Library of Congress Control Number: 2011937196

Unless otherwise noted, Scriptures taken from the NEW AMERICAN STANDARD BIBLE, Copyright © 1960, 1962, 1963, 1971,1973, 1975, 1977, 1995 Used by permission. www. Lockman.org.

Other Scripture references, especially in the Personal Accountability Program, are from the HOLY BIBLE, NEW INTERNATIONAL VERSION, Copyright © 1973, 1978, 1984 by International Bible Society. Used by permission of Zondervan. All rights reserved.

Unless otherwise noted, transliterations of all Greek and Hebrew words were taken from The Exhaustive Concordance of the Bible: Showing Every Word of the Text of the Common English Version of Canonical Books, and Every Occurrence of Each Word in Regular Order by James Strong. electronic ed., Ontario: Woodside Bible Fellowship, 1996.

For information on other materials by Dr. James M. Cecy contact JARON Ministries International, Inc., 4710 North Maple Ave., Fresno, California 93726. www.jaron.org.

Cover Design and Book Layout Design by Sarah O'Neal | www.evecustomartwork.com
Background cover canvas image courtesy of iStockphoto and artist Ranplett

Printed by Snowfall Press
www.snowfallpress.com

Printed in the United States of America

condeo press

WHAT OTHERS ARE SAYING

"Dr. Cecy's *The Purity War* is phenomenal! Beautifully written, and strikingly persuasive. This book is full of candid and compelling illustrations, and unique insights into the Scriptures. More than a guide to moral purity in an immoral world; it is a straight-to-the heart invitation to radical Christian obedience that will transform life on every level. It is a book we will get behind, and circulate around the globe."
　　—DR. DAVID W. DORRIES, Academic Dean and Professor of Historical and Theological Studies, Oslo International Bible College, Oslo, Norway

"Excellent from cover to cover. . . . I may make it required reading for all the men at our church. Thoroughly biblical. Thoroughly insightful. Thoroughly convicting. Thoroughly practical. And thoroughly redemptive. This book is a must read!"
　　—PASTOR GEORGE POSTHUMUS, Senior Pastor-Teacher, Riverpark Bible Church, Fresno, California

"*The Purity War* provides a biblical foundation for understanding and overcoming the struggle of soul in sexual matters. Thoughtful, practical, and encouraging, Dr. Cecy offers a clear strategy for holiness. If there is one book to read on this subject, you are holding it in your hands."
　　—PASTOR GREGG CANTELMO, Bridgeway Community Church, Phoenix, Arizona

"From his heart to ours, Pastor Jim Cecy has poured his life message into this book. It is written with passion and conviction overflowing from his ministry focus of the last two-plus decades. While so many Christians are straying from God's standards, this book is a clarion call to righteousness—like the voice of a prophet, calling us back to God."
　　—DR. KEN ROYER, Director of Pastoral Counseling, Link Care, Fresno, California

"Pastor Jim Cecy goes far beyond equipping and teaching about personal purity; he goes to the very heart of the matter. For many years I have witnessed how numerous lives have been impacted by the biblical principles taught through his seminars. Every Christian can have these solid and practical guidelines as a personal manual . . ."
　　—PASTOR JOBY SORIANO, Christ's Commission Fellowship, Manila, Philippines

"Dr. James Cecy has set forth a biblical blueprint on sexual purity that will greatly benefit men as well as women in the body of Christ. Dr. Cecy has consistently taught on this subject in seminars all around the world. I believe he is the leading Christian authority on this issue. He has exemplified this truth in his own life and has been an inspiration to me and other Christian leaders to be ambassadors of purity in our own lives and ministries. I had the privilege of teaching this material to church leaders in central India where the positive response was overwhelming, even among the women. May God be glorified through the distribution and reading of this book. May it bring about repentance, renewal and the refreshing of zeal for the holiness of God within the Church."

—**DR. RANDALL L. BRANNON**, Senior Pastor, Grace Community Church, Madera, California and Adjunct Missionary, JARON Ministries International

"Reading through *The Purity War* is a fresh reminder of what we learned in the live seminars. I especially appreciate the connection between theological accuracy and practical application. Dr. Jim Cecy's personal concern for those who are struggling is apparent. I am really looking forward to the book being translated into Czech for I know that many are struggling with the issues he addresses."

—**PETER LUPTON**, Church Planter, Svitavy, Czech Republic

"This book is different! The world of Christian publishing has recently produced piles of books on sexuality and purity. Many of these volumes exchange scriptural perspective for personal testimonies and descriptions of the battle for purity that can border on voyeurism. The biblical description of the cause of moral failure and the practical plan of attack laid out in Part Three through Five will make this book a valuable tool in the believer's library. "

—**PASTOR JUSTIN GREENE**, Senior Pastor, Salem Heights Church, Salem, Oregon

"This is a refreshing treatise on the Biblical call to personal purity. It is well known that God will use the greatest likeness to His Son in the ministry of Kingdom work. As our Lord Jesus was pure for us, so are we to be for Him as His faithful servants."

—**DR. DARRYL DELHOUSAYE**, President, Phoenix Seminary, Phoenix, Arizona

"Your book on purity was very readable and I enjoyed the way it flowed and challenged me as I read it. Because of the balance between biblical content and relevant illustrations, the book was clear and personal. In several places it was academic, however it needed to be to fully explain the text. The entire book held my interest and the worksheets at the end of the book were very helpful and relevant. It should translate well into any other language. This book is a "must read" for all ages. Pastor Jim Cecy has taught these principles for many years, but even more importantly, has lived out these principles in his own personal life. The balance between biblical truth and practical application is extremely helpful. This is one the most reliable and relevant books written on the subject of purity."

—**PASTOR RON SCHAFER**, Executive Director of S.T.E.P.S., Monument, Oregon

"*The Purity War* equips us to march together with our fellow Christian soldiers and to win this battle with a combat knowledge of the Word of God."

—**PASTOR GIL HARDER**, Missionary to Africa, JARON Ministries International

"*The Purity War: A Biblical Guide to Living in an Immoral World* is a very practical guide to living with purity in today's world. Dr. Cecy writes with refreshing honesty, giving personal examples of both success and failure, and interweaves it all around the centrality of Scripture for our central focus, reference, and commitment. With the included *Study Guide and Personal Accountability Program*, there is a wealth of resources for immediate application. This book should be part of each of our personal library for our own purity journey, as well as a reference for those we work with, whether it be in church, school or counseling setting."

—**DR. BRENT LINDQUIST**, Clinical Psychologist and President, Link Care Center, Fresno, California

"This book obviously comes from one who is deeply concerned for people's well-being. It is eminently timely since our society is plunging toward its demise in large part because of flouting our Creator's ways. It may be 'too little too late' for society as a whole, but it can certainly help many individuals avoid, and many others find significant healing from violation of basic sexual morality."

—**DR. GARY TUCK**, Professor of Biblical Literature and Academic Coordinator Western Seminary, San Jose, California

"Open. Direct. Highly useful. *The Purity War* is a living text, filled with rich examples from Scripture and personal testimonies. It is a highly useful and much-needed book, especially in Eastern Europe where the sexual revolution has resulted in our part of the world becoming a major center for the sex-trade industry and 65% of all pregnancies ending in abortion."

—**JAROSLAW LUKASIK**, Director of the Eastern European Leadership Forum

"James Cecy's book *The Purity War* powerfully addresses one of the most important topics in the world wide church – purity and holiness. I read chapter after chapter of biblically rich and insightful insights and was convicted time and again. This is a wonderful book which caused me to turn to the Lord and his Word. I am convinced that every Christian leader should read this book first for their own walk with the Lord and then read it again to learn how to help others. Jim has been teaching this content across Europe and is powerfully being used by the Lord to inspire and teach thousands to a closer walk with the Lord!"

—**DR. GREG PRITCHARD**, Director, European Leadership Forum and Communication Institute, Lisle, Illinois

"I have no advanced degrees. No fancy titles. However, I am married to the man who wrote this book. I have seen these sound biblical guidelines and practical principles work in his life for forty years of marriage. I can think of no higher endorsement."

—**KARON CECY**, Jim's wife

CONTENTS

PART FOUR: THE WAY OF ESCAPE

PART FIVE: THE WAY BACK

PART SIX: THE WAY FORWARD

STUDY GUIDE

APPENDICES

DEDICATION

Heroism is an extraordinary feat of the flesh; holiness is an ordinary act of the spirit. One may bring personal glory; the other always gives God the glory.
 —Chuck Colson—

As a Vietnam War veteran, I was honored to visit Washington, D.C. and the memorial listing over 58,000 fellow soldiers, sailors, and airmen who paid the ultimate price.

Semper fidelis—Always faithful.

As I stood at attention, unable to control the tears, I could see my own reflection behind the etched names on the polished black granite. I asked myself that all-too-common question many war veterans ask:

Why not me, Lord?

A few years later, I returned. This time, however, I was in the middle of my research related to why Christian leaders fall morally. As I stood again at the memorial, I imagined the names of too many of my fellow Soldiers of the Cross who fell in the battle with sexual immorality. As I reflected on the consequences, I thought:

What a horrible price to pay for a few minutes of sinful pleasure.

There, in that solemn moment of dedication and remembrance of all Christ had done for me, I stood at attention and reflected on the apostle Paul's words:

For you have been bought with a price: therefore glorify God in your body (1 Corinthians 6:20).

This book is dedicated to the tens of thousands of men and women on five continents who have participated in some form of our purity seminars. With humbled hearts, they dedicated themselves to become champions of personal purity in their homes, in their churches, and in their communities. Their names are etched on the heart of Christ, the Holy One who called His disciples to be Soldiers of the Cross and Ambassadors of Purity. Together, may our lives cry out:

Gloria in excelsis Deo—Glory to God in the highest.

Dr. Jim Cecy
Fresno, California

A WORD TO PARENTS, PASTORS, & OTHER UNDERSTANDABLY SENSITIVE PEOPLE

TABOO?

When I first taught Building Personal Purity seminars overseas, I was warned by well-meaning missionaries that talking about sexual matters was completely off-limits—a highly taboo subject. I especially remember my first time in the Philippines teaching pastors at the Word of Life Camp just south of Manila. I was surprised at how responsive the Filipino pastors were to the scriptural instruction on sexual purity. I felt the freedom to share my concern, "I thought this was a taboo subject about which missionaries have avoided speaking." Their response encouraged me, "That's exactly why we need to hear it!"

I am a Pastor-Teacher, deeply committed to my calling to feed and equip God's people, especially by teaching the inspired Word of God (2 Timothy 3:16-17; Ephesians 4:11-16). I believe it is as appropriate for me to communicate what the Bible teaches about the doctrines of holiness and moral purity as it is to preach about heaven and hell. I take my lead from the apostle Paul's personal testimony when he wrote, "For I did not shrink (i.e. "draw back in fear," Greek: hupostello) from declaring to you the whole purpose (i.e. "counsel, will," Greek: boule) of God (Acts 20:27).

However, I am also fully aware of my responsibility to be sensitive to the sensitive. I have endeavored to present this subject biblically and pastorally without being unnecessarily specific. My deep concern over some of the current materials on the market is that they border on conversational or literary voyeurism. Perhaps unintentionally, the authors are too graphic and stimulate the very thoughts and behaviors they are trying to teach people to avoid. Rest assured, this book is written from the heart of a shepherd to the souls of God's precious flock. Even so, my pastoral recommendation is for parents, teachers, counselors, and shepherds to be like those noble-minded believers in Paul's day who "received the word with eagerness" but also examined the Scriptures "to see whether these things were so" (Acts 17:11).

A WORD FROM THE AUTHOR

WELL, STOP IT!

In the early years of JARON Ministries, I moved to Fresno, California. I wish I could say it was easy for this life-long city boy to move to the agriculturally blessed San Joaquin Valley. I have since learned to deeply love the people and this city. I am especially grateful to God for the unity of the churches in this community. It truly is a great place to live, raise a family, and minister.

Actually, my dramatic change of heart began one morning at the local Salvation Army Thrift Store. I was standing at the door waiting for my wife and daughters to finish looking through row after seemingly endless row of used clothing. They were having a great time; I was not. My face must have revealed my misery.

A little girl, who looked about seven years old, approached me at the door. She gazed up at me with her beautiful brown eyes and without any shyness proclaimed, "Jesus died for your sins!" Frankly, I was not in the mood to have this little girl witness to me. I gave a dismissive mumble, "I know." Undaunted, she continued, "Well, you're a sinner!" My sour face turned to a smile and I responded, "I know that, too!" Then to my amazement, she put her hands on her hips and raised her voice, "Well, stop it!" She turned on her heels and sauntered away. I decided that day I wanted to live in a city where a seven-year-old is used by God to confront a Pastor-Sinner like me.

In that same spirit, I am asking you to receive these words from one who cares enough about you to stand toe-to-toe and communicate heart-to-heart with fellow sinners about the immorality in all our lives. In fact, like that little thrift store messenger from God, I want to look into the eyes of your heart and just as boldly shout, "Well, stop it!" My fervent prayer is that the rest of this book will clearly and biblically show you why and how.

INTRODUCTION

CALLING ALL AMBASSADORS OF PURITY

When I was thirty years old, I took my first overseas ministry trip to India. I will never forget the sights and sounds (and even the smells) of what was for me an incredibly foreign country. Towards the end of our month-long trip, we walked into the American Embassy in New Delhi, the Indian capital. There, my senses were filled with reminders of home: an American flag, American Marines, American music, and American art. Although it may have been my famished imagination, I could even smell American hamburgers and fries! All thirty fellow pastors sang "God Bless America" in the echoing rotunda of the beautiful, American-style building. What a memorable experience! I have thought often about that welcome taste of home in a foreign land.

As one who has trusted in Jesus Christ alone for his salvation, I do not consider this world my home. The Bible is clear that, as born-again Christians, we are aliens and strangers in this foreign land. Our true citizenship is in heaven (Ephesians 2:19; Philippians 3:20-21). Therefore, our primary allegiance is to the King of Kings under whom we serve as emissaries. The apostle Paul reminds us of our unique calling: "Therefore, we are ambassadors for Christ, as though God were making an appeal through us" (2 Corinthians 5:20).

A TASTE OF HEAVEN IN A FOREIGN LAND

As ambassadors of Jesus Christ, our job description is to live in this foreign land, Earth, as representatives of our home country, heaven. Though our heavenly citizenship comes with tremendous privileges, it also comes with substantial responsibility to live in such a way that reflects the values of the King we represent. Furthermore, each Christian family and local church is to be an Embassy of Heaven where those godly virtues exist and are readily seen by all people, so they will glorify our Father in heaven (Matthew 5:16). Put simply, my life is to be an embassy, a taste of heaven on Earth.

I hasten to admit that being an ambassador and representing eternal values is certainly not easy. In his letter to the Ephesians, the apostle Paul spoke about being an "ambassador in chains" (Ephesians 6:20). He was, in my opinion, talking about the physical chains that bound him during his imprisonment in Rome. There are, however, many Christians who are ambassadors living in chains brought about by their own sinful choices— shackles of lust, fornication, adultery, pornography, and other sexual sins of mind and body. They are still ambassadors of Christ but, nonetheless, ambassadors in chains.

Much of this material has been presented in live sessions to thousands in many countries. This book is now written to enable and equip even more fellow ambassadors to be freed from the fetters of sexual immorality. It is also a call for every Ambassador of Jesus Christ to become an Ambassador of Purity, a diplomat representing God's holiness in an immoral world. To change the metaphor, this also means serving as a Soldier of the Cross (2 Timothy 2:3-4), fighting trench-warfare against this never-ending battle with ungodliness.

Our training isn't going to be easy. Ask anyone who has served in the Foreign Service or the military. Beyond the initial education needed, it takes years of on-the-job training to properly represent a country and battle an enemy. Our instructions on how to be effective Ambassadors of Purity and Soldiers of the Cross are as close as our Bible. Most of our training, however, will be in the trenches as we live out these biblical principles as resident aliens on foreign soil. Our orders are clear: "Beloved, I urge you as aliens and strangers to abstain from fleshly lusts which wage war against the soul" (1 Peter 2:11).

PART ONE:

THE NEED

chapter 1

THE LAND IS FULL OF ADULTERERS

It can sound like a question for a seminary-level Bible quiz: "What did Lot's daughters, Reuben, Judah, Samson, David, Amnon, Absalom, Hophni, Phinehas, and Abner have in common?" The simple answer is that they were all Old Testament Bible characters. The sad answer is that they all fell victim to sexual temptation. Their names are forever inscribed on the list of "Moral Failures in the Bible"—a veritable Hall of Shame:

- Lot's daughters, who committed incest with their father (Genesis 19:30-38)
- Reuben, the son of Jacob, with Bilhah, his father's concubine (Genesis 35:22)
- Judah, the son of Jacob, with his daughter-in-law, who pretended to be a prostitute (Genesis 38:15-23)
- Samson, the Judge of Israel, with the prostitute (Judges 16:1-2)
- David, the King of Israel, with Bathsheba (2 Samuel 11:1-5)
- Amnon, the son of David, who raped Tamar, his half-sister (2 Samuel 13:1-20)
- Absalom, the son of David, with his father's concubines (2 Samuel 16:22)
- Hophni and Phinehas, the Priests, the sons of Eli, with the women in the Tabernacle (1 Samuel 2:22)

- Abner, the Commander of Saul's army, with Rizpah, Saul's concubine (2 Samuel 3:6-7)[1]

A second Bible quiz question follows: "To what local churches did the New Testament writers give clear instructions regarding immorality?" The answer is also quite lengthy. Understanding our human propensity to compromise God's holy standards, the New Testament writers presented their prohibitions against the sins of impurity, fornication and adultery:

- To the Church in Rome (Romans 6:19)
- To the Church in Corinth (1 Corinthians 5:1)
- To the churches in Galatia (Galatians 5:19)
- To the Church in Ephesus (Ephesians 5:3)
- To the Church in Colossae (Colossians 3:5-7)
- To the Church in Thessalonica (1 Thessalonians 4:3-8)
- To the Church in Pergamum (Revelation 2:14)
- To the Church in Thyatira (Revelation 2:20-22)

Moreover, from the mandate given by the Jerusalem Council around AD 50, we have a wide-sweeping admonition to *all* the churches in *every* city and in *every* generation to "abstain from ... fornication (Greek: *porneia*, the general word for illicit sexual activity)" (Acts 15:29; Acts 21:25).

Twenty-seven hundred years ago, the Weeping Prophet, Jeremiah, lamented the spiritual and moral condition of his fellow Hebrews with these indicting words: "For the land is full of adulterers" (Jeremiah 23:10).[2] This was certainly not unique to Israel. Demosthenes, the famous Greek orator, described the lifestyle of his fellow fourth-century BC Greeks: "We keep prostitutes for pleasure, we keep mistresses for the day-to-day needs of the body ..."[3] Ancient Egypt, Babylon, Medo-Persia, and Rome were no better.

In the ancient world, it was not uncommon to find temples of worship next to houses of prostitution. You were expected to enter one door to worship with your spirit and exit the other after worshiping with your body. Imagine the pressure on a young man in first-century Rome, walking down some Via Desideratio (Road of Desire) and being propositioned by a temple prostitute urging him to do his *religious duty*.

THE NEW MORALITY?

There is little need to review the obvious struggle with immorality in every century since the fall of Adam and Eve. We are well into this twenty first century, facing our own culturally unique pressures. One wonders what Jeremiah would write if he were alive today. Perhaps his headline would read, "The Land is Still Full of Adulterers: The 'New Morality' Is Really Just the 'Old Immorality' With a New Name."

Sadly, the new morality of our day may have even surpassed the old immorality of Jeremiah's day. This shouldn't surprise us. Two millennia ago, the apostle Paul forewarned:

> But realize this, that in the last days difficult times will come. For men will be lovers of self . . . unholy . . . without self-control . . . haters of good . . . lovers of pleasure rather than lovers of God (2 Timothy 3:1-4).

I am unimpressed with the false hopes humanists and new-agers offer. Although they try to convince us we are evolving into *better* people, I believe modern man is hardly deserving of such a high grade. The evidence in our day suggests the opposite.

Over thirty years ago I was shocked to read the appalling conclusions made by Wardell Pomeroy, the co-author of the original Kinsey Report. In an April 4, 1980 *Time Magazine* article entitled, "Sexes: Attacking the Last Taboo," Pomeroy is quoted as saying: "It is time to admit that incest need not to be perversion or a symptom of mental illness. . . . Incest between . . . children and adults . . . can be beneficial."[4] In the same article, another clinical professor of psychiatry added this ridiculous remark: "Children have the right to express themselves sexually, even with members of their own family."[5] The article went on to describe the sex-research establishment's view that, "all forms of consensual sexuality are good, or at least neutral; problems arise not from sex, but from guilt, fear and repression."[6] That was three decades ago. Given our society's current acceptance of the view that some people may be genetically pre-disposed to such things as adultery and homosexuality, I expect we will soon be asked to be even more tolerant of pedophiles and other deviants, arguing, "It's not their choice; they were born that way."

We have moved far beyond the widespread acceptance of *consensual* sex as the expression of the human libido. We are becoming increasingly more open to the *non-consensual*. Besides the substantial increase in the number of cases of sexual assault, incest and rape (most of which are unreported or discounted), it is no surprise to read the reports of millions of children, teenagers, and adults who are abducted and forced to become part of the multi-billion dollar sex-slave industry. On a personal note, my wife and I have cared for twenty-three foster children. Many were the innocent victims of sexual assault. It was hardly consensual and very few of the perpetrators suffered the punishment they deserved.

With this devilish philosophy of toleration being espoused by so-called experts and becoming even more acceptable, it is no surprise we are seeing such an increase in all forms of blatant immorality today, including the rise of sadomasochism, bestiality and a host of other deviant sexual activities. Modern man is hardly getting *better*. To paraphrase an old saying, "If God doesn't deal with us soon, He may have to apologize to Sodom and Gomorrah." I am reminded of the words of Jude and the apostle Peter:

> Sodom and Gomorrah . . . indulged in gross immorality and went after strange flesh . . . [they] are exhibited as an example in undergoing the punishment of eternal fire (Jude 7).

> He condemned the cities of Sodom and Gomorrah to destruction by reducing them to ashes, having made them

an example to those who would live ungodly lives thereafter
(2 Peter 2:6-7).

SO WHAT'S WRONG WITH A LITTLE PORN?

Most of us reading this book are committed to a life of fidelity. We believe sexual sins such as adultery, fornication, homosexuality, and incest to be offensive to God, regardless of what our generation might say. We are certainly repulsed by modern man's growing acceptance of immoral behavior and we are doing our best to not be stained by the degrading values of the world. However, we must also admit a common struggle, even among the most faithful among us, with the most intrusive invasion in our day—pornography. It has quite possibly become the "drug of choice" for this new millennium.

We live in a "pornified culture"[7] in which we are constantly bombarded with immoral enticements from every imaginable media. Invitations to view sexually explicit materials fill our senses and threaten to entangle us even more. Sexting (sending sexually explicit text messages) has become common-place communication. Social networks have become playgrounds for conversational voyeurism. We are being offered increasingly more sophisticated technological opportunities for "cyber-cheating in electronic bedrooms."[8] Under rapid development, and soon to be offered to the masses, are a number of multi-sensory sexual experiences, even beyond the current availability of holographic pornography and 3D sex. High tech porn or low-tech smut. Their selling points are the same: Accessibility. Affordability. Anonymity. And no cuddling!

Some argue that pornography (in all its forms) is just the natural expression of our human need to enjoy sexual *fantasy*. Let's talk about *reality* instead. I won't exhaust you with a mountain of statistics regarding the huge numbers of *real* illicit affairs, *real* rapes, *real* cases of incest and sexual abuse, resulting in *real* unwanted pregnancies, *real* cases of sexually transmitted diseases, and *real* "crimes of passion" that have been stimulated by this so-called *harmless fantasy*. Must I quote the recent figures concerning the high numbers of *real* divorces that are caused by *real* affairs that began with *real* emotional bonding in a seemingly innocent chat room or while interacting on a social network? Even the unexpected but inevitable disillusionment in this new wave of sexual disconnection is becoming increasingly more *real*. These aren't *fantasies!* The countless stories of destroyed lives aren't *fiction!* In the words etched on the gravestone of the hypochondriac, "Now will you believe I was sick?"

SURELY OUR SIN HAS FOUND US OUT

Perhaps you remember not too many years ago when "dial-a porn" was a new phenomenon. A law enforcement officer who attended one of our purity conferences sent me the following account of his own unforgettable experience. It brought a dramatic principle to the forefront of his life and mine:

> One night at about quarter past midnight, while my wife and kids were asleep in the other side of the house, I was flipping through the cable channels on the TV and came across a 900 number. . . I decided to call the number, completely knowing that it was wrong. After listening to a girl on a recording for about four or five minutes, I heard a door open in my house. Fearing that I'd be discovered by either my wife or one of my kids, I quickly hung up the phone. Little did I know that the 900 number had a ten-minute minimum and an automatic call-back feature if less than ten minutes had elapsed on the phone call. Consequently, the phone rang and my wife picked it up on the bedroom extension. She answered the call and was greeted by the seductive voice of a young centerfold talking of what she would do to the man of her dreams in a hot tub. My wife called out to me, "Hey, it's for you; it's your whore!" and locked the bedroom door. The next morning,

humiliated, I asked forgiveness from my wife and from God. Trust is hard enough to build in a marriage, but it is so easy to shoot down. Please share this story as you may see fit, and let others know that surely their sin will find them out.[9]

The Bible clearly speaks of the "passing pleasures of sin" (Hebrews 11:25). As this brother found out, God also warns that our sin will surely find us out (Numbers 32:23). I will not pretend that the pleasures of illicit sexual activity are not immensely attractive. They are. I also agree with this dear comrade in arms. It just isn't worth it.

This unsuspecting man wasn't actively looking for an opportunity to trade years of marital trust for a few unfulfilling moments of illicit pleasure. Opportunity came knocking at his door. That's what makes today's walk of purity so challenging. Sin is crouching at the door of our lives. In this technologically advanced world of illicit opportunity, it is becoming increasingly more difficult—even for the people of God—not to open that door.

JUDGMENT BEGINS WITH THE HOUSEHOLD OF GOD

Perhaps you are thinking, *Of course the land is filled with immorality. What do we expect from the unbelieving world?* I agree. Consider the ancient and prophetic words of the apostle John: "The world is passing away *and also its lusts*" (1 John 2:17, emphasis added).

We would certainly do well to discuss the need for personal purity in this immoral, unbelieving world. Oftentimes, that's the context in which Christians express their greatest concerns. However, as a Pastor-Teacher called to "equip the saints" (Ephesians 4:11-12), I am more concerned with the problem of immorality in the rank and file of those who claim to be born-again believers. The apostle Peter expressed it this way: "For it is time for judgment to begin with the household of God; and if it begins with us first, what will be the outcome for those who do not obey the gospel of God?" (1 Peter 4:17).

In his booklet, *Sexual Temptation*, Randy Alcorn, founder of Eternal Perspectives Ministries, states what is, sadly, very familiar: "Much as we hate to admit it, the evangelical landscape is littered with the carcasses of lives and ministries decimated by sexual sin."[10] The church is suffering from the carnage of its men, women, youth and even its leaders falling into immorality's deadly trap.

AS THE LEADERS GO, SO GO THE PEOPLE

You've heard the stories, read the newspapers, and listened to the cruel and shameful jokes of late night comedians, as they mock fallen Christian leaders. We can almost hear Nathan's words as he confronted King David's immorality: "By this deed you have given occasion to the enemies of the LORD to blaspheme" (2 Samuel 12:14). For many of us, this matter hits too close to home. We have experienced first-hand the devastation of a fallen Christian leader—a pastor or missionary we trusted, a parent we looked up to as a role model, a friend or relative with whom we confided, a fellow Christian with whom we worked, witnessed, and worshiped.

I spent five years doing research on why Christian leaders fall morally. I gathered the statistics, collected the sad stories, analyzed the problem, and presented some biblical solutions.[11] Frankly, we don't need to be convinced by any more statistics or stories. We have felt the pain and disappointment, up close and personal. We have experienced the anger and outrage, deep within our souls. We are the multitude of victims, crying out, "When will this stop?" Unless this matter is dealt with openly and honestly in the community of faith, we will continue to face an ever-building wave of immorality that threatens to wipe out more of the church's leadership and subsequently, even more of the people of God. Judgment must begin with the household of God, especially its pastors, missionaries, elders, deacons, teachers, and leaders. We who are leaders in Christ's church must be willing to examine that painful beam in our own eyes before we can ever hope to make any headway in dealing with the specks in the eyes of the people around us (Matthew 7:1-5).

PEACEFUL CO-EXISTENCE?

The story is told of a tourist visiting a foreign zoo, accompanied by an official government tour-guide. He was directed to an enormous glass enclosure where a large bear was fast asleep. In the bear's paws was a little lamb. It too was asleep. The visitor remarked, "That's amazing." The official replied, "Yes, here in my country we call that peaceful co-existence." "How do you do it?" asked the tourist. The guide whispered, "Well, the truth is that every morning we have to put in a new lamb." In the life of the believer, especially one who desires to be an Ambassador of Purity, there is no peaceful co-existence with immorality. Never has been. Never will be.

chapter 2

KILLING SPIDERS. PREVENTING FIRES.

The old man was known for standing at every prayer meeting and with uplifted hands shouting, "O, Lord, clean out the cobwebs." It needed no explanation. We all know the things that entangle our lives throughout the week. However, a young man had grown weary of hearing the same old plea. One evening, as the elderly saint stood and prayed, the young man shouted, "No, Lord, don't do it! Kill that spider!"

If we are going to be effective in stopping the immorality in our own lives and in the lives of those around us, we must learn to be proactive and not just reactive. It is much easier to prevent a fire than it is to stop one. It's a life-impacting lesson I learned while attending U.S. Navy basic training and the mandatory shipboard fire-fighting school. It became even more personal when I poured gasoline in the open carburetor of my foster daughter's car. Flaming vehicles have a way of making us ask, "What could I have done to prevent this?"

Our basic training for living pure lives in an immoral world begins with a detailed examination of one of those life-impacting, spider-killing, and fire-preventing Bible passages:

> Finally then, brethren, we request and exhort you in the
> Lord Jesus, that as you received from us instruction as
> to how you ought to walk and please God (just as you

actually do walk), that you excel still more. For you know what commandments we gave you by the authority of the Lord Jesus. For this is the will of God, your sanctification; that is, that you abstain from sexual immorality; that each of you know how to possess his own vessel in sanctification and honor, not in lustful passion, like the Gentiles who do not know God; and that no man transgress and defraud his brother in the matter because the Lord is the avenger in all these things, just as we also told you before and solemnly warned you. For God has not called us for the purpose of impurity, but in sanctification. So, he who rejects this is not rejecting man but the God who gives His Holy Spirit to you (1 Thessalonians 4:1-8).

We often challenge those who attend our seminars to read this passage at least forty times in a span of two weeks. I encourage you to do the same. The next time you are faced with temptation you will have this passage written on the doorpost of your heart and you can readily say: "For this is the will of God, your sanctification; that is, that you abstain from sexual immorality." I can tell you from experience that it will stop the fire before it gets out of control.

AN ANCIENT TEXT WITH A CONTEMPORARY MESSAGE

Whenever I have the opportunity to minister in Naples, Italy, I make it a priority to visit the uncovered ruins of the ancient city of Pompeii lying at the base of Mount Vesuvius. It is an irrefutable testimony to what Roman life was really like in the first century AD.

I walk the streets, enter the homes, and visit the area museums filled with innumerable artifacts. But I do so with caution. For on the streets and in the buildings my eyes are affronted with the still vivid colors of pornographic frescoes and statuary that would compare with anything we could ever see on television, in movies, magazines, or on the internet.

One would expect that of the local brothels still visible in Pompeii. I was surprised to find images just as profane in the entry ways and kitchens of private homes displayed in a décor I refer to as "Early Roman Debauchery."

This is the world the apostle Paul faced as he entered the homes of pagan Romans and as he traveled from city to city spreading the gospel. The Appian Way from Naples to Rome is still lined with the ruins of pagan temples and inns where it was common for a weary traveler, like Paul and his fellow missionaries, to be approached with an invitation to *worship* with a temple prostitute or *rest* in the arms of a sex-worker for hire. First-century Roman culture was as debased as our own. Clearly, the apostle Paul's instructions to the ancient Thessalonians are both timely and relevant for us today.

Most of the Thessalonians to whom the apostle Paul wrote had been converted from Macedonian paganism within that very year. They had "turned to God from idols to serve the living and true God" (1 Thessalonians 1:9). As such, they were well acquainted with the vile practices of immorality and their painful consequences.

Although this letter was written almost 2,000 years ago, Paul's passion is to have all of us heed his instructions regarding how to walk in obedience and please God. He wants all of us to excel even more as Christians living in an immoral world. Living a pure life is more than a choice; it is our calling. It is more than a wish; it is God's will.

I have been in pastoral ministry for over thirty-five years. I wish I had a dollar for every time I have been asked about God's will. I might have bought myself a houseboat! In the past, I have been known to tease, "I don't know God's will for your life. I'm too short to play Holy Spirit!" I have since recognized that I really *can* know God's specific will for people's lives. Simply stated: It is God's will that we do exactly what He commands us to do!

We are right to seek out God's will in such areas as relationships, education, employment, and ministry. Of the specifics for each of our lives, the Bible is not clear. There was no specific verse telling me to marry my wife or to attend seminary. In order to make such decisions, we must wait upon the Lord's direction as He leads us through instruction in His Word, the influence of His indwelling Holy Spirit, the counsel of others, and the working out of specific opportunities and circumstances. Not so here in this text. It is perfectly clear what God's specific will is for all of our lives. It's His will that we live pure lives. Sadly, its clarity has been clouded by our self-centered desire to do whatever pleases us.

FOR THIS *IS* THE WILL OF GOD

In December 1998 U.S. President Bill Clinton faced impeachment by the House of Representatives for charges of perjury and obstruction of justice stemming from his false statements regarding his immoral relations with White House intern Monica Lewinsky. During one part of the grand jury questioning, Clinton bantered over the meaning of the word "is." He contended that his statement that "there [is] nothing going on between us" had been truthful since, at the time of questioning, he was no longer involved with her. In another interview he had also denied having "sexual relations" with her, limiting the definition to sexual intercourse. He did, however, admit his actions (sexual, by every legal definition), were "wrong" and "inappropriate."

I am still amazed at the influence of this man's shameful actions, not only in perjuring himself but in re-defining sexual sin. We now have a generation of young people, even my fellow Christians, who believe that "anything goes as long as we do not have sexual intercourse."

Shortly after those proceedings I was teaching a purity seminar to a group of men. While explaining the phrase, "For this *is* the will of God" (1 Thessalonians 4:3), one of the participants interrupted me, "What does the word 'is' really mean?" I laughed, thinking he was being facetious. Then I noticed he was very serious. In his mind, when a brilliant man like William Jefferson Clinton questions a word, he was inclined to do so, as well—even as it relates to the will of God!

What does the word "is" really mean? Don't miss that powerful little verb! Abstaining from sexual immorality *is* the will of God for everyone who desires to follow the Lord Jesus Christ. It doesn't say that this *might* be, this *should* be, or even that this *could* be. God's will regarding our personal purity and holiness is a matter that needs no further explanation, no more special counsel, and no additional illumination of Scripture. This isn't a subject for debate nor is it a matter of personal interpretation. The apostle Paul didn't stutter. In the familiar words of my first-year seminary professor, "If the plain sense makes sense, make no other sense." This is sound advice not just for studying this text but for applying it to our lives daily.

So what is it that is so clearly the will of God? Our *sanctification* (1 Thessalonians 4:3). That's what my seventh grade English teacher would have called "a fifty-cent word." Actually, it's worth far more. The Greek word *hagiosmos* speaks of the special condition of being set apart as a pure vessel, like one of God's fine golden masterpieces that He wants to display to the world. The counterpart to this word (the Greek word *koinos*) speaks of being ordinary, unclean, and even vulgar or profane. Later, in his second epistle to Timothy, and his last written words, the apostle Paul states the importance of being a pure, and therefore, useful vessel:

> Now in a large house there are not only gold and silver vessels, but also vessels of wood and earthenware, and some to honor and some to dishonor. Therefore if anyone cleanses himself from these things, he will be a vessel for honor, sanctified, useful to the Master, prepared for every good work. Now flee youthful lusts and pursue righteousness, faith, love and peace, with those who call on the Lord from a pure heart (2 Timothy 2:20-22).

One of my favorite authors, A.W. Tozer, wrote that the holy man is not one who *cannot* sin; but one who *will* not sin.[1] I may not yet know God's will when it comes to many things in my life but I do know God's will when it comes to this one very critical matter. It is His will that I be set apart—sanctified. Put even more succinctly, "It is God's will that I be pure." A simple emphasis on each of these words proves helpful:

- It *is* God's will that I be pure. It is not up for debate.
- It is *God's* will that I be pure. Even if it is not my desire; it is His.
- It is God's *will* that I be pure. It is not just His wish.
- It is God's will that *I* be pure. It is not just for others; it is also for me.
- It is God's will that I *be pure.* It is an on-going process.
- It is God's will that I be *pure.* It is His desire that I be "a vessel for honor, sanctified, useful to the Master, prepared for every good work" (2 Timothy 2:21).

IT'S NOT ONLY GOD'S WILL, DEAR!

After declaring that it is our Holy God's divine will that we be pure, I invited one of the men at a seminar to bring his cell phone to the front. I asked permission to call his wife in front of that group of 400 men in Phoenix, Arizona. I spoke into the phone, "Your husband has just declared before hundreds of men that it is God's will that he be a pure man." She was quick to respond, "It's not only God's will. Tell him that it's my will as well!"

It is not only our heavenly Father's will that we be pure; it is also the heartfelt desire of those on earth who care for us the most. Stop to consider the devastation our sexual sin will produce in the lives of those who love us. Imagine the impact on our family, our friends, our fellow Christians, and a host of others. I expect our great-grandchildren looking back at our moral history would add, "It was also *our* desire that you led a pure life!" Even our distant descendants need us to live holy lives.

chapter 3

COMMANDS, NOT SUGGESTIONS

It was a slow news day. The newspaper had some space to fill, so one of the editors decided to print the Ten Commandments in a small corner of the front page. They didn't expect such a negative response. Many of their subscribers complained, "You're getting too pushy!" Some even canceled their subscriptions. We humans just don't like to be told what to do. We want suggestions, not directions. However, our Creator has every right to command His creation.

Here in the fourth chapter of 1 Thessalonians, the apostle Paul gives three very specific and urgent directions regarding our personal purity. Much like the Ten Commandments, these verbs carry the sense of lifestyle-commands. They are "functional imperatives" that are indicative of a life in continuous submission to the will of God.[1]

LIFESTYLE COMMAND #1
STOP YOUR IMMORALITY . . . NOW

The concerned apostle Paul gets even more specific regarding this divinely mandated sanctification that God wills for all believers calling us to "abstain from sexual immorality" (1 Thessalonians 4:3). A closer look at the original text reveals a much more dramatic expression than translated here in English. In essence, the apostle Paul is shouting with his pen, "Continue to stop the sexual immorality in your life and do it now!" He assumes all his readers are struggling to some degree or another. How right he is.

A very elderly-looking gentleman sat in the front row of my seminar, very attentive to all I was saying about dealing with lust. I could not resist asking him, "Sir, what are you doing here?" The crowd exploded with laughter when he replied, "Son, I ain't dead."

After reading one of my published magazine articles on moral purity[2], a 93-year-old man wrote a letter to the editor thanking me for helping him deal with a struggle with pornography that plagued him from the time he was 13 years old. Do the math. Eighty years battling this secret war.

The Russian Czar, Peter the Great, expressed it well, "I have conquered an empire but I have not been able to conquer myself." Young or old, male or female, married or single, king or common folk—all of us need to stop our immorality and stop it now! In the words of the great nineteenth-century preacher, Charles Haddon Spurgeon, "Learn to say 'No;' it will be of more use to you than to be able to read Latin."[3]

RED LIGHT!

While going on hikes, my children and I used to play the familiar game called, "Red Light, Green Light." When I yelled, "Green light!" they would run at will and then stop immediately when I gave the command, "Red light!" One unforgettable day, one of my daughters was about to run directly into a speeding truck's path. I certainly didn't have time to explain what would happen to her tiny human frame when it came in fatal contact with a twelve-ton truck. In the intensity of that life-threatening moment, I yelled, "Red light!" She heard the command and stopped in her tracks just as the truck barreled past her. Postponed obedience to that command could have cost her life!

This is the apostle Paul's exact point. Many of us are on a collision course with deadly moral disaster. With the intense fervor of a protective father, the desperately concerned apostle shouts, "Red light! Stop! Obey now, even before you understand all the whys and wherefores." If we are presently involved in any sexual activity that we know displeases God, hear His Holy Spirit shout, "Red light!" Postponed obedience could cost us our lives!

I was in Hawaii, teaching a purity seminar in a beautiful beach-front home on the North Shore of Oahu. After our morning session, I encouraged the men to go outside for some fresh air. As the men walked out on to the porch, a number of them rushed back into the house. They mumbled under their breath, "Red light! Red light!" I was impressed how quickly they wanted to rehearse the principles I just taught. Little did I know that on the beach, in clear view of all, a crew was filming a bikini commercial with a number of scantily-clad models. "Red light!"

LIFESTYLE COMMAND #2
LOOK AT OTHERS THE WAY GOD DOES

In his letter to the Thessalonians, the apostle Paul continues his challenge by pointing out that we have two major choices. With great concern for us, he writes, "that each of you know how to possess his own vessel in sanctification and honor, not in lustful passion, like the Gentiles who do not know God" (1 Thessalonians 4:4-5).

Let me get a little technical, especially as it relates to the phrase, "possess his own vessel." Many fine Bible scholars suggest that this passage refers to controlling one's own body. Some translations even favor this view.[4] Although I have great respect for many teachers who teach this, I lean toward the view of another, equally credible group of scholars. In particular, I believe this phrase primarily speaks of acquiring one's spouse God's way (i.e. "in sanctification and honor") rather than man's way (i.e. "in lustful passion, like the Gentiles who do not know God"). Here are my reasons, very briefly:

The word *possess* (Greek: *ktaomai*) is most often used to *acquire* or *gain* something.[5] Here in 1 Thessalonians 4:4, the apostle Paul speaks of possessing one's own *vessel* (Greek: *skeuos*), a word that admittedly can refer to one's *body* (2 Timothy 2:21) or a *wife* (1 Peter 3:7). However, prior to the writing of the New Testament the word *acquire* (*ktaomai*) when used with *vessel* (*skeuos*) was mostly used in the context of marriage.[6] How does one *acquire* and *gain possession* of one's own body? Scripture is clear that our bodies are not our own. They belong to God (1 Corinthians 6:19) and to our spouse (1 Corinthians 7:3-4). Certainly there are plenty of other passages in Scripture that call us to a life of self-control, but I am not certain 1 Thessalonians 4:4-5 is one of them. Also, I believe it is a stretch to suggest we engage in *lustful passion* toward our *own* bodies.

Okay, thanks for reading the technical stuff, but what does this have to do with our lifestyle? Fundamentally, I believe the apostle Paul is presenting a lifestyle command that prepares us even before we are ready to find a spouse. In particular, he presents the two opposing ways to view people— God's way or man's way.

Consider the Lord's words to the prophet Samuel regarding young David, whom no one suspected could ever be a candidate to become the anointed monarch of Israel. He just didn't look kingly enough. But God had a different view: "Do not look at his appearance or at the height of his stature . . . for God sees not as man sees, for man looks at the outward appearance, but the LORD looks at the heart" (1 Samuel 16:7). Simply put, Paul suggests two approaches to people:

- The Divine Approach: To view people *in sanctification and honor* like those who know God.
- The Human Approach: To view people *in lustful passion* like those who do not know God.

Men, what are we looking for in a woman? A perfect ten? Maybe we'd settle for an eight or a nine. However, when God puts His measuring tape around a woman He doesn't put it around her breasts or buttocks (or whatever other body part you fancy); He puts it around her heart! Women, when God measures a man He doesn't measure his biceps, his wallet, or even his personality; God measures his character. (Remember ladies, personality is often what a man shows you; character is what he really is behind the closed doors of his life).

To possess your vessel *in sanctification and honor* is to view your spouse (or future spouse) the way God does. In general, it is to view all people through the eyes of the Creator, regardless of outward appearances. It is to focus on the internal and not the external. To revise the old expression: Beauty is in the eye of the beholder and the Ultimate Beholder is God. Does this mean we cannot appreciate physical beauty or be attracted to that which is handsome? Of course not. It is just not the priority. Love at first sight is hardly the biblical expectation for those who are committed to look for a person whose life is pleasing to the Lord. An accurate assessment of someone's true character takes time.

We would avoid much heartache and pain if we learned from the shortsighted foolishness of two famous Bible characters. Both suffered the severe consequences of being consumed by the physical and acting like those *who do not know God*. First there was Samson, whom I once heard Dr. Charles Swindoll call, "a he-man with a she-weakness." Samson sees a gorgeous but ungodly Philistine woman and commands his father, Manoah: "Get her for me, for she looks good to me (literally, 'she looks right in my eyes')" (Judges 14:3). His *lustful passion* blinds his heart and he marries this idolatrous woman. Imagine those confused parents, ordered to facilitate the sin of the son whose birth was miraculous and who had been dedicated to God from the womb (Judges 13:5). Later, Samson has an encounter with a prostitute (Judges 16:1-2), followed by his infamous and fatal relationship with Delilah (Judges 16:4-20). The familiar story ends with Samson's moral blindness costing him his eyes and his life (Judges 16:21, 30).

Sadly, King David did not learn from Samson's blindness. One night, while walking on the roof of his palace, he sees an exceptionally beautiful woman taking a bath. David immediately sends his servants to go find out who she is and learns that she is Bathsheba, the wife of one of his faithful soldiers, Uriah (2 Samuel 11:2-3). King David's heart is already filled with *lustful passion* and he commands his servants to bring the woman to him (2 Samuel 11:4). More about David's sin in Chapter 42.

Imagine those perplexed servants ordered to take part in the sin of the very one who had been appointed their king because he was a man after God's own heart (1 Samuel 13:14). What would they say to Bathsheba? We can only guess: "Mrs. Uriah, the King wants to see you—in his bedroom. Oh no, don't bother getting dressed!" How history would have changed if the King had only remembered the psalm he wrote as a young shepherd in the fields of Bethlehem: "The LORD is my shepherd, / I shall not *want*" (Psalm 23:1, emphasis added).

Neither Samson nor David cared about the spiritual condition of these women. They had other issues in mind. Samson wasn't planning on having a prayer meeting with this godless Philistine woman. David had no intention of writing a psalm with Bathsheba. What a price they paid for their *lustful passion*, the kind we would expect in those "*who do not know God*" (1 Thessalonians 4:5, my emphasis).

LIFESTYLE COMMAND #3
STOP MESSING WITH SOMEONE ELSE'S

A wise Sunday school teacher was trying to get the attention of a number of high school young people who she feared were treating her lesson on abstinence too lightly. She took a beautiful rose and handed it to the young men in the front row of her class asking each one to pluck off one petal. When the last petal had been removed, she handed the "manhandled" stem to a boy in the back of the room and said, "Here's your wife." Her point became clear.

An even wiser apostle Paul directs our attention beyond the momentary pleasures of immorality to a lifelong consideration of one of the often overlooked consequences of our sexual sin. His charge is "that no man transgress and defraud his brother in the matter" (1 Thessalonians 4:6). If we have been sexually involved with anyone other than our spouse, we have not only sinned against our spouse (or future spouse), we have also sinned against God, that person, and their present and future family. We have also sinned against our church family, our brothers and sisters in Christ, who rely on us to be examples of personal purity and holiness. Frankly, if that person *with whom* we have sinned is considering his or her moral purity before God, we are the person *about whom* they have to ask God's forgiveness. Most likely we are also not the person *from whom* they would seek godly counsel. Defrauding bears life-long consequences.

Lifestyle Command #3 is preventative. It reminds us that there is no such thing as a private sexual affair. As we will discuss in greater detail later, there are hundreds who are affected by our sexual sin. Most likely, many who get hurt will be our brothers or sisters in Christ.

CAN'T YOU MAKE THEM STOP?

When I was in my second year of seminary, a young woman came into our church office and shared the wonderful story of her conversion to Christ from her former life as a prostitute and "porn queen." As she spoke about the transforming grace of God, she sobbed uncontrollably for two or three very long and uncomfortable minutes. I didn't know what to do. When she finally pulled herself together, she spoke words I have never forgotten, "Do you know the hardest thing about all of this? I realize that even today there are a number of men, some who might even be my brothers in Christ, who are looking at photos and films of my nude body and sinning against the Lord and their families. Don't they know I'm their sister in Christ? Don't they know that I will be with them in heaven? Don't they know that I am not just a bunch of body parts? Why are they looking at me that way? Can't you make them stop?"

I have thought about that conversation many times. Often it has stopped me from being tempted to peek at something inappropriate. When I start to notice a beautiful woman walking down the street, I imagine that she has just given her life to Christ and is my fellow citizen of heaven. Even if she is not yet my sister in Christ, I know that by God's grace she soon might be.

One of the ways to deal with that "wandering eye" is to personalize what we are tempted to gawk at. It helps to remind ourselves that these are real people with real families. It is not a stretch to consider the great possibility that there may be family members and friends who are praying for the salvation of that very person upon whom we are lusting. In fact, maybe that one upon whom we are disrespectfully gazing is at this very moment repenting of sin and committing his or her life to Jesus Christ. Daily, we must take to heart Paul's command "that no man transgress and defraud his brother in the matter" (1 Thessalonians 4:6).

ONE FINAL SHOT

I invited a young man who was courting my daughter to go to the pistol range. Since it was his first time, I was careful to pay close attention to all he was doing and did not do any shooting myself. Toward the end of our time, he asked if I would take the final shot. I reluctantly picked up the .45 caliber pistol and placed a small target sixty-six feet down range. I fired quickly without taking time to aim. I brought the target back and discovered a perfect bull's-eye, every shooter's dream and the luckiest shot I ever made. His eyes were as wide as the target itself. As much as I wanted to give a victory shout, I kept calm. I looked intently at this young man, who was now falling in love with my little girl, and quietly said, "Good shot, huh?" I quickly added, "Now, as long as you stay about seventy feet away from my daughter until you're married, you should be just fine." He laughed. I did too. His was a nervous laugh and rightly so.

Don't mess with someone else's. That girl with whom we are fooling around doesn't belong to us. She belongs to her parents. That boy belongs to his spouse or future spouse. They both, especially, belong to God. We don't want to be messing around with that which is His. He's an even better shot.

chapter 4

BECAUSE . . . JUST BECAUSE

My wife and I have raised three daughters and helped to raise a number of foster-children, mostly girls. We obviously had our share of rules, especially concerning their developing relationships with boys. (I was unsuccessful in trying to enforce the rule that every new boyfriend attend my all-day seminar on personal purity, go to the pistol range with me, or spend a weekend with my 350-pound cousin, Guido the Enforcer!) Rules are rules, not general guidelines. Commands are commands, not suggestions. Sometimes rules come without explanation: "Because . . . just because." However, there were times, rare, to be sure, that our girls truly wanted to try to understand the reasons behind the rules. In those teachable moments, this father's heart leapt for joy. My hope was that they would see the rules for what they were: safeguards. So it is with our heavenly Father.

Perhaps we need to be reminded that there is a God, and we're not Him! God, the Creator, has every right to command us, His creation, to be morally pure. Yet, God, our heavenly Father, also chooses to lovingly give us three of the many reasons why He calls us to abstain from sexual immorality. In other words, He goes beyond the "because" and gives us the "why"—why we need to stop our immorality, why we need to acquire a mate His way, and why we must not sexually transgress and defraud one another. His rules protect us. His reasons make sense.

REASON #1
BECAUSE . . . GOD AVENGES IMMORALITY

One afternoon I received a call from a Christian brother whom we, as elders, desperately tried to restore. Because of his refusal to repent of continued adultery, he was removed from formal membership in our local church. It broke our hearts. The elders and pastoral staff attempted regular conversations with him, begging him to repent of his sin, but to no avail. His defiance continued. Two years passed. However, on the phone that afternoon, his demeanor was completely different. This time, instead of defending his actions, he described his life as one of complete devastation, "I've lost my wife. I've lost my children. I've lost my health. I've lost my position as a ministry leader, and my business is going bankrupt." He went on to say what I have heard many times from people in similar situations, "I married the woman with whom I had the affair, but I don't love her. I want back what I had before!" Finally he yelled into the phone, "Pastor Jim, I've repented of the sin, but it still hurts. When will it stop hurting?"

The apostle Paul reminds his readers that God is not fickle or arbitrary. The reason behind his passionate and repeated appeals for sexual purity is clear. It is "because the Lord is the avenger in all these things, just as we also told you before and solemnly warned you" (1 Thessalonians 4:6). This wasn't news to the Thessalonians; it isn't news to us. God hates sin, and He disciplines those who willfully violate His holy standards.

How does our Holy God avenge immorality? In some cases, He allows the natural consequences of sin to come to fruition, such as guilt and a troubled conscience, public disgrace, entrapment into habitual sin, physical disease, spiritual emptiness, social ostracism, financial disaster, and emotional trauma, to name a few. King Solomon warned his son and us about the life-long consequences of sexual sin:

> The one who commits adultery with a
>   woman is lacking sense;
> He who would destroy himself does it.

Wounds and disgrace he will find,
And his reproach will not be blotted out
(Proverbs 6:32-33).

The old adage rings true in the ears of too many: "If you play, you're going to pay!" We must never ignore the age-old principle of sowing and reaping: "Do not be deceived, God is not mocked; for whatever a man sows, this he will also reap" (Galatians 6:7). Folks, I am not a legalist trying to impose my own arbitrary standards on your life. I am a realist who has seen the devastation in those I have counseled over the years. There is a price to pay for immorality. Although we hope not to experience all of the possible consequences, the time may come when we will.

Yes, we hold to the great truth of God's lovingkindness. Yes, there is forgiveness for sin and restoration to fellowship with our heavenly Father (Psalm 103:1-14; 1 John 1:9). This does not necessarily remove all the physical, emotional, relational, and spiritual consequences of sin. Pull a nail from a wall and the hole is still left behind. Holy God is still the great avenger of immorality. Only Merciful God knows to what degree He will regulate the flow of lovingkindness or corrective chastisement toward His children (Hebrews 12:5-11). What I do know is that we deserve the full measure of consequences, even if it means our physical death (Romans 6:23). I thank God daily for His mercy, don't you?

REASON #2
BECAUSE . . . GOD CALLS BELIEVERS TO BE PURE

I was teaching a course on *A Theology of Ministry* and one of my seminary students came to me with great concern: "How do I know what I'm called to be? A pastor? A missionary? A Bible scholar?" I remember thinking, as I recalled his recent grades, *Well, not a Bible scholar!* Fortunately, I didn't say what was initially on my mind. Instead, I quoted 1 Thessalonians 4:7 and said to him, "I really don't know what God is calling you to do as a vocation. However, I am absolutely certain of God's calling for your life. God is calling you to be pure. Whether a *pure* plumber, a *pure* painter, or a *pure* pastor, I don't know. Whatever the Lord calls you to do; He calls you to do it as a *pure* vessel." Personal purity is not only His *will* for all our lives; it is His *calling*. We have been ordained to holiness!

The apostle Paul reminds this group of believers who were so recently converted from the moral poverty of Macedonian paganism, "For God has not called us for the purpose of impurity, but in sanctification" (1 Thessalonians 4:7).

REASON #3
BECAUSE . . . GOD HIMSELF IS HOLY AND EMPOWERS US TO BE HOLY

One Sunday morning, after guest-preaching on one of the many Scriptures related to sexual purity, an elderly church leader came to me and exclaimed, "I heard you use the word 'sex' this morning. Well, we don't talk dirty in our pulpit!" I attempted to point out the references in Scripture that use the term, but it was no use. If I had been quicker in my thinking, I would have started with the apostle Paul's powerful words: "So, he who rejects this is not rejecting man but the God who gives His Holy Spirit to you" (1 Thessalonians 4:8). His point in this verse couldn't be more straightforward. We can try to find offense in the directness of Paul's words. We can even accuse him of being a narrow-minded cleric, a pharisaic extremist, an unenlightened simpleton or even a pre-Victorian-age prude. However, I believe the apostle Paul would respond with: "If you don't like what I'm saying, talk to the Author!"

HERE'S MY HOLY SPIRIT. NOW BE HOLY.

Notice the special provision Our heavenly Father has given His children to live pure lives in an immoral world. The apostle Paul reminds his readers that it is "God who gives His Holy Spirit to you" (1 Thessalonians 4:8). If we are truly born-again believers, saved by grace alone through faith alone, then we have God's promise that we are indwelt by His Holy Spirit

(Romans 8:9). As such, we have *everything* we need to live pure lives. The apostle Peter echoes the thoughts of his fellow apostle: "Grace and peace be multiplied to you in the knowledge of God and of Jesus our Lord; seeing that His divine power has granted to us everything pertaining to life and godliness, through the true knowledge of Him who called us by His own glory and excellence" (2 Peter 1:2-3).

What a great God we have. He commands us to be holy and then empowers us to be holy. How? He provides His Holy Spirit to live inside of us. In our own power, do we have the capacity to be holy? No! Does the Holy Spirit who indwells us have the capacity to be holy? One does not need a seminary course in the doctrine of the Holy Spirit to answer. Of course He does! It's as if our Holy God is saying that we owe Him a million dollars and then He reaches into His pocket and hands us the money and says, "Here. Now pay me back. Be holy for I am Holy. Oh, by the way, here's my indwelling Holy Spirit."

Don't miss the point of 1 Thessalonians 4:1-8. God wills that I be pure. God calls me to be pure. God enables me to be pure. Then what's the only issue? Do I want to be pure? Some of us may not be ready to take this giant step. Perhaps we need to take a baby step and ask ourselves, Do I even <u>want</u> to <u>want</u> to be pure? You decide; I have.

I, Jim Cecy, want to live a pure life.

I, _____, *want to live a pure life.*
   (Sign your name)

AND EVERYONE SAW HIMSELF

This amusing story has been making the rounds for many years. After much struggle over the lack of response by the congregation, a new pastor came to the sad realization that his local church was dead. From his ministerial training he understood that when things die, they deserve a proper burial. In his mind, this also applied to his church. He announced in the local newspaper there would be a funeral service for "The Dead Church" on Saturday evening. To his surprise, that night the church auditorium was packed with people, far more than ever before. The pastor arranged for a flower-covered coffin to be placed in front of his pulpit. From there he preached about the greatness of the church in the past and sadly bowed his head as he announced that the church was now gone. As he finished his eulogy, he stepped in pastoral fashion to the head of the casket. He opened the coffin and invited the congregants to file by and pay their last respects to "the dearly departed church." As they sheepishly viewed the contents of the coffin, many stared in disbelief while others broke into tears. At just the right angle he had placed a mirror. Everyone saw himself, the real reason why the church was dead!

There is no question in my mind; Christ's church is still very much alive. Given the excuses and compromises I have witnessed in the body of Christ, my only question is whether Christ's church is both alive and *well*. Although she is not doing as well as she could or should be doing, my great hope is that someday Jesus will, as promised, present to Himself His bride, the church "in all her glory, having no spot or wrinkle or any such thing; but that she would be holy and blameless" (Ephesians 5:27).

I was once asked at a conference, "Why doesn't somebody do something about the immorality in the church?" My answer was simple, "You're a somebody. Do something!" If a true revival of purity is to occur in our lives and in our churches, all of us who know Christ as Savior and Lord must take an honest look at the mirror of God's Word. We must keep the timeless words of Jesus at the center of our focus:

> Blessed are those who hunger and thirst for
>   righteousness, for they shall be satisfied. . . .
> Blessed are the pure in heart, for they shall see God
> (Matthew 5:6, 8).

PART TWO:

GOD'S DESIGN

chapter 5

SEX REALLY IS GOD'S IDEA

WHERE DID I COME FROM?

"Mommy, where did I come from?" His mother always knew that some day she'd have to face this fundamental question, but was surprised her son was asking at such an early age. She sat him down and explained, as best she could, the "facts of life." The little guy listened attentively, but after about fifteen minutes he interrupted her, "But Mommy, where did I come from? My friend said he's from Toledo."

Like this well-intentioned mother, many of us are guilty of answering questions not really asked. When asked why there is such a problem with immorality in our day, we are quick to speak of the bombardment of a sexually charged media or the sagging morality of a society gone wild. However, the deeper problem with immorality in our world has, as its foundation, a widespread ignorance of God's design for human sexuality. Whereas, we may understand the basics of biological function, many of us are unaware of the fullness of the Creator's divinely ordained purpose for sexual union in marriage. Where did I come from? I came from a loving Creator who designed me as a sexual being.

WHO WROTE THAT DIRTY WORD

I was preparing for an adult Sunday school class in a church where I had never before spoken. All alone in the classroom, I wrote the word "SEX" on the whiteboard. Before I could complete the title of my message, my marker broke. I left to find another and returned as the custodian was frantically erasing the board. I could hear his intense grumbling, "Who wrote that dirty word? These kids! Wait until I tell the pastor!" I thought it prudent to claim my right to anonymity.

SEX. What is it about that word that elicits such a wide range of responses? There are those who devalue it by wanting us to believe sex is just biological, simply "the urge to merge." Some over-emphasize it by holding that sex is the driving force of the human psyche, and therefore, "if it feels good, do it." Then there are those who treat sex as a necessary evil, carrying the deep-seated attitude, "Well, if I have to."

The Christian community has its own hang-ups about the subject. Many of my fellow believers have admitted an especially hard time integrating their sexuality with their faith. One pastor friend of mine, whose theology I trust and whose understanding of God's Word impresses me, expressed what I have since learned is a common sentiment: "I just can't imagine God watching when I am making love to my wife! I know He does, but . . ."

Many years ago, I attended a pastors' seminar led by a well-known Christian leader. I was shocked at what I heard. He stood before 600 of my fellow clergymen and taught that ministers should never be sexually involved with their wives the night before preaching. He actually declared that such activity would sap us of our spiritual strength, the very power we need to effectively preach the glorious gospel. What is the only thing that can sap a believer of spiritual strength? Sin. Was this man really intending to say that sexual union in marriage is sin? God forbid!

As Bible-believing people, we must seek to understand the wonder and mystery of "the way of a man with a maid" (Proverbs 30:19), especially our heavenly Father's part in creating sex as a special gift to humanity. In her book, *A Christian Guide to Sexual Counseling*, MaryAnn Mayo writes:

> God, in His sovereignty, could have made mankind any way He wished. Cloning or some process that left sexual relations out completely could have accomplished

reproduction. Men and women could have been created without the need for relationship as well. But God chose to do otherwise. He created us to be two distinct sexes and to need and want one another for reproduction, for comfort, and for communion. Sex is, therefore, a God-given mandate.[1]

HOW DOES GOD SPELL SEX?

In one of our early seminars, I asked the question, "Biblically speaking, how does God spell 'sex'?" With my back to the audience, I wrote on the board as they responded, "God spells 'sex' L-O-V-E." Another shouted from the back, "He spells it M-A-R-R-I-A-G-E." One "armchair theologian" seemed rather proud of himself as he spoke, "God spells sex K-N-O-W." He was certainly right. As we'll see, Adam *knew* his wife. However, theologically speaking, I would have hoped to hear someone say, "God's favorite spelling of the word 'sex' is O-N-E." In other words, when we talk about sex from God's point of view, we are speaking of that God-given desire for physical, emotional, and spiritual oneness.

THE *echad* OF GOD

In Deuteronomy 6:4-9 we find one of the central passages in all of Old Testament Scripture. Some consider it the theme passage. Our Jewish friends refer to it as the *Shema,* taken from the first word in the Hebrew text, translated, "Hear." Wherever Hebrew prayers are spoken, expect to hear: "*Shema Yishrael, Adonai Elohenu, Adonai echad.*" Translated in English, it reads: "Hear, O Israel! The LORD, our God, the LORD is one" (Deuteronomy 6:4). In Orthodox Judaism, that passage is reverently placed in wooden boxes, called phylacteries, and worn on the forehead and on the wrist to help them remember its importance. I encourage you to memorize it, in any language you choose, as long as you write it on "the tablet of your heart" (Proverbs 7:3).

The last word in Deuteronomy 6:4 (*echad*) is of special interest. It speaks of a compound unity, or many things in one. Besides pointing to the existence of the one and only God (*Adonai Echad*), we Christians believe it also speaks of the Trinity—i.e. the tri-unity of Father, Son, and Holy Spirit—three persons in one—the *echad* of God. With this in mind, I suppose it could be said that in the mathematics of the Godhead (Father, Son, and Holy Spirit), $1 + 1 + 1 = 1$.

Where else in the universe are persons that are separate still viewed by God as mysteriously one? In marriage. The same Hebrew word *echad* that is used to describe the oneness of God in Deuteronomy 6:4 is also used to describe the oneness of Adam and Eve in Genesis 2:24. They joined (i.e. "cleaved," Hebrew: *dabaq*) in sexual union and became "one flesh" (*basar echad*). Jesus Himself spoke of this unity:

> And He answered and said, "Have you not read that He who created them from the beginning made them male and female, and said, 'For this reason a man shall leave his father and mother and be joined to his wife, and the two shall become one flesh'? So they are no longer two, but one flesh. What therefore God has joined together, let no man separate" (Matthew 19:4-6).

Therefore, it can also be said that in the mysterious mathematics of marriage (husband and wife), $1 + 1 = 1$ (Ephesians 5:31-32). We must quickly add that the church, the body of Christ, is also a reflection of the *echad* of God (Galatians 3:28; 1 Corinthians 12:20; Ephesians 5:32). Just as we see in the Trinity and in marriage, in the mysterious mathematics of the church (all born-again believers of every age), $1 + 1 + 1 + 1 + 1 + 1$ (and so on) $= 1$.[2]

While teaching at the 2010 European Leadership Forum in Eger, Hungary, I was privileged to sit in on a couple of seminars taught by Dr. Richard Winters. I appreciated his quiet demeanor and his profound words, "The union of the sexes is a foretaste of our even higher union."[3] It reminded me of an older quote from Lewis Smedes, "Sexuality is the human drive toward intimate communion."[4]

The One God, *Adonai Echad*, designed sex within marriage as a picture of oneness. Thus, the many admonitions against premarital and extramarital relations also make theological sense. In the mathematics of premarital sex, $1 + 1 = 2$. In the mathematics of an extra-marital affair, $1 + 1 + 1 = 3$. In both cases, the unity math is wrong. Because of the *echad* of God, we were designed for one-ness, not two-ness or three-ness, or in the case of one boastful sports figure, twenty-thousand-ness![5] The familiar command to not commit adultery (Exodus 20:14) is more than an injunction against extra-marital intercourse. It is a lifestyle command against anything that desecrates, distorts, or minimizes the doctrine of the *echad* of God.

THE DEVIL: THE ENEMY OF ONENESS

The New Testament clearly identifies the greatest adversaries of oneness: "You believe that God is one (Greek: *heis*). You do well; the demons also believe, and shudder" (James 2:19). The demons tremble in fear (Greek: *phrisso*) at the reality of the *echad* of God. It now becomes understandable why the Lead Demon, the Devil, so actively tries to distort our understanding of marital oneness. His ultimate goal is to divide not unite. His name in Greek (*diabolos*) quite literally means "one who throws through (i.e. divides or separates)" and later came to mean "false accuser, maligner, divider." He certainly is true to his name.

Satan is the evil agent of division, the anti-oneness Devil. He hates the *echad* of God, the oneness in the true Godhead. This hatred may have motivated him to tempt Jesus to sin (Matthew 4:1-11). He, of course, failed to move the impeccable Son of God to such oneness-severing action. However, he does prompt us to many forms of idolatry (spiritual adultery) such as "immorality, impurity, passion, evil desire, and greed, which amounts to idolatry" (Greek: *eidololatreia*) (Colossians 3:5). The Devil also abhors oneness in the church and works hard to divide believers. (Put two

Christians together and we are bound to hear three opinions). Thus, Jesus prayed that we, as His disciples, would be *one* even as He and the Father are *one* (John 10:30; 17:21-22). Satan also loathes the *echad* of marriage. What God has joined together (Greek: *suzeugnumi*), *Diabolos*, the Divider tries to pull apart (Greek: *chorizo*) (Mark 10:9). He applauds every instance of infidelity in marriage counting it as a left jab to the face of God Himself.

Certainly, one of the Devil's highest goals would be to stimulate us to violate our marriage covenant through adultery (1 Corinthians 6:12-20). He also takes every advantage when we are not enjoying the sexual union God designed for marriage. Heed the apostle Paul's warning against this diabolical plot: "Stop depriving one another (i.e. sexually) . . . and come together again *so that Satan will not tempt you* because of your lack of self-control" (1 Corinthians 7:5, emphasis added).

Idolatry in our lives, disunity among believers, and adultery in our marriages are all anti-oneness sins motivated by Diabolos. It helps to know the Enemy's tactics if we are going to do battle effectively:

> Be of sober spirit, be on the alert. Your adversary, the devil (Greek: *diabolos*), prowls around like a roaring lion, seeking someone to devour. But resist him ("stand against," Greek: *anthistemi*), firm ("steadfast," Greek: *stereos*) in your faith, knowing that the same experiences of suffering are being accomplished by your brethren who are in the world (1 Peter 5:8-9).

chapter 6

WHAT IS THIS FEELING ANYWAY?

As we consider God's design for human sexuality, we must make a fundamental distinction between sexual *nature* and sexual *drive*. Very simply, sexual *nature* relates to gender ("male and female He created them" Genesis 1:27). Sexual *drive*, however, is the God-given quest for oneness with a covenantal partner (i.e. a spouse) as a reflection of the *echad* of God, His oneness. It is far more than the desire for sexual intercourse.

Is it therefore true, as is often observed, that men have a stronger sexual *drive* than women? If we are thinking biologically (i.e. physical sex), many think so. However, given our biblical understanding, men and women were created with the same God-given desire for oneness. As we'll see later in our study, women may find physical or emotional fulfillment differently than men, but they have just as much need for oneness. Desire for unity is not gender-determined.

IT IS GOOD. IT IS VERY GOOD!

I don't know how to say it any more simply. Sex is God's idea, and it's a really good idea. Therefore, each of us must come to a point when we accept our sexuality as a gift of God and say with our Creator, "It is good. It is very good" (Genesis 1:31).

Frankly, some are exclaiming, "It's not so good. It's frustrating, disappointing and a big hassle." However, the Scriptures call us to a different mind-set: "I will give thanks to You, for I am fearfully and wonderfully made" (Psalm 139:14). The general instruction the apostle Paul gave to young Timothy can also be specifically applied to our sexuality: "For everything created by God is good, and nothing is to be rejected if it is received with gratitude; for it is sanctified by means of the word of God and prayer" (1 Timothy 4:4-5). Some of us need to rehearse these words often, as a statement of faith and not feeling: "Everything created by God is good . . . including my sexuality."

I WAS MADE TO RUN ON ONENESS

I used to be the happy owner of a completely restored classic 1955 Chevrolet. Equipped with a 327 cubic inch Corvette engine, that shiny red and white "blast from the past" could really move down the road—at about five miles per gallon of expensive fuel. If only I could have figured out a way to convert the engine to run on sand. However, my Chevy simply wasn't designed by General Motors to run on anything but gasoline.

Likewise, our Master Designer has specifically fashioned us to function a certain way sexually. He designed us to run on unity. The fullest sexual pleasure is experienced when it is used for its designed purpose. To violate that supernatural design is to end up damaged, like a classic car engine filled with sand. Let's consider the many purposes for sexual union in marriage.

chapter 7

COVENANTAL ONENESS

LET'S MAKE A DEAL

My early morning men's group was resisting my statement that studying systematic theology early in the morning can be invigorating. One of them, a lawyer, handed me the classic law text, *Prosser on Torts*. He said, "Try reading this and feel our pain." Early the next morning, I tried. Within minutes, I was asleep! Lengthy law discussions can be as tedious as lengthy theological discussions.

I remember the first time I stood before a crowd and declared with confidence, "God designed sexual union to ratify the binding marriage covenant." I was not expecting the blank looks and the confused stares. It certainly is a theological mouthful. Let's make a deal. I will do my best to simplify this. You do your best to let this sink in. I assure you it will be well worth the time spent.

MARRIAGE IS A COVENANT

In the last book of the Old Testament, God speaks through the prophet Malachi to His wayward people. In particular, in Malachi 2:13-16, the Lord rebukes the rebellious husbands who were dealing treacherously and divorcing the women who had been their "wife by covenant." With great concern for more than just their marriages, God says:

This is another thing you do: you cover the altar of the LORD with tears, with weeping and with groaning, because He no longer regards the offering or accepts it with favor from your hand. "Yet you say, 'For what reason?' Because the LORD has been a witness between you and the wife of your youth, against whom you have dealt treacherously, though she is your companion *and your wife by covenant.* But not one has done so who has a remnant of the Spirit. And what did that one do while he was seeking a godly offspring? Take heed then to your spirit, and let no one deal treacherously against the wife of your youth. "For I hate divorce," says the LORD, the God of Israel, "and him who covers his garment with wrong," says the LORD of hosts. "So take heed to your spirit, that you do not deal treacherously" (Malachi 2:13-16, emphasis added).

Perhaps this word "covenant" (Hebrew: *bariyth*) is not very familiar to you. Fundamentally, a covenant refers to an agreement, a contract, or a partnership.[1] The word is also used to describe a treaty between enemies who have now joined together as allies. It's an especially important word when used to describe a marriage contract. Tim Alan Gardner, in his book, *Sacred Sex: A Spiritual Celebration of Oneness in Marriage,* reminds us that marriage is, in fact, more than a contract:

> It's a relationship you choose to enter into, and by entering this relationship you make the commitment to meet the terms of the covenant. Unlike a purely human arrangement, a covenant is authorized by God, supported by God, and ratified by God.[2]

Husbands, she is your wife "by covenant." Wives, he is your husband "by covenant." Whether you are still allies is another matter!

MARRIAGE IS A BINDING COVENANT

There are far too many, even of my fellow Christians, who are casting off their spouses like old pairs of shoes. Sadly, pollsters report that the divorce rate among those who claim to be born-again believers is about equal to those who do not. We can remove the words "until death do us part" from our wedding *vows*, but the marriage *covenant* is nonetheless binding. Speaking in general about all contracts and covenants, certainly including marriage, King Solomon wrote succinctly:

> When you make a vow to God, do not be late in paying it; for He takes no delight in fools. Pay what you vow! It is better that you should not vow than that you should vow and not pay (Ecclesiastes 5:4-5).

You might now be asking what happens if people do not say their vows *to God*. Perhaps they are *legally* married in some other way. Does this mean they are not in a binding covenant *in the eyes of God*? Take to heart the pithy words of the apostle Paul: "Are you bound ("under obligation to the law," Greek: *deo*) to a wife? Do not seek to be released " (1 Corinthians 7:27). In other words, if you are *legally* married, you are married *in the eyes of God*, as well as the eyes of men.

There is much debate in Christian circles regarding the biblical grounds for divorce. Some allow for the possibility of divorce for causes of adultery (Matthew 5:32; 19:9) or desertion by an unbelieving spouse (1 Corinthians 7:15). Others respectfully disagree and argue for no grounds, using as proof such passages as Malachi 2:14-16 and 1 Corinthians 7:27. There are, of course, a wide range of other views. Let the debate continue. It has for centuries. However, I would hope we all agree that marriage is a *binding covenant* and vows are not to be taken lightly: "What therefore God has joined together (i.e. "fastened to one yoke," Greek: *suzeugnumi*), let no man separate (i.e. "depart," Greek: *chorizo*) (Mark 10:9).

MARRIAGE IS A BINDING COVENANT RATIFIED BY THE SEXUAL UNION

Today, if we want to enter into a contractual agreement to buy a house, take out a loan, or enter a partnership, we will be shown papers that have, most likely, been reviewed by an able contract attorney. That agreement will contain clearly stated conditions as well as the consequences if those conditions are breached. In order to "seal the deal" both parties will inscribe their signatures, which, in most cases, will be notarized and authenticated by a qualified witness.

This is not how it was done in some parts of the ancient Middle East. After discussing the specific terms, sacrificial animals would be cut in half and placed on the ground. Both parties would then walk between the bloody animal parts, reciting vows that would, in essence, declare to the other party and the world, "May it be as difficult to break our agreement as it would be to put these animal parts back together, and may what happened to this animal, happen to either of us who breaks this covenant." It was a very bloody reminder that contracts, partnerships, and covenants are serious matters. I did glean something from what little I read in that civil law book. Breaking a contract reaps substantial consequences. So it is with the marriage covenant.

DO YOU WANT TO WALK BETWEEN THE PARTS WITH ME, DEAR?

In Ezekiel, Chapter 16, we find a curious passage that concerns God, as He enters into symbolic marital union with His bride, Israel. I've included some clarifying notes in parentheses:

> Then I *(God)* passed by you *(Israel),* and saw you, and behold, you were at the time for love; so I spread My skirt over you and covered your nakedness *(a very sexual expression).* I also swore to you and entered into a covenant

(a marriage contract) with you so that you became Mine,'
declares the Lord GOD (Ezekiel 16:8, emphasis and notes
added).[3]

In the Old Testament Scriptures, the Hebrew words often translated
"make a covenant" (*karath bariyth*) originally meant "to cut in half" and
later meant, "to cut an agreement." Throughout the Bible, the practice of
cutting was often seen as the seal on the contract. For example, the Noahic
covenant was sealed by cutting the sky with a rainbow as a "sign of the
covenant" (Genesis 9:12-17). The Abrahamic covenant was symbolized
by cutting a heifer, goat, and ram in half and God alone passing between
the parts in this unilateral agreement (Genesis 15:7-18; Hebrews 6:13-
14). The Mosaic covenant was later affirmed by circumcision, the ritual
cutting of the foreskin as the sign of that covenant (Genesis 17:10-11).
Reflecting on His body that would soon be crucified (i.e. "pierced,"
Zechariah 12:10), Jesus declared: "This cup which is poured out for you
is the *new covenant in My blood*" (Luke 22:20, emphasis added).

What has all this to do with marriage? I believe it is significant that
the marriage covenant is consummated by sexual union, a union involving
cutting or piercing (Genesis 2:24; Ezekiel 16:8; Matthew 19:5; Ephesians
5:31). Quite frankly, this principle of "cutting the agreement" may be
one of the reasons why God designed men and women as He did—a
man's body to pierce; a woman's to be pierced.[4] It is reminiscent of both
parties of an ancient contract walking between the bloody parts. Sexual
intercourse has been divinely designed to ratify the initial marriage
covenant. It is the spiritual signature on the marriage contract that "seals
the deal." Tim Gardner, in *Sacred Sex*, says it clearly:

Since marriage has always been defined by God as two
becoming one, the sexual union of a wife and husband is
the perfect, God-intended oath sign that a marriage has
been established. We speak an oath with our vows; we

> seal that oath with our bodies. Together, our words and
> our action form a covenant. . . . Sex is not only part of the
> covenant of marriage, but it functions in the *creation* of the
> covenant. Sex is the divine seal.[5]

I'm not, in any way, suggesting that the act of sex by itself and apart from legally recognized marriage vows constitutes a biblically-binding marriage covenant. People are not married in the eyes of God simply because they have engaged in sexual intercourse. Besides the biblical requirement to obey the laws of the land, including the legal requirements for entering into marriage (Romans 13:1-7; 1 Peter 2:13-17), we must also ask, "Where are the qualified witnesses? Where is the binding contract? Where are the promissory vows?"

Wearing a wedding ring does not make one married; nor does having sex. Both are symbols. In a legally-binding marriage sexual union can be likened to reviewing the printed signatures on an official marriage license. It is a constant reminder that this man and woman are husband and wife "by covenant."

YES, YOU HAVE TO; GOD SAYS SO

Where does sexual union after that first legal consummation fit in with all this? Are we not to look at the rainbow and be reminded of God's *covenantal* faithfulness? (Genesis 9:11-13). Are we not to partake of communion "often" (1 Corinthians 11:25-26) in remembrance of the *new covenant* in Christ's blood? Why is it therefore hard to grasp that marriage involves the regular and continual expression of *covenantal love and loyalty* through sexual union (1 Corinthians 7:5)? Again, Tim Gardner comments:

> Oneness and the mystery of Christ are proclaimed each
> time we join ourselves intimately with our mate. Our
> coming together as wife and husband, the two becoming
> one in order to jointly represent God's divine image, is

to be a regular reminder of the promises we made in our marriage covenant, just as a rainbow is to be a reminder of God's promise in His covenant with Noah after the flood.[6]

Many men have come to me and complained how infrequently they enjoy sexual relations with their wife. One man even admitted what many men have thought, "My experience with foreplay involves thirty minutes of begging!" Another understandably frustrated brother shared with me his anguish over only having had relations with his wife twelve times in seventeen years of marriage. Something was certainly amiss here!

The Bible does not specifically speak of sexual frequency in marriage. Since far too many married couples use sex as a means of reward or punishment, the apostle Paul's ancient instructions to the Corinthian believers couldn't be more timely: "Stop depriving one another, except by agreement for a time" (1 Corinthians 7:5). Sex is not to be used as a weapon nor as a tool of manipulation. It was not designed as a means of getting what we want from our partner. Sex in marriage is to be a mutual expression of covenantal oneness and a reflection of the unity of the Father, Son and Holy Spirit. It is also a picture of the oneness of Christ and His Church, as well as the unity of the members of His church with each other. In other words, regular sexual union with our spouse is not only good for us—it's biblical.

chapter 8

RESTORATIVE ONENESS

"BUT WHAT IF . . . ?"

What if our partner breaks our marriage vows? Theologically speaking, when adultery occurs, it violates the marriage covenant and grieves the heart of Adonai Echad. Perhaps this is why the apostle Paul speaks about the devastation of adultery with such severity, as compared to "every other sin a man commits" (1 Corinthians 6:18). King Solomon spoke of "the adulteress . . . that leaves the companion of her youth / And forgets the covenant of her God" (Proverbs 2:16-17). Here we have a woman that, by committing adultery, *leaves* ("forsakes," Hebrew: *azab*) the covenant with her husband and *forgets* ("ceases to care about," Hebrew: *shakach*) the covenant with her Creator. The apostle Paul's words state it succinctly: "Or do you not know that the one who joins himself to a prostitute is one body with her?" (1 Corinthians 6:16).

In Matthew's gospel, Jesus makes reference to immorality (i.e. the Greek word *porneia* which includes the sin of adultery) as separating what God has joined together (Matthew 5:32; 19:4-6, 9). I believe adultery breaks the *conditional marriage covenant*; it need not sever the *legal marriage*. Restoration is the goal.

YOU BROKE THE COVENANT, BUT ALL IS NOT LOST

A young couple sat in the front row of a seminar I was teaching in Mexico

City. By the way they were seated, it was obvious something was very wrong. As I spoke through the interpreter about the devastating consequences of sexual immorality, I could see her getting angrier. She ran out of the auditorium, leaving him sitting alone. No translation was needed to figure out what was happening.

At the end of the session, I approached them and heard the all-too-familiar story of his infidelity and her intense bitterness at his blatant betrayal. He also had issues about her. I spoke gently to them about the possibility of restoration and prayed with them, asking God to give them the grace to forgive each other, once they asked His forgiveness (Ephesians 4:32). I ended our conversation, expressing the hope that someday soon they would be willing to renew their marriage vows. By the look on both of their faces, I did not expect to see them again. To my surprise, they came early the next night, once again sitting in the front row. It was obvious by their countenance and their body language that things were very different. Before the teaching session began, they held hands as they shared with me that they not only asked forgiveness from God and each other but they also renewed their wedding vows. I will never forget their tears of joy. From my podium I watched this broken couple, humbled by God's grace and mercy, fall in love once again. Did renewing their vows solve all their problems? Of course not. Was further marriage counseling needed? Certainly. But, this was the re-start they needed.

IT'S NOT OVER WHEN IT'S OVER

Although adultery violates the marriage covenant, it does not mandate that the marriage be over. Though restoring the marriage *relationship* will take time, I believe the marriage *covenant* can be renewed *immediately*. We find our example in God's relationship with His people. Once again we look to Ezekiel 16 and see the mercy and lovingkindness of God as He renews His covenant with His bride, Israel, even though she committed blatant spiritual adultery by chasing after other gods:[1]

But you trusted in your beauty and played the harlot because of your fame, and you have poured out your harlotries on every passer-by who might be willing . . . you who have despised the oath by breaking the covenant. Nevertheless, I will remember My covenant with you in the days of your youth, and I will establish an everlasting covenant with you (Ezekiel 16:15, 59-60).

We see this same covenant-renewing mercy and lovingkindness of God demonstrated throughout the Old Testament and exemplified in the story of Hosea and his relationship to his adulterous wife.

When counseling couples that have experienced the pain of infidelity, I strongly urge them to formally renew their vows. Some choose to do it privately while others need to hold a more public ceremony, especially if the adultery was well known. Many of the couples then go on a second honeymoon to re-establish their marriage union. Although renewing vows reforms the foundation immediately, I am quick to remind couples that they will then have to spend years rebuilding the damaged relationship.[2]

Perhaps some of us need to do this, especially if there has been adultery that has occurred any time in our marriage. Frankly, it's a good idea to renew our wedding vows regularly, even if adultery hasn't occurred. After all, who among us hasn't been tempted or looked at another with lust, thereby committing adultery in our hearts (Matthew 5:27-28)? Thankfully, my wife and I have never suffered through the pain of infidelity in our marriage. We have, however, enjoyed renewing our wedding vows on numerous occasions, privately and publicly. I would do it again in a moment. Why not pull out those old wedding vows or work together on writing new ones? Make sure you include a commitment to be faithful to your marriage covenant and to each other. Then, enjoy the reunion!

chapter 9

SACRED ONENESS

"HONEY, LET'S WORSHIP!"

"If I were to ask you to worship the Lord for the next thirty seconds, what would you do?" The responses at the men's conference came back to me more quickly than usual. "I'd sing." "I would pray." "I'd study my Bible." "I would serve someone." "I think I'd go fishing in the mountains." One man stopped us in our tracks, when he unashamedly shouted, "I would make love to my wife!" Most of the men laughed in agreement. Some, however, shook their heads, as if to say he was some twisted, heretical reprobate. Far from it.

The essence of true worship is any thought, word, or deed that declares who God is. It is often defined as the adoring response of the creature to the infinite majesty of God. I have learned to understand that worship is not primarily about art; it is about heart. In other words, if my heart is right with the Lord then any way that I declare God's majesty or character can be a form of worship. If I sincerely declare His oneness in song or in some other form of praise, that is worship. So it can be with sexual union in marriage.

In Psalm 46:10 the Lord exhorts us to "Cease striving and *know* that I am God." Later in Proverbs 3:6 we are commanded in all our ways to *acknowledge* Him. In both passages we find the Hebrew word *yada* which speaks of knowing a person intimately, relationally, and experientially. In some cases it can even refer to knowing someone *sexually*. Thus, Genesis 4:1 uses the same Hebrew word *yada* to declare that Adam *knew* his wife. In other words, he had sexual relations with her and she conceived and bore her first son. Sexual intercourse in the covenant of marriage can be the body language of sacred worship, a private and intimate declaration of the *echad* of God, His infinite oneness. Sex in marriage can point to "a higher ecstasy."[1]

Does this mean that sex in marriage is *always* a form of sacred worship? Not necessarily. Sadly, there are times when I have sung "How Great Thou Art" and yet my soul has been quite distant from the Lord. I have publicly prayed words not spoken from my heart. I have engaged in the rote practice of worship forms without a genuine passion for God who is worthy of sincere praise. So it is with sexual union in marriage. It is not always worship but it *can* be, especially when our hearts are right and when the unity is evident. That's what makes sexual relations in marriage so very different. Sex outside of marriage can never, under any circumstances, be true worship. It can never reflect the *echad* of God.

IS GODLINESS REALLY SEXY?

If God designed sexual union in marriage as a sacred worship experience, the implications in our marriages are certainly far-reaching. Proper preparation for a corporate worship experience has, fundamentally, the same elements as proper preparation for a private sexual experience with our spouse.

Over the three and a half decades of our ministry, my wife has demonstrated her special ability to set the worship atmosphere for our home, especially on Sunday mornings. As I would rise early to prepare to preach, she would get me a cup of coffee, prepare my clothes, play soft music, and try to keep the child-noise to a minimum. If she saw that I was especially apprehensive, she would calmly soothe the moment by praying with me and expressing her support. By setting an atmosphere of love, joy, and peace, she helped prepare me not only to preach but also to corporately worship with my fellow believers. Love, joy and peace can also set the mood for other forms of worship.

I once wrote the nine fruit of the Spirit, mentioned in Galatians 5:22-23, on a whiteboard at a women's counseling training seminar:

- *Love*
- *Joy*
- *Peace*
- *Patience*
- *Kindness*

- *Goodness*
- *Faithfulness*
- *Gentleness*
- *Self-control*

Without stating what these were, I quickly asked the ladies, "Suppose you were to meet a man who demonstrated all of these. What kind of man would he be?" One of the women slipped and said, "A really sexy one!" She was embarrassed until I publicly agreed with her.

Besides being the essence of Christlike character, these are certainly attractive qualities that are the essence of romantic love—spiritual foreplay, if you will. I think walking in the Spirit and manifesting these nine fruit of the Spirit should become the new textbook definition of the word *sexy*!

BEWARE OF OVER-SPIRITUALIZING SEX

Let's be careful. Yes, sex in marriage can be a sacred form of worship. Even so, there are obviously real dangers of over-spiritualizing this concept. We are certainly well aware of the abuse of this doctrine by false teachers and the cults. Sadly, we have even witnessed abuses of this "doctrine of sacred sex" in some of our once-trusted Christian leaders. Lewis Smedes makes a profound observation:

> Why have people often associated sex with religion, as though somehow sex were the gateway to God? What distorted vision of reality led those ancient Canaanites to their shrines of prostitution. . . . But the ecstasy of sexual fulfillment is not absolutely unlike the ecstasy of religious experience, otherwise it would not have been so often identified with it.[2]

Beyond the horrific sexual abuse, there have also been some of the rank and file believers who have distorted this great truth and used it to put intense spiritual pressure on their marriage partner—"Honey, let's worship!" I suppose others could even distort this teaching and make it an excuse to skip church. "Let's stay in Bedside Bible Church this morning." Once again, it is *a* form of worship, not the *only* form.

chapter 10

PROCREATIONAL ONENESS

BE FRUITFUL AND MULTIPLY

> God blessed them (Adam and Eve); and God said to them,
> 'Be fruitful and multiply, and fill the earth (Genesis 1:28).

I grew up in a large Italian family. I suspect that, without knowing it, Genesis 1:28 was my father's life verse. Perhaps Dad thought of himself as an Italian Adam or a Mediterranean Noah, personally commissioned by God to "Populate the earth abundantly and multiply in it" (Genesis 9:7).

It has been well over fifty years since I heard "the facts of life." I have gotten over the youthful shock of what had to occur between my parents in order for me and my many siblings to be born. It was God's plan from the beginning: "Now the man *had relations with his wife Eve, and she conceived* and gave birth to Cain, and she said, 'I have gotten a manchild *with the help of the LORD*" (Genesis 4:1, emphasis added).

Our magnificent Creator made it possible for us lowly humans to help Him fill the earth. He sovereignly designed sexual intercourse between a man and a woman to make this happen. As almighty God, He certainly could have populated the world without our help. He might even have used us to accomplish this purpose without us ever having to engage in sexual union. He could have designed us to shake hands with our mate, wait ten seconds, and a baby drops out of the sky. Instead, our omnipotent Lord chose sexual union to not only declare His oneness but to bless our lives.

We get the pleasure of sexual union, the joy of having children, and the thrill of knowing that we have been used of God to populate the earth. Making babies is a win, win, and win adventure. Solomon, the author of Psalm 127, wrote these familiar words:

> Behold children are a gift of the LORD;
> *The fruit of the womb* is a reward.
> Like arrows in the hand of a warrior,
> So are the children of one's youth.
> How blessed is the man whose quiver is full of them
> (Psalm 127:3-5, emphasis added).

IT'S NOT ONLY FOR MAKING BABIES

Danger lies not so much in viewing sex as God's plan for having children but in seeing this as the only purpose of the sexual union. Around AD 350, Saint Augustine taught that sex was the bitter fruit of the fall, rather than the sweet gift of creation.[1] Jerome, the fourth-century theologian, spoke of anyone who was too passionately in love with his wife as an adulterer.[2] In the early part of the last century, the widely held Christian view was that God would bless marriage only if sex was primarily used for procreation. As wonderful as it is to have children, to make reproduction the ultimate and only goal of sex is to distort what God created.

Some today teach that Christians are expected, even *commanded*, to have large families in order to populate the earth with "godly offspring," an abuse of Malachi 2:15. Some embrace a dogma that declares that any form of birth control is sinful disobedience to God's Word. Although I do agree that we should not use those forms of birth control that *terminate pregnancy*, I personally support a couple's prayerful decision to, upon counsel of their physician, use safe forms of *prevention of pregnancy* (i.e. contraception). I can find no Bible reference to the contrary. However, should you decide to have *many* children, do so as your God-given right, not as an irrefutable biblical mandate.

chapter 11

PHYSICAL AND EMOTIONAL ONENESS

MALE AND FEMALE HE CREATED THEM

One Christmas, my wife and daughters presented me with a book they were certain I had never read, *Everything Men Know About Women*. Frankly, no one had ever *read* it. All the pages were blank.

I recall hearing many years ago that there are only two ways to understand women and no one knows either of them! The same sentiment is widely held by women about men. We are marvelously different. Consider these timeless words: "You husbands likewise, live with your wives in an understanding way, as with a weaker vessel, since she is a woman; and grant her honor as a fellow heir of the grace of life, so that your prayers may not be hindered" (1 Peter 3:7, New American Standard Version, 1977).

Speaking man to man, the apostle Peter reminds us guys of three very important *gender facts* that, if more fully understood, will make living with our wives so much easier. In essence, he is saying that there really are *three* ways to understand a woman and we *can* know all of them.

> *Gender Fact #1*
> *Husbands and wives are <u>different physically</u>.*
> *She is "a weaker vessel" (1 Peter 3:7).*

God created human beings in two very different and distinct packages.

"God created man in His own image, in the image of God He created him; *male and female* He created them" (Genesis 1:27, my emphasis). Besides the obvious differences in genitalia, men were created with larger muscular and skeletal properties; women with bodies that bear children as well as cradle and nurse babies.

Even though they are physically different, men and women were designed to unite in physical oneness. When God created Eve, He designed a partner that was a "suitable helper" (Hebrew: *'ezer neged*) for Adam's loneliness (i.e. his "separateness," Hebrew: *bad*) (Genesis 2:18). I find it curious that God, *after* declaring it not good for man to be alone but *before* creating Eve, brings all the animals to Adam (Genesis 2:18-25). Might this have been God's way of showing Adam that there was no suitable partner— no one that fits!

Sexually speaking, men and women fit. God designed them to be united as "one flesh" physically in marriage, as male and female. Not human and animal. Not female and female. Not male and male.

Even the timing of their sexual desire and response is different. In general, God created men like quick-heating microwave ovens; women like slow-cooking crock pots. He is fast heat, fast cool. She takes time for both. That certainly makes for an interesting combination. Frankly, the marriage bed needs both. In most marriages, if men waited for women to initiate, very little would happen. On the other hand, if the woman's physical needs are ignored by the man, sex becomes a forgettable few minutes of intimacy.

> *Gender Fact #2*
> *Husbands and wives are <u>different emotionally</u>.*
> *She is "a woman" (1 Peter 3:7).*

Try as we may to create a unisex society, the truth is that women are wired differently than men. Most men are like simple pieces of mechanical equipment. It doesn't take much to figure them out. Push a button here, pull a switch there and off to work they go. Many women, on the other hand, are like multi-functioning electronic equipment. Daily fine tuning and adjustments are required.

I could fill this book with evidence from scores of writers on the subject of his needs, her needs, male traits and female characteristics. However, after almost forty years of marriage, raising daughters and foster-daughters and thirty-five years of pastoral ministry, I have a lifetime of my own observations.

One evening, at dinner with another couple, my wife stood and asked the other woman, "Would you like to go to the restroom with me?" I was perturbed at her for interrupting our four-way conversation. I blurted, "Can't you go alone?" She calmly replied, "Sure, but this way the two of us ladies can continue the conversation."

I can assure you that, in the span of my life, I have never asked a man, "Would you like to go to the restroom with me, so we can finish our conversation?" I'm told that women even talk over the stalls! Gentlemen, I am sure you agree that if a man tries to have a lengthy conversation with us in the restroom, it's time to get out of there! Oh, how different women are from men, especially when it comes to romance.

OH YEAH! DEFINE ROMANCE!

One supposedly romantic weekend away, my wife and I got in what I have since learned is a typical argument between even the most seasoned husbands and wives. My wife complained, "You are just not romantic anymore," I retorted like a true professional (?), "Oh, yeah! Define romance!" She wasn't about to be intimidated and asked, "Will you listen to me, if I do?" I smugly agreed. Three hours later (sigh!), I finally figured out what she was really saying.

To my wife, romance is defined as giving her what costs me the most, especially my valuable time. Nothing "rings her bell" more than when I spend a day with her. To me, romance is defined as her giving me what costs her the most, her beautiful body. Nothing "rings my bell" more.

True love costs! Isn't that what the apostle Paul said so succinctly when he commanded: "Husbands, love your wives, just as Christ also loved the church and *gave Himself up for her*" (Ephesians 5:25, emphasis added). Christ's *agape* love[1] toward His bride, the church, was sacrificial and expensive. Husbands, your love for your wife will also cost you:

> So husbands ought also to love their own wives as their own bodies. He who loves his own wife loves himself; for no one ever hated his own flesh, but nourishes and cherishes it, just as Christ also does the church (Ephesians 5:28-29).

God did not design sex just for physical union. The Creator also designed sex in marriage to produce emotional oneness in very different emotional creatures. Lewis Smedes comments, "Our sexuality, on all of its graduated levels, is our deeply human drive toward and our means of discovering human communion at its intimate peak."[2]

In general, a woman experiences sex as an emotional act enhanced by physical union. Men experience sex as a physical act enhanced by emotional union. There are exceptions, of course. Some women are more physical than their spouse; some men are more emotional. However, as we are about to see, God designed sex to be a spiritually unifying event for both.

chapter 12

SPIRITUAL ONENESS

There is something special about a marriage where the husband and wife are both born-again believers who have trusted in Jesus Christ alone for their salvation. Let's take another look at the apostle Peter's profound words: "You husbands likewise, live with your wives in an understanding way, as with a weaker vessel, since she is a woman; and grant her honor as a fellow heir of the grace of life, so that your prayers may not be hindered" (1 Peter 3:7). In the last chapter we considered:

> *Gender Fact #1*
> *Husbands and wives are <u>different physically</u>.*
> *She is "a weaker vessel" (1 Peter 3:7).*

> *Gender Fact #2*
> *Husbands and wives are <u>different emotionally</u>.*
> *She is "a woman" (1 Peter 3:7).*

The third is the clincher:

> *Gender Fact #3*
> *Husbands and wives are <u>the same spiritually</u>.*
> *They are each a "fellow heir of the grace of life" (1 Peter 3:7).*

My wife and I are fellow believers in Jesus Christ. She trusted in Christ when she was eighteen; I did at twenty-one. That makes us more than fellow church-goers. We have the *same* heavenly Father and are indwelt by the *same* Holy Spirit. We are recipients of the *same* grace, heirs of the *same* promise, headed for the *same* heaven, and saved from the *same* hell. Both of us have the *same* Spirit-led illumination of the Bible from which to draw wisdom and instruction in order to love and appreciate each other. We made the *same* vows and entered the *same* marriage covenant before God.

Although we will only be husband and wife "until death do us part," we will be brother and sister in Christ for eternity. The apostle Paul reminds us, "there is neither male nor female; for you are all one in Christ Jesus. And if you belong to Christ, then you are Abraham's descendants, heirs according to promise" (Galatians 3:28-29).

Our male and female, physical and emotional differences shouldn't matter much. Whereas, we may never fully understand each other's physical and emotional differences, we can relate to each other spiritually as joint heirs of God's grace. That is more than *common ground*; it is the *spiritual ground—the holy ground* upon which we, as very different physical and emotional people, place the firm footing of our marriage. It makes me want to sing my wife's favorite old hymn of the faith, "On Christ, the solid rock, I stand. All other ground is sinking sand." It is what I believe to be the essence of what King Solomon was driving at when he wrote this popular portion of Ecclesiastes:

> Two are better than one because they have a good return for their labor. For if either of them falls, the one will lift up his companion. But woe to the one who falls when there is not another to lift him up. Furthermore, if two lie down together they keep warm, but how can one be warm alone? And if one can overpower him who is alone, two can resist him. A cord of three strands is not quickly torn apart (Ecclesiastes 4:9-12).

I am one strand; my wife, Karon, is another. We believe the center strand in our marriage is our commitment to the lordship of Jesus Christ in our daily lives. Without Him we would most certainly fray and break when rubbing against each other's differences. Instead, as a Christian couple, we are able to cast all our cares and anxieties on Jesus Christ, Our Center Strand (1 Peter 5:7). He is the only One who can hold us together; the only One who can produce amazing unity amidst our substantial diversity.

THE TWO OF US IN THE SAME CANOE

I have experienced the joy of traveling and ministering in the Republic of the Philippines some twenty-five times. On one of those trips I traveled to the Ifagao area, in the northern part of the island of Luzon. I was teaching on the beauty of *fellowship* in the Christian marriage.

After the session a tribal chief approached me and explained his view of marriage: "In the Ifagao language, since we have no ships, the phrase we use for fellowship is 'two guys in a canoe.' We use the same word to speak of two Christians who marry." At first I chuckled over his need to be so literal, thinking the word fellowship referred to two people in the same ship. Then, I reflected on what he was really saying, especially about marriage.

Marriage really is two people in the same canoe. When one partner paddles in a different direction than the other or stops paddling altogether, the vessel goes in circles. True biblical *fellowship* in marriage is a husband and wife paddling in the same direction, with Christ as the Navigator.

"ONE ANOTHER-ING"

God designed sexual union as an even more special type of fellowship between married believers. The nature of true biblical *fellowship* (Greek: *koinonia*) is meeting one another's needs. It seems to me that all those "one another" verses in the Bible that apply to our relationships with our fellow church-going Christians would be even more important in our private *fellowship*—our personal *koinonia*—our sexual intimacy with our spouse. After all, isn't our Christian marriage partner, with whom we are in *covenant* together (Malachi 2:14), to be the one who God desires to be our closest brother or sister in Christ? I love what King Solomon said to his wife: "You have made my heart beat fast, *my sister, my bride*" (Song of Solomon 4:9, emphasis added).

I often counsel couples to consider how practicing the "one-another" verses in the New Testament would not only help resolve their relational conflicts[1], but make their hearts beat faster for their born-again husband (their brother in Christ) or their born-again wife (their sister in Christ). Take a moment to not only reflect on your last intense disagreement with your spouse, but to consider the romantic side of *fellowship*—of "one another-ing."

- Loving one another (John 13:35)
- Not fighting with one another (Acts 7:26)
- Being devoted to one another (Romans 12:10)
- Honoring one another (Romans 12:10)
- Sympathizing with one another (Romans 12:15; 1 Corinthians 12:26)
- Being of the same mind (i.e. living in harmony) with one another (Romans 12:16)
- Not passing judgment on one another (Romans 14:13)
- Accepting one another (Romans 15:7)
- Admonishing (i.e. warning) one another (Romans 15:14; Colossians 3:16)
- Greeting one another (Romans 16:16)
- Being considerate of one another (1 Corinthians 11:33)
- Caring for one another (1 Corinthians 12:25)
- Serving one another in love (Galatians 5:13)
- Not biting and devouring one another (Galatians 5:15)
- Bearing one another's burdens (Galatians 6:2)
- Being patient, showing tolerance for one another (Ephesians 4:2)

- Being kind and tender-hearted toward one another (Ephesians 4:32)
- Submitting to one another (Ephesians 5:21)
- Being honest with one another (Colossians 3:9)
- Forgiving one another (Colossians 3:13; Ephesians 4:32)
- Encouraging one another (1 Thessalonians 5:11)
- Stimulating one another to love and good deeds (Hebrews 10:24)
- Not slandering one another (James 4:11)
- Not grumbling or complaining against one another (James 5:9)
- Confessing your sins and faults to one another (James 5:16)
- Praying for one another (James 5:16)
- Offering hospitality to one another (1 Peter 4:9)
- Treating one another with humility (1 Peter 5:5)
- Having fellowship with one another (1 John 1:7)

That tribal chief was right. Paddling in the same direction sure makes for a smoother trip, even through the rapids of marriage. It also makes it possible for marital "shipmates" to enjoy a lifetime of truly romantic fellowship.

chapter 13

RECREATIONAL ONENESS

Regardless of what evolutionists would have us believe, we are not merely members of the animal kingdom. We humans are the pinnacles of God's creation (Psalm 8:5). Sexually, we have more than the primal "urge to merge."

Animals mate; humans cleave (Genesis 2:24). In nature, mating is hardly intimate. In fact, it is often accompanied by brutality, even cannibalism. The black widow spider is so named because the female sometimes eats the male after mating. (This gives a whole new meaning to the idea of going out for dinner afterwards!)

Animals primarily mate for one reason and one reason only—procreation. As we have seen, we humans cleave for reasons of covenantal, restorative, sacred, procreative, physical, emotional, and spiritual oneness. We also cleave for fun!

Sadly, some of my fellow Christians might think that *fun* is a dirty word when used in the context of the Christian marriage bed. Not so with God! Our Creator designed sexual union to be mutually enjoyable for husbands and wives. Before sin entered their lives, Adam and Eve "were both naked and were not ashamed" (Genesis 2:25). The Hebrew word speaks of not delaying because of embarrassment or disappointment.[1] That's right, both of them unashamedly enjoyed the union—post-haste!

When promised she would conceive a son in her old age, Sarah, the wife of Abraham, asked the question, "After I have become old, shall I have *pleasure* (Hebrew: *'adnah*) . . .?" (Genesis 18:12, emphasis added). Although bearing a son would bring great delight (Genesis 18:13), I also believe that conception was not the only *pleasurable* thing on her mind!

SIZZLE! SIZZLE!

Even a glancing look at the words King Solomon and his Shulamite bride wrote about each other should give us the clear impression that those two lovers were regularly enjoying each other's bodies. Such was God's design for them and for all married couples. Let's listen in on their love-talk—sizzling dialogue, straight from the pages of Holy Scripture. We begin with Mrs. Solomon:

> May he kiss me with the kisses of his mouth!
> For your love is better than wine (Song of Solomon 1:2).

> My beloved is to me a pouch of myrrh
> Which lies all night between my breasts
> (Song of Solomon 1:13).

> Let his left hand be under my head
> And his right hand embrace me (Song of Solomon 2:6).

> Let me see your form.
> Let me hear your voice;
> For your voice is sweet,
> And your form is lovely (Song of Solomon 2:14).

> May my beloved come into his garden
> And eat its choice fruits! (Song of Solomon 4:16).

And my feelings were aroused for him
(Song of Solomon 5:4).

For I am lovesick (Song of Solomon 5:8).

He is wholly desirable.
This is my beloved and this is my friend
(Song of Solomon 5:16).

I am my beloved's,
And his desire is for me (Song of Solomon 7:10).

Let us rise early and go to the vineyards. . . .
There I will give you my love (Song of Solomon 7:12).

Hurry, my beloved,
And be like a gazelle or a young stag
On the mountains of spices (Song of Solomon 8:14).

Gentlemen, how would you like your wife to talk to you like that? Hopefully, in the eyes of your bride, you are still a young stag and not an old goat!

Now it's King Solomon's turn to sweet-talk his wife:

Your two breasts are like two fawns,
Twins of a gazelle
Which feed among the lilies (Song of Solomon 4:5).

My dove, my perfect one is unique (Song of Solomon 6:9).

The curves of your hips are like jewels,
The work of the hands of an artist (Song of Solomon 7:1).

How beautiful and how delightful you are,
My love, with all your charms!
Your stature is like a palm tree,
And your breasts are like its clusters.
I said, 'I will climb the palm tree,
I will take hold of its fruit stalks,'
Oh, may your breasts be like clusters of the vine,
And the fragrance of your breath like apples,
And your mouth like the best wine!
(Song of Solomon 7:6-9).

Ladies, imagine him referring to you as his perfect and unique dove. Hopefully, you have not become his squawking chicken!

We have an all-wise, all-loving, Holy God who designed sexual union in marriage to be exhilarating. King Solomon, whose expression about his bride we just read, wanted his son to know that if he followed God's guidelines for romantic love in marriage, the Lord would grant him the same enjoyment. His fatherly instruction is born out of his own experience:

Drink water from your own cistern
And fresh water from your own well. . . .
Let your fountain be blessed,
And rejoice in the wife of your youth.
As a loving hind and a graceful doe,
Let her breasts satisfy you at all times;
Be exhilarated always with her love (Proverbs 5:15, 18-19).

That Hebrew word *shagah,* translated *exhilarated,* can literally mean to be intoxicated. The ancient Greek playwright, Antiphanes, is known to have said that there are two things a man cannot hide—when he is drunk and when he is in love. God prefers we experience the intoxicating excitement of the latter.

chapter 14

RULES FOR THE MARRIAGE BED

When it comes to sexual enjoyment and expression in marriage, there is a great need for us to understand the balance between biblical freedom and restriction. The words seem mutually exclusive, but they are not. Remove a locomotive from the track and place it in the middle of a field. It may look free, but it has now become a slave to its liberty.

Pay particular attention to the following passages. They have as much to do with the bedroom as they do the other rooms in our lives:

> For everything created by God is good, and nothing is to be rejected if it is received with gratitude; for it is sanctified by means of the word of God and prayer (1 Timothy 4:4-5).

> Marriage is to be held in honor among all, and the marriage bed is to be undefiled (Hebrews 13:4).

> Whatever you do, do all to the glory of God (1 Corinthians 10:31).

> Glorify God in your body (1 Corinthians 6:20).

> But immorality or any impurity or greed must not even be named among you, as is proper among saints; and there must be no filthiness and silly talk, or coarse jesting, which are not fitting, but rather giving of thanks (Ephesians 5:3-4).

With these passages in mind and in order to help us stay on track, here are some rules for the marriage bed. Don't worry, I promise I will not need to get too specific.

RULES FOR THE MARRIAGE BED

RULE #1

THOU SHALT HAVE FUN WITHIN LIMITS.

Speaking in general terms, the apostle Paul expressed a principle that can easily be applied to sexual relations in marriage: "For *everything* created by God is *good* and *nothing* is to be rejected" (1 Timothy 4:4, emphasis added). The marriage bed need not be just a place of consummation and procreation; it can also be a place of recreation. If you are not finding mutual pleasure in the relationship, get some much-needed help.[1] Nothing is to be rejected—nothing, as long as it doesn't violate the rest of the rules. I agree with Lewis Smedes, "Sexuality is developed within the playground and workspace of human creativity: this is why it has limits as well as liberty."[2]

RULE #2

THOU SHALT NOT DO ANYTHING YOU BELIEVE WILL PRODUCE REGRET OR COMPROMISE YOUR RELATIONSHIP TO GOD.

What we do sexually must be "received with gratitude" (1 Timothy 4:4) by both partners. That means there needs to be unpressured mutual agreement. If what we are about to do, though not expressly forbidden in Scripture, is still not right for either partner, then we must not do it.

Actually, I often counsel that, in sexual matters, the wife gets two votes. She is often the better barometer when it comes to questionable matters. The apostle Paul's instructions help clarify this guideline:

> It is good not to . . . do anything by which your brother stumbles. . . . Happy is he who does not condemn himself in what he approves. . . . But he who doubts is condemned . . . and whatever is not from faith is sin (Romans 14:21-23).

> Whatever you do, do all to the glory of God (1 Corinthians 10:31).

RULE #3
THOU SHALT NOT DO ANYTHING FORBIDDEN IN SCRIPTURE OR THAT VIOLATES GOD'S DESIGN FOR SEX.

Whatever we do sexually must be *"sanctified by means of the Word of God"* (1 Timothy 4:5). The world's philosophy of "Anything goes!" has to go. Admonitions against a number of illicit sexual activities abound in Scripture. As we have also seen, anything contrary to God's design for oneness is, by definition, immoral. For example, watching or reading pornographic materials certainly does not promote God's design for marital union and fidelity. It will also do long term damage to the marriage. If you are unclear about what is forbidden in Scripture, consult a concordance, other Bible references, or the help of a competent biblical counselor.

The writer to the Hebrews expressed what I hope is also our desire: "Marriage is to be held in *honor* (Greek: *timios*) among all, and the marriage bed is to be *undefiled*" (Hebrews 13:4, emphasis added). The Greek word translated *undefiled* is *amiantos*. It refers to those things that are not soiled, deformed or abnormal. Of course, this can refer to those things that Scripture clearly commands against but it can also refer to those that our spirit, moved by God's Holy Spirit, also senses are dishonoring, defiling, and degrading.

RULE #4
THOU SHALT NOT BE CRUDE, VULGAR OR INAPPROPRIATE IN YOUR CONVERSATIONS ABOUT SEX.

> The marriage bed is to be held in honor *among all* (Hebrews 13:4, emphasis added).

We must never cheapen our God-given intimacy. This includes obscene or vulgar conversation and foul joking that are not fitting (Ephesians 5:3-4) and do not present a high view of the beauty of sex, as designed by our Creator. This rule also includes being careful when sharing intimate details of our sexual activities with others. We must keep our private fellowship private. What we do behind the closed doors of our lives should remain there. This rule certainly does not apply when we are in private consultation with a doctor, pastor, or skilled counselor.

RULE #5
THOU SHALT PRAY ABOUT EVERYTHING YOU DO.

What we do sexually must be "sanctified by . . . prayer" (1 Timothy 4:5). God's Holy Spirit is ready, willing and able to guide us in this (Psalm 32:8). Don't leave Him out. After all, He not only lives in our heart; He also lives in our bedroom (Psalm 139:1-7).

God created us to enjoy sexual intimacy with our spouse. When we do, we are to receive it "with gratitude" (1 Timothy 4:4). Covenantal intimacy, accompanied by sexual pleasure in marriage, should result in an abundance of prayer and praise.

chapter 15

SEX AND THE SINGLE PERSON

Too many persons have managed a beautifully whole existence without sexual intercourse to let us suppose that only nonvirgins need apply for full humanity. And too many unwhole and distorted people have jumped into almost any available bed to let us suppose that sexual intercourse is a magic carpet to personhood.
—Lewis Smedes—[1]

WHY DIDN'T GOD GIVE US AN 'ON-OFF' SWITCH?

During my seminary years in Southern California, my wife and I had the privilege of ministering to a wonderful group of about 400 career-age singles. Those were some of the most precious years of our early ministry. They were also some of the most challenging. The questions these single men and women asked put my newly-developing shepherd's heart to the test:

- "Why does our loving God allow single people to have such an intense sexual drive?"
- "Why didn't God give us an 'on-off' switch that can be activated when we get married or turned off if we remain single?"
- "I was once married. How do I deal with all my sexual memories?"

- "I believe the Lord has called me to be single. What do I do about my sexual feelings and impulses?"

In his book, *Sins Of The Body: Ministry In A Sexual Society,* Terry Muck comments on Mark Twain's observation about sex: "Mark Twain railed against God for parceling out to each human a source of universal joy and pleasure, at its peak in teenage years, then forbidding it until marriage and restricting it to one partner."[2]

The fact that we now reach puberty much earlier and get married much later makes being single much harder. The challenges are even greater for the higher number of divorcees and substantial number of widows and widowers. These precious folks now battle with sexual desires that they once righteously fulfilled in marriage. Single people's sexual feelings matter greatly to our loving heavenly Father. He has not left us in the dark as to how to deal with them.

GOD'S ALARM SYSTEM FOR SINGLES

We have a very loud security alarm system in our home that warns us of intruders. When our girls were single, it also served as a very handy curfew monitor. At least, that's what I thought. After she was married, one of my daughters admitted to knowing how to by-pass the alarm and slip back into the house unnoticed. She and her husband enjoy making me guess how many times they violated curfew. She says only once; he just laughs. The alarm is now fixed, ready for our grandchildren.

Almighty God has a built-in alarm system for singles, a monitor we call the sex drive, that desire for oneness. Unless He replaces it with a special calling to be single, God designed most of us with a desire for an intimate partner, especially expressed in the covenant of marriage:

> It is not good for the man to be alone;
> I will make him a helper suitable for him (Genesis 2:18).

He who finds a wife finds a good thing
And obtains favor from the LORD (Proverbs 18:22).

A SEVEN ALARM FIRE

Single people, when you begin to feel that God-given urge for sexual union, when those passions flame up, God is sounding some life-saving fire alarms in your heart. Don't run from them or ignore them. Certainly don't try to bypass them. They are there for your protection.

ALARM #1
GOD IS CALLING YOU TO WALK IN ONENESS WITH HIM.

Blaise Pascal, the seventeenth-century French philosopher is well-known for his statement that every one of us is born with a God-shaped vacuum. In his *Confessions*, written in the late fourth century, Augustine cried out in praise to the Lord: "The thought of you stirs [man] so deeply that he cannot be content unless he praises you, because you made us for yourself and our hearts find no peace until they rest in you" (*The Confessions of St. Augustine 1.1*). The Lord has built us with a desire for intimacy with Him. It is a relationship that is made possible through His Son, Jesus Christ.

The first response when your passion for oneness is stimulated is to be certain that you have trusted in Jesus Christ alone for your salvation and are enjoying a personal relationship with your heavenly Father:

This is eternal life, that they may know You, the only true
God, and Jesus Christ whom You have sent (John 17:3).

Therefore, having been justified by faith, we have peace
with God through our Lord Jesus Christ (Romans 5:1).

Jesus told us we will all be single in heaven (Matthew 22:28-30). There, face to face in intimate fellowship with Him, singleness tops marriage!

Intimacy with Him surpasses intimacy with any human being here or there. Therefore, as a born-again child of God you can now let the fires of sexual passion stir you to walk in the Spirit and manifest the fruit of the Spirit and not the deeds of the flesh (Galatians 5:16-23). You can let them motivate you to, "Be still" and know that He is God, your heavenly Father. (Psalm 46:10). You can let the heat of the moment become the fire of passion that opens your heart to Him. You can let your songs of praise flow from your lips.

A widow was expressing to me, her pastor, how a recent devotional time with the Lord had been especially rich and meaningful. It was a conversation I would fully expect from this godly woman. She very carefully whispered, "Pastor, I don't know how to say this any other way. That time of worship with God made me feel the way I felt when I was sexually intimate with my husband!"

ALARM #2
GOD IS CALLING YOU TO WALK IN ONENESS WITH FELLOW CHRISTIANS.

Many years ago I read one of the most indicting observations about my fellow members of the body of Christ. This non-Christian man, quoting what he declared to be the words of Mahatma Gandhi, suggested that if you persecute Christians, they'll unite. Leave them alone and they'll die fighting among themselves. Though sadly true to some degree, this is quite contrary to God's intention and design for Christ's church:

> The glory which You have given Me I have given to them, that they may be one, just as We are one; I in them and You in Me, that they may be perfected in unity, so that the world may know that You sent Me, and loved them, even as You have loved Me (John 17:22-23).

> Therefore I, the prisoner of the Lord, implore you to walk in a manner worthy of the calling with which you have been called, with all humility and gentleness, with patience,

showing tolerance for one another in love, being diligent to preserve the unity of the Spirit in the bond of peace. There is one body and one Spirit, just as also you were called in one hope of your calling; one Lord, one faith, one baptism, one God and Father of all who is over all and through all and in all (Ephesians 4:1-6).

Beloved singles, when those sexual feelings kick in, consider them as another reminder to walk in godly unity with your fellow Christians. Let that inward passion stir you to treat others as more important than yourself (Philippians 2:3). Let it push you to assemble with God's people as you stimulate them to love and good deeds (Hebrews 10:24-25). Let that drive for oneness lead you to take special care of the unlovely and unlovable people in your midst (1 Corinthians 12:20-26). When you do, you will be amazed at the deep and abiding fulfillment you will feel.

ALARM #3
GOD IS CALLING YOU TO PRAY REGARDING YOUR MARITAL FUTURE.

Marriage is not fundamentally a matter of one's personal choice; it really is a matter of God's calling. God calls some to be single; others to be married. Both conditions are equally precious in the sight of the Lord. To those called to be single, the apostle Paul writes that "it is good for a man not to touch a woman" (1 Corinthians 7:1). To those called to be married, he exhorts "each man is to have his own wife, and each woman is to have her own husband" (1 Corinthians 7:2).

Most scholars believe that at the time of his writing of his epistles the apostle Paul was not married. Whether he was never married, a widower or a divorcee rejected by an unbelieving spouse remains a matter of debate. However, what he wrote to his fellow singles moves us from the academic to the personal:

Yet I wish that all men were even as I myself am. However,

each man has his own gift from God, one in this manner, and another in that. But I say to the unmarried and to widows that it is good for them if they remain even as I (1 Corinthians 7:7-8).

Single people, when the passion alarm sounds, don't ignore it. See it as God drawing your attention to pray for His will regarding whether you are to marry or remain single. In those moments of increasing sexual passion pray for the strength to honor the Lord in your singleness. Pray also for your future spouse and for the maturity you will need to be a responsible, caring marriage partner. In other words, P.U.S.H.—Pray Until Something Happens!

If you feel that your God-given desire for sexual union cannot be fully satisfied in singleness, then God may be calling you to get married. Either way, married or single, can be God's best for you as long as you follow His will and not your own. That, of course, means marrying someone who is also a born-again believer (2 Corinthians 6:14. Also read 1 Corinthians 7:39 where "in the Lord" refers to a fellow believer). In the words of Tevye in *Fiddler on the Roof*, "A bird may love a fish, but where will they build their home together?" When God does call you to marry, He also will expect that you find a spouse His way, which is "in sanctification and honor, not in lustful passion, like the Gentiles who do not know God" (1 Thessalonians 4:4-5).

ALARM #4
GOD IS CALLING YOU TO LEARN SELF-CONTROL.

I define maturity, at least in part, as the ability to delay gratification. Mature people wait; immature people don't. Our graveyards are filled with people who were in a hurry to get somewhere and were killed while speeding. Our prisons are packed with murderers who couldn't wait to see certain people dead. If they just had a little self-control, nature would have eventually done the job for them. Our bankruptcy courts are jammed with people who didn't have the self-discipline to save the money. Instead, they charged, leveraged, or borrowed themselves into financial ruin.

In this "hook up" culture, too many singles have bought the lie that waiting until marriage for sexual intimacy serves no purpose. Many prefer "casual friendships with benefits." The world has convinced them that it is possible to have instant casual sex, devoid of intimacy and commitment, only to have them realize there is no lasting joy in this kind of culture of disconnection. Too many have paid the heavy price for their impulsive immaturity and have suffered the long-term physical, emotional, and spiritual consequences brought on by their lack of self-control.

Possibly considering the lesser of two evils, the apostle Paul was bold enough to say, "if they do not have *self-control*, let them marry; for it is better to marry than to burn with passion" (1 Corinthians 7:9, emphasis added). He was not teaching that uncontrolled lust constitutes God's special permission to marry. He was acknowledging that if you truly believe God is calling you to a life of physical intimacy, then don't fight it. Better to marry than to be burning with passion. Celibacy is simply not for you! However, don't be in too big of a hurry.

Biblically speaking, *waiting* is a form of *worship*. It expresses your strongest hope in the timing of God (Psalm 37:3-7; Isaiah 40:27-31). While you wait for His will to unfold concerning a marriage partner you have a major life lesson to learn: self-control. It is one of the qualities the indwelling Holy Spirit is continually seeking to develop in you (Galatians 5:22-23). Frankly, it is an attribute that is fundamental to success in every area of life, whether in the home, the community, the workplace, or in the church. It is also a major life skill you want to have in your life and the life of a potential marriage partner! Learn it well. When it comes to wanting sexual intimacy just say, "No, not yet! I'm waiting for God's perfect timing."

ALARM #5
GOD IS CALLING YOU TO IMMEDIATE CHRISTIAN SERVICE.

To some, singleness feels more like a closed door than a divine opportunity. However, that same divinely created drive for sexual fulfillment produces specific energy in a single person that can be rightly used in very effective Christian service. In fact, the apostle Paul describes the spiritual and ministerial advantages of being single:

> But I want you to be free from concern. One who is unmarried is concerned about the things of the Lord, how he may please the Lord; but one who is married is concerned about the things of the world, how he may please his wife, and his interests are divided. The woman who is unmarried, and the virgin, is concerned about the things of the Lord, that she may be holy both in body and spirit; but one who is married is concerned about the things of the world, how she may please her husband. This I say for your own benefit; not to put a restraint upon you, but to promote what is appropriate, and to secure undistracted devotion to the Lord (1 Corinthians 7:32-35).

Whereas I thank God for the *holy distraction* that marriage and family bring to those He calls to be married, I also praise the Lord for the many *undistracted* single servants of God who are free to serve in the local church and in other ministries around the world.

As a pastor, I have observed that the degree to which a single person backs off from Christian service, to that degree his sexual frustration increases. Conversely, the degree to which a married person backs off from his responsibility to be effective in his marriage and family, to that degree his Christian service is negatively affected.

Single people, when the sexual passions flare up, don't suppress them. Get busy serving the Lord. Your God-given desire for unity can be expressed and fulfilled in effective service and undistracted devotion to Christ.

ALARM #6
GOD IS CALLING YOU TO LEARN TO BUILD INTIMATE RELATIONSHIPS.

If the truth were told by those who promote this new wave of disconnection, jumping from one meaningless relationship to another is actually very empty. Almighty God created us for much more. In His wisdom He gave each of us a sex drive (a desire for oneness) to stimulate a desire for more substantial relationships.

In the Hebrew language of the Old Testament there are different words that refer to varying levels of friendship. More than word studies, these provide practical insights as we seek to develop life-long friendships, whether single or married.

LEVEL 1: THE CASUAL ACQUAINTANCE (HEBREW: REA')

> You shall love your neighbor ("acquaintance," Hebrew: *rea'*) as yourself (Leviticus 19:18).

Unless we live on some remote island, our lives are filled with people-sightings. Most of us could list hundreds of neighbors, fellow students, co-workers, and others we would consider casual friends or, at least, passing acquaintances. Think of the people on this planet we have yet to meet—about seven billion of them! And whatever number of people God allows to come directly into our path deserve to be loved and valued as He has loved and valued us. As we learn to love all our *neighbors* in such a way, God singles out some of those relationships to go even deeper.

LEVEL 2: THE SACRIFICIAL FRIEND (HEBREW: 'AHAB)

Contrary to what many think, popularity—i.e. being stuck in an endless pile of Level 1 casual relationships, is a dead end street. King Solomon's observation in Proverbs 18:24 is sadly true:

> A man of too many friends (i.e. "acquaintances," Hebrew: *rea'*) comes to ruin (i.e. "shattered or broken," Hebrew: *ra'a*), But there is a friend (i.e. "a loving friend," Hebrew: 'ahab) who sticks closer than a brother (Proverbs 18:24).

Without a deeper emotional connection with others our lives become shattered and broken. Who among us has not felt a sense of loneliness, even in a stadium with 30,000 sports fans? We develop more meaningful relationships with our *neighbors* (i.e. our casual friends) by taking the time to learn their likes, dislikes, values, and dreams. This information then allows us to make our own self-sacrificial decisions regarding how to best meet their needs, thus treating them as more important than ourselves (Philippians 2:3). When they do the same we move from being casual acquaintances to being sacrificial friends "that stick closer than a brother" (Proverbs 18:24). Besides bringing greater fulfillment to our lives, these relationships prepare us for the most intimate level of friendship, the trusted companion.

LEVEL 3: THE TRUSTED COMPANION (HEBREW: CHABER)

> [Your wife] is your companion (i.e. "guide," Hebrew: *chabereth*) and your wife by covenant (Malachi 2:14).

This is the level of inter-personal relationships that speaks of being knit together as trusted companions and guides. In modern terms, these are fellow life coaches who are committed to each other's growth. Obviously, this kind of relationship certainly does not happen quickly. It is the fruit of long-term love and loyalty that produces a true and lasting companionship. These are also the intimate friendships that cause the greatest joy or, if broken, the greatest heartache. Real *chaber* friendships are rare but attainable. In fact, they are the goal.

I read many years ago that the ancient wedding vows of a Jewish couple, even those whose marriages were arranged, contained a promise to continue the life-long work required to become a *chaber,* a trusted companion.

What has this to do with the driving passions of our libido? Each of us is created with a God-given vacuum for authentic intimacy with God and our fellow humans. The sex drive is a call to learn how to effectively develop relationships from fact-finding, loving acquaintances (*rea'*) to self-sacrificial friends (*'ahab*) and, ultimately, to trusted companions and life coaches (*chaber*). Certainly these are lessons that need to be learned prior to marriage. So, when the alarm sounds, go build a friendship, one level at a time.

ALARM #7
GOD IS CALLING YOU TO A LIFE OF CONTENTMENT.

Loneliness breeds a gnawing restlessness that can consume; an unrelenting vacuum that seems to never fill. It is truly the disease of emptiness that can attack any of us whether we are married or single, male or female, young believer or mature saint. Even the apostle Paul honestly admitted his seasons of loneliness (2 Timothy 1:4). He also shared the secret of his contentment, no matter what happened in his life. I have added my thoughts as to what I believe he is saying:

> Not that I speak from want *(God has provided all my needs)*, for I have learned to be content *(strong enough to stand alone)*[3] in whatever circumstances I am. I know how to get along with humble means *(in the hard times)*, and I also know how to live in prosperity *(in the easy times)*; in any and every circumstance I have learned the secret of being filled and going hungry *(being empty)*, both of having abundance and suffering need. *(And here's the secret, the key to contentment)* I can do all things through Him who strengthens me (Philippians 4:11-13).

I appreciate Dr. John MacArthur's exhortation to singles. Frankly, it's a good reminder to us married folks, as well:

> The message of 1 Corinthians 7 is that those who possess God's special care for singleness will be happier if they remain single, and all others will be happier if they marry as God leads. Marriage does not prevent great devotion to Christ, nor does singleness guarantee it, but by definition it

is easier for a single person to be singleminded in the things of the Lord. Perhaps God will call or has called you to experience "the grace of life" (1 Peter 3:7). Perhaps He will not spare you "trouble in this life" (1 Cor. 7:28). Whatever your situation, be content to remain as you are—a point Paul makes four separate times in 1 Corinthians 7 (vv. 17, 20, 24, 26)—all the while doing your best to serve God and His people in this life. The bonds of love you cultivate now will spill over to perfection in the next life.[4]

Stop trying to find ways to sidestep the alarms. When the passions fire up, realize:

- God is calling you to walk in oneness with Him—today!
- God is calling you to walk in oneness with fellow Christians—today!
- God is calling you to pray regarding your marital future—today!
- God is calling you to learn self-control—today!
- God is calling you to immediate Christian service—today!
- God is calling you to learn how to build intimate relationships—today!
- God is calling you to a life of contentment—today!

Do this today and God will take care of tomorrow. Be comforted by the words of Jesus: "So do not be anxious for tomorrow" (Matthew 6:34). Your singleness, whether temporary or permanent, is a tremendous gift to the body of Christ. Even more so, it is God's gift to you. Thank Him for it—today!

A WORD ABOUT DATING

There are many fine books about the moral cautions that need to be taken should you decide to date. Some have chosen the road of courtship rather than dating.[5] Having raised three daughters and many foster-children, I can assure you of the need for clear guidelines. Fail to plan and you truly are planning to fail.

Rather than list my own guidelines, I want to share those I gleaned from Randy Alcorn's book, *The Purity Principle*. Frankly, they are strikingly similar to the ones I used with my daughters and foster-daughters.

Heed these words, not just from two shepherds, but from two concerned and experienced fathers. In fact, I suggest you post them on your mirror and review them every time you are preparing to go out with someone of the opposite sex, whether you call it a date or not:

- If you're a Christian, date only Christians (see 2 Corinthians 6:14).
- If you're a committed disciple, date only committed disciples.
- Christ is with you all evening—wherever you go and whatever you do.
- Remember your date is your brother or sister, not your "lover" (see 1 Timothy 5:1-2).
- Go out in groups, not alone.
- Focus on talk, not touch; conversation, not contact.
- Avoid fast-moving relationships or instant intimacy.
- Plan the entire evening in advance, with no gaps.
- Avoid set-ups—never be alone: on a couch, in a car late at night, in a house or bedroom.
- Be accountable to someone about your purity.
- Imagine your parents and church leaders are watching you through the window. God *is* watching (see Jeremiah 16:17).
- Don't do anything with your date you wouldn't want someone else doing with your future mate.
- Beware of the "moral wear down" of long dating relationships and long engagements. Once young people and parents agree

on marriage, it's dangerous to wait longer than necessary (see 1 Corinthians 7:8-9).[6]

A WORD ABOUT MASTURBATION

The subject is bound to come up, not just as it relates to singles but also to those who are married. Rather than discuss it here, I am choosing to place my thoughts about this controversial subject in the Appendix, just in case some of those married folks skipped this chapter related to singles. Feel free to jump ahead now, with an open heart, mind, and Bible. Then join us back here as we move on to consider *Part Three: Man's Abuses*.

PART THREE:

MAN'S ABUSES

chapter 16

MISSING THE TARGET

As one who does a lot of target shooting, I enjoy telling the story of the half-blind farmer who was purported to be a phenomenal marksman. In fact, he never missed hitting the bulls-eye. People could see clear evidence of his incredible accuracy on fence posts and barns all over town. At least, that's what it seemed. However, when asked by a young admirer how he accomplished this amazing feat, he finally whispered the truth: "Son, I shoot first and draw the circle later."

What Holy God creates, sinful man confuses and abuses. This is especially true of God's design for human sexuality. Keeping divinely created sexuality separate from sin's distortions is no easy task. To do so, we must have a fixed target—a clearly biblical understanding of what is of God and what is not. That way, we can know how close we have come to His righteousness.

Sadly, for those of us who think we can live a life of moral relativity ("Anything goes"), there is no fixed target. Even among those who believe that almighty God has laid out standards of holiness, there is far too much subjectivity ("You do your thing; I'll do mine"). Fundamentally, both approach life the same way. Ready! Fire! Draw the circle! Declare myself, "Right on target!" It's so much easier that way.

MISSING HIS GLORY

The Greek word for sin, *hamartia*, speaks of missing the mark. In essence, sin is any thought, word, or deed that misses the target of God's impeccable attributes, His holy standards, His righteous character, and inexplicable majesty. The sum total of these are sometimes referred to as the *glory* of God. They are the fixed target of our lives. However, when it comes to hitting the target of God's perfections in our own lives, none of us are perfect shots. The apostle Paul reminds us that "all have sinned and *fall short* of the glory of God" (Romans 3:23, my emphasis). The apostle John adds his concern that we not try to fake our accuracy: "If we say that we have no sin, we are deceiving ourselves and the truth is not in us. . . . If we say that we have not sinned, we make Him (i.e. God) a liar and His word is not in us" (1 John 1:8, 10). The writer to the Hebrews also warns of the danger of drawing the circle after the shot and becoming "hardened by the deceitfulness of sin" (Hebrews 3:13).

MISSING HIS ONENESS

What has this to do with immorality? One of the *glories* of God is His oneness (Deuteronomy 6:4). As described previously, our Creator designed us as sexual beings in order to reflect that attribute. In particular, the sin of immorality is any thought, word or deed that misses the target of God's oneness—the *echad* of God. It shows up as a number of oneness-missing lustful thoughts and immoral behaviors. As such, we need to spend a lifetime focusing on the target and learning how to improve our aim.

chapter 17

LUSTFUL THOUGHTS AND IMMORAL BEHAVIORS

SOW A THOUGHT, REAP A WORLD OF TROUBLE

Who hasn't heard it? Samuel Smiles' famous quote is well worth repeating:

> Sow a thought and you reap an act.
> Sow an act and you reap a habit.
> Sow a habit and you reap a character.
> Sow a character and you reap a destiny.

The old clichéd saying became that way because it is so true. Lustful thoughts, if left unchecked, become the immoral acts and habits of life that influence our character and, eventually, our destiny.

YOU ARE WHAT YOU THINK

> As in water face reflects face,
> So the heart of man reflects man (Proverbs 27:19).

I once read that the average man has a lustful thought every seven seconds. I have not seen the research. However, if it is true, then that's some pretty active brain function for the gender that is often accused of being a bit brain-dead. The current thinking is that since lust is such a common human event, we shouldn't expend any effort fighting the urge. After all, lust doesn't hurt. I hold a different view, both from my experience and my theology. Our Creator cares about every thought. He knows they do more than lead to action; they represent who we really are. We will become what we let our minds dwell on. The book of Proverbs expressed it this way: "For as he thinks within himself, so he is" (Proverbs 23:7). Whether it's every seven seconds or every seven hours, it's those little thoughts that we must not ignore. Samuel Johnson said it well, "The chains of habit are too weak to be felt until they are too strong to be broken."

THE BRIGHT SIDE OF LUST

This is not to say that all lust is evil. Lust, in and of itself, is amoral; neither right nor wrong, good nor bad. The word *epithumeo* used in the New Testament for lust denotes strong desire of any kind. It clearly describes the apostle Paul's eagerness to see his beloved converts in Thessalonica (1 Thessalonians 2:17) and his deep desire to depart from this world and be with Christ (Philippians 1:23). It is even used of Jesus, who earnestly desired (literally, "lustfully lusted") to eat the Passover with His disciples, before He was crucified (Luke 22:15).

The issue, then, is not whether we lust or not, but what it is we are lusting after. To have a strong desire for God is right. To have a deep and eager desire for my wife is certainly appropriate, even every seven seconds.

THOU SHALT NOT COVET

Sinful lust is quite different. It is the strong, inward passion to possess that which God has not permitted us to possess. We lust sinfully after things that do not belong to us: "You shall not covet ("delight in," Hebrew: *chamad*) your neighbor's house; you shall not covet your neighbor's wife or his male servant or his female servant or his ox or his donkey or anything that belongs to your neighbor" (Exodus 20:17, emphasis added)

Though sinful lust comes in many forms, for our purposes, we will be primarily talking about sinful sexual lust. In particular, I will be addressing the kind of lust that is the selfish, unchecked search for counterfeit fellowship that steps outside the bounds of God's design for the sexual union. It is desiring sexually that which God does not permit us to have. Randy Alcorn summarizes it well, "Lust is mental promiscuity"[1]

In the New Testament, we find a number of words and phrases that give us an overview of the character of inward lust:

- Lust of the heart (Matthew 5:27-28; Romans 1:24)
- Degrading passion/shameful lust (Romans 1:26)
- Burning (evil) desire (Romans 1:27; 1 Corinthians 7:9; Colossians 3:5)
- Depraved mind (Romans 1:28)
- Impurity (Galatians 5:19; Colossians 3:5)
- Sensuality (Galatians 5:19)

They form a multi-faceted obstacle, clouding our view of the *echad* of God.

WE GET TO BLAME ADAM

How did sinful lust even get here? Who's to blame? Initially, we get to kick Adam for our struggle with lust, since it was through him that sin, in general, entered the world (Romans 5:12). Because of him, each of us was born with a sin nature that has an evil bent to violate all of God's holy standards. I appreciate the way the New English Translation expresses King David's words as he repented of his sin of adultery. He wasn't making excuses for his choices. He was, however, showing where it all started: "Look, I was prone to do wrong from birth;/I was a sinner the moment my mother conceived me (Psalm 51:5, The New English Translation). Shortly after, David's son, Solomon, added: "Foolishness is bound up in the heart of a child" (Proverbs 22:15).

Sinful lust is fundamentally an innate heart issue in every man, woman, and child. Jesus Himself said:

> That which proceeds out of the man, that is what defiles the man. For from within, out of the heart of men, proceed the evil thoughts, fornications... adulteries, deeds of coveting... deceit ... sensuality... pride and foolishness. All these evil things proceed from within and defile the man (Mark 7:20-23).

Without the redemptive and sanctifying work of God in our lives, it is impossible for any human being, living on this side of heaven, to avoid sinful lust. Because of Adam's sin in the garden, it is like an alien seed implanted in our heart, ready at any moment to pop out its ugly head.

WE ALSO GET TO BLAME OURSELVES

Put a three-year-old boy and girl in a bathtub. No problem. However, it would certainly be foolish to permit them to bathe together fifteen years later. It's not that children, even at three years old, are completely innocent; they are just less experienced. In time, while their natural sexual development occurs, their sin natures will also gain more sinful experience. Solomon was not exaggerating when he wrote that "a child who gets his own way brings shame to his mother" (Proverbs 29:15).

Although, at the moment of our conception, sinful lust became a deep-seated part of our Adamic sin nature, it is also something we develop over a lifetime. Given the influence of our sinful flesh within us, the twisted values of the world around us, and the attacks of Satan toward us, it is no wonder we learn quickly. Therefore, we must daily confront the sinful lust that abides deep within our sinful hearts. If we do not, it is just a short step until we are engaging in immoral behavior in all its anti-oneness forms.

LUSTFUL THOUGHTS. IMMORAL BEHAVIORS. WHAT'S THE DIFFERENCE?

Simply stated, *lustful thoughts* are any *thoughts* that violate the oneness that is God's intended design for our sexuality; *immoral behaviors* are any *actions* that do the same. Is there, therefore, any substantial difference between sinful lust and immoral behavior? Before I answer, let me tell you about one of the strangest phone calls I have ever received.

The call came from a gas station attendant who apparently attended my local church. He refused to give his name. He confessed that he had been looking out the window of his cash booth and was, at that very moment, lusting after a beautiful female who was pumping gas. He then added, "Pastor, doesn't the Bible say that when you lust after a woman you have committed adultery with her already in your heart?" I affirmed what I knew to be the words of Jesus in Matthew 5:28. So far things seemed pretty normal. He then asked, "Since I have already committed the sin of adultery with her in my heart, would it be okay if I went ahead and had sex with her?"

Even though I doubted it was a real possibility, I hastened to give him my answer. I explained, "There is a vast difference between lust in the heart and immorality in the flesh. Sinful lust is between you and God. Sinful behaviors impact you, God, and a host of others. Do you really think that Jesus would give you permission to have sexual intercourse with anybody you are lusting after?" Hopefully, it made sense to him.

GOD HATES IMMORALITY

The Bible does not mince words about God's passionate hatred of immorality in all its forms. It is so very contrary to who He is and what He designed for us, especially as believers. A few reminders:

> Flee immorality. Every other sin that a man commits is outside the body, but the immoral man sins against his own body. Or do you not know that your body is a temple of the Holy Spirit who is in you, whom you have from God, and that you are not your own? For you have been bought with a price: therefore glorify God in your body (1 Corinthians 6:18-20).

But immorality or any impurity or greed must not even be named among you, as is proper among saints. . . . Let no one deceive you with empty words, for because of these things the wrath of God comes upon the sons of disobedience. Therefore do not be partakers with them (Ephesians 5:3, 6-7).

Therefore consider the members of your earthly body as dead to immorality, impurity, passion, evil desire, and greed, which amounts to idolatry. For it is because of these things that the wrath of God will come upon the sons of disobedience (Colossians 3:5-6).

For this is the will of God, your sanctification; that is, that you abstain from sexual immorality . . . the Lord is the avenger in all these things. . . . For God has not called us for the purpose of impurity. . . . So, he who rejects this is not rejecting man but the God who gives His Holy Spirit to you (1 Thessalonians 4:3, 6, 8).

Therefore be imitators of God, as beloved children; and walk in love, just as Christ also loved you and gave Himself up for us, an offering and a sacrifice to God as a fragrant aroma. But immorality or any impurity or greed must not even be named among you, as is proper among saints; and there must be no filthiness and silly talk, or coarse jesting, which are not fitting, but rather giving of thanks. For this you know with certainty, that no immoral or impure person or covetous man, who is an idolater, has an inheritance in the kingdom of Christ and God. Let no one deceive you with empty words, for because of these things the wrath of God comes upon the sons of disobedience.

Therefore do not be partakers with them; for you were formerly darkness, but now you are Light in the Lord; walk as children of Light (for the fruit of the Light consists in all goodness and righteousness and truth), trying to learn what is pleasing to the Lord (Ephesians 5:1-10).

chapter 18

FILLING THE BUCKET ONE GRAIN AT A TIME

Earlier I spoke of how wrong it would be to put a bucket of sand in a classic 1955 Chevy's gas tank. It simply wasn't designed for it and would immediately destroy that high performance engine. However, what if I suggested trying to gradually acclimate the car to run on sand by putting a tiny grain in the tank each day? Of course, this would be equally as foolish. I would only be delaying the inevitable. The only difference between the impact of a bucket of sand and a grain of sand is t-i-m-e.

This illustrates the attitudes I've found in many Christians. Most who claim to be born-again followers of Jesus Christ understand God's prohibitions against sexual immorality. Many have already experienced some of the painful consequences and hope to never repeat the offense. Never again will they pour a bucket of sand in the gas tank. Sadly, too many unsuspecting members of God's family are nonetheless filling their spiritual tanks with little grains of sand—those small indulgences and miniscule compromises that, if left unchecked, turn into a bucket of life-destroying immorality.

THE PERISHING PRINCIPLE

Snowflakes can be dangerous. Ask anyone who has lived in snow country, especially those who have seen the destructive force of an avalanche. I once heard, "A tiny snowflake isn't much by itself, but it takes a bulldozer to move them when they cooperate."

Sin also accumulates. Even the smallest of abuses of our God-given sexuality can result in a continuous hunger and thirst for more frequent and diverse expressions of our sexuality, which simply cannot be quenched. It's what many of my fellow pastors refer to as The Perishing Principle. James, in his epistle, describes this deadly progression:

> But each one is tempted when he is carried away and enticed by his own *lust*. Then when *lust* has conceived, it gives birth to *sin*; and when sin is accomplished, it brings forth *death*" (James 1:14-15, emphasis added).

Lust results in *sin*, which results in *death*. At one of our purity seminars, one man rightly observed the first letter of each of these key words—L.S.D., the same initials as the deadly drug that destroyed so many minds in the 1960s. However, more than any illicit drug, we must be on guard against this deadly process of *lust, sin* and *death*.

The apostle Paul spoke of many in his day who, "having lost all sensitivity, they have given themselves over to sensuality so as to indulge in every kind of impurity, *with a continual lust for more*" (Ephesians 4:19, New International Version, emphasis added). He also described this perishing principle as he pointed out the former condition of the Roman Christians, "you presented your members as slaves to impurity and to lawlessness, *resulting in further lawlessness*" (Romans 6:19, emphasis added).

One of the ancient writings of the early second century, called the Didaché, embodies the teaching of the apostles. It also offers its warning concerning the danger of ignoring sin:

> My child, flee from every evil thing, and from every likeness of it. Be not prone to anger, for anger leads to murder. Be

neither jealous, nor quarrelsome, nor of hot temper, for out of all these murders are engendered. My child, be not a lustful one, for lust leads to fornication. Be neither a filthy talker, nor of lofty eye, for out of all these adulteries are engendered.[1]

THERE IS NO SUCH THING AS CONTROLLED LUST

What we think about today could become a behavior tomorrow. The behaviors that excite us tomorrow will bore us the day after tomorrow. In his book, *Sins of the Body*, Terry Muck presents the testimony of an anonymous church leader who discovered this truth too late:

> I learned quickly that lust, like physical sex, points only in one direction. You cannot go back to a lower level and stay satisfied. Always you want more. A magazine excites, a movie thrills, a live show really makes the blood run. . . . Lust does not satisfy; it stirs up. I no longer wonder how deviants can get into child molesting, masochism, and other abnormalities. Although such acts are incomprehensible to me, I remember well where I ended up was also incomprehensible to me when I started.[2]

There is no such thing as controlled sinful lust. It always degenerates. Just as the New Testament presents a number of facets of sinful lust, it also presents a number of facets of immoral behavior. Often, these lead into each other. Some are grains of sand, the rest buckets. All of them mess up the engine of our lives:

- Impurity (Greek: *akatharsia*) (Ephesians 5:3,5; Colossians 3:5; Galatians 5:19)
- Sensuality/lasciviousness/licentiousness/unbridled lust (Greek: *aselgeia)* (Galatians 5:19; Ephesians 4:19; 2 Peter 2:6-8)

- Degrading, vile passion (Greek: *atimia pathos*) (Romans 1:26)
- Evil desire (Greek: *kakos epithumia*) (Colossians 3:5)
- Passion/inordinate affection (Greek: *pathos*) (Colossians 3:5)
- Impure, filthy, disgraceful, obscene talk or actions (Greek: *aischrotes*) (Ephesians 5:4,12)
- Coarse joking (Greek: *eutrapelia*) (Ephesians 5:4)
- Indecent, unseemly, shameful acts (Greek: *aschemosune*) (Romans 1:27)
- Lewd behavior (Hebrew: *zimmah*) (Leviticus 18:17; Ezekiel 23:21)
- Shameful nudity/indecent exposure (Hebrew: *'ervah*) (Leviticus 18:6-18)
- Immorality/fornication (Greek: *porneia*) (Galatians 5:19; Colossians 3:5; 1 Corinthians 6:18)
- Adultery (Hebrew: *na'aph*; Greek: *moicheia*) (Exodus 20:14; Mark 7:21)
- Prostitution/harlotry (Hebrew: *zanah*; Greek: *porne)* (Leviticus 19:29; 1 Corinthians 6:16)
- Rape (i.e. to ravish/violate someone) (Hebrew: *'anah*) (Lamentations 5:11; 2 Samuel 13:1-19)
- Effeminism (Greek: *malakos*) (1 Corinthians 6:9)
- Homosexuality (Greek: *arsenokoites*) (1 Corinthians 6:9; 1 Timothy 1:10; cf. Leviticus 18:22;   20:13; Romans 1:18-32)
- Incest (Leviticus 18:6-16; 2 Samuel 13 and possibly 1 Corinthians 5:1)
- Bestiality (Exodus 22:19; Leviticus 18:23; 20:16; Deuteronomy 27:21)

The problem with these sins is that they not only corrupt us, they also de-sensitize us. They not only unleash the passion, they also cripple our repulsion against all sin, like a mind-altering drug that destroys the inhibitions in our brains.

I AM A POTENTIAL SEX OFFENDER

In 1989 serial killer Ted Bundy was executed in the electric chair by the State of Florida. In a public interview he declared that his life was one of uncontrolled lust and engaging in sexual activities that eventually resulted in murdering over thirty people:

> It happened in stages, gradually. My experience with pornography generally, but with pornography that deals on a violent level with sexuality. . . . I would keep looking for more potent, more explicit, more graphic kinds of material . . . you reach a point where the pornography only goes so far, you reach that jumping off point where you begin to wonder if maybe actually doing it would give that which is beyond just reading it or looking at it.[3]

In 1991 the world was shocked to learn of Jeffrey Dahmer, who confessed to raping, killing, dismembering and later consuming the flesh of some of his seventeen victims. How very repulsive! Sentenced to fifteen life terms, totaling almost a thousand years, he was eventually bludgeoned to death by a fellow prison inmate. His life was also the story of lust, sin, and death.

Why speak of such gruesome matters? Every time we lust, we are putting a grain of sand in the tank that could eventually turn us into another Ted Bundy. Every time we allow impurity to control us, we are on the road to becoming a Jeffrey Dahmer.

I am grateful for the convicting work of the indwelling Holy Spirit of God in the life of every believer. Without Him, our sinful lust would grow into behaviors beyond imagination. As difficult as it may seem, we must *all* admit, "I am a potential sex offender."

chapter 19

WALK INTO MY PARLOR

Every immoral act begins with deception. We face an on-going attack from three cruel, unrelenting enemies.

1. *WE ARE DECEIVED BY OUR OWN FLESH, WITH ITS NATURAL BENT TOWARD SIN.*

    Now the deeds of the flesh are evident, which are: immorality, impurity, sensuality . . . (Galatians 5:19).

2. *WE ARE DECEIVED BY THE WORLD, WITH ITS TWISTED VALUES.*

    For all that is in the world, the lust of the flesh and the lust of the eyes and the boastful pride of life, is not from the Father, but is from the world (1 John 2:16).

3. *WE ARE DECEIVED BY THE DEVIL, WITH HIS SPECIFIC PLAN TO OPPOSE ANYTHING GODLY.*

    Be of sober spirit, be on the alert. Your adversary, the devil, prowls about like a roaring lion, seeking someone to devour (1 Peter 5:8).

> You are of your father the devil, and you want to do the desires
> of your father. He was a murderer from the beginning, and
> does not stand in the truth, because there is no truth in him.
> Whenever he speaks a lie, he speaks from his own nature, for
> he is a liar, and the father of lies (John 8:44).

Whether faced with an attack from our flesh, the world, or the Devil, we need to honestly admit to God, each other, and ourselves that we are more vulnerable to immoral behavior than we think:

> Pride goes before destruction,
> And a haughty spirit before stumbling (Proverbs 16:18).

> Therefore let him who thinks he stands take heed that he
> does not fall (1 Corinthians 10:12).

Most of us do not enter marriage in hopes of someday breaking our marital covenant or vows of fidelity. Most of us in full-time Christian service do not enter the ministry with the dream of someday falling into immorality and destroying what we have worked so hard to build. I would like to believe that most Christians don't begin their day with a specific plan to fall morally. But it happens—to Christian singles, Christian married people, Christian pastors, and Christian church leaders. In the time it takes you to read this book, a shamefully large number of God's family will succumb to immorality's temporary pleasure and suffer life-long consequences.

The old poem by Mary Howitt, entitled, *The Spider and the Fly*, describes the subtle process of deception and seduction quite well. Though it was written two centuries ago and the spelling is a bit archaic, it's message is still relevant:

> "Will you walk into my parlour?" said the Spider to the Fly,
> 'Tis the prettiest little parlour that ever you did spy;

The way into my parlour is up a winding stair,
And I've a many curious things to shew when you are
   there."
"Oh no, no," said the little Fly, "to ask me is in vain,
For who goes up your winding stair can ne'er come down
   again."

The poem continues. Although the fly resists, little by little the cunning spider entices her toward the web of destruction until she is stuck and ultimately eaten alive—cast away as a dried carcass, as the spider awaits its next victim. The last part of this old rhyme gives the moral of the story:

And now dear little children, who may this story read,
To idle, silly flattering words, I pray you ne'er give heed:
Unto an evil counsellor, close heart and ear and eye,
And take a lesson from this tale, of the Spider and the Fly.[1]

My friends, that which is true of that unsuspecting little fly is happening to many of us today. Countless thousands of unsuspecting Christians are being caught in the web of immorality and are being eaten alive by the wickedness of sin.

How then does it happen? For most, it does not happen overnight. It is very much a degenerating process, a slippery slope to moral defeat.

Step #1: *Faltering in the Search for Biblical Wisdom*
   Step #2: *Failing in the Development of a Healthy
      Marriage*
      Step #3: *Fantasizing in the Arena of the Mind*
         Step #4: *Flirting with the Forbidden
            World of Seduction*
            Step #5: *Falling into the Trap of
               Immorality*

In the next chapters we will examine these five steps down to the horrible, muck-filled pit of immorality; the subtle walk into the parlor of life-consuming, death-producing immorality.

chapter 20

STEP #1
FALTERING IN THE SEARCH FOR BIBLICAL WISDOM

GETTING THINGS RIGHT WITH GOD

Falling into the trap of immorality begins with a fouled-up relationship with our Creator and a blockage of the free-flowing wisdom He offers His children (James 1:5; 3:13-18; 2 Timothy 3:16). It makes sense. When we turn away from God, we look for intimacy in all the wrong places. Randy Alcorn is spot on when he writes, "Ultimately, the battle for purity is won or lost in quietness, on our knees with God..."[1]

If you've walked the hallowed halls of Christianity for any length of time, you know the plan. You must grow in wisdom if you want the moral protection needed to avoid the wiles of immorality. It doesn't happen quickly. I wholeheartedly agree with Alan Redpath, evangelist and former pastor of Moody Memorial Church in Chicago: "The conversion of a soul is the miracle of a moment, the manufacture of a saint is the task of a lifetime."[2]

WHOSE VOICE AM I HEEDING TODAY?

I have the joy of being a senior pastor, a Bible teacher, a conference speaker,

117

and the president of JARON Ministries International. I also do a great deal of pastoral counseling and ministry consulting. My days are often filled with verbal, written, and electronic voice messages vying for my immediate attention. Although I love what I do, it sometimes causes my heart to shout, "No more, please!" Even so, there are two voices that call out to me every day which must never be ignored. To do so would mean moral disaster, not only for me, but also for my loved ones and my ministry.

King Solomon reminded his son that every day of his life there would be two women crying out for his undivided attention (Proverbs 7:4-5). On one side of the street is Wisdom. She is calling, "Come, spend the day with me and enjoy the pleasures I have to offer. They lead to abundant life" (Proverbs 8:1-36). On the other side of the street is Immorality. She too is calling, "Come, spend the day with me. I have many pleasures to offer, as well." What she fails to mention is that they lead to death (Proverbs 2:18). (I encourage you to read Proverbs 5-9 for the complete picture).

The wisdom to walk in purity comes from the Spirit of God as He uses the Word of God He desires to richly dwell in us (Colossians 3:16). In those often-repeated words, "Either the Bible will keep us from sin or sin will keep us from the Bible." The message is simple, yet so often discounted.

Whose voice are we heeding today? Are we listening to our Bible lying on a distant shelf, dusty, and unused? Do we hear it crying out to us, "Come, spend some time with me. I will show you the path to life." Or are we hearing the familiar call of our television remote control or our computer mouse, so worn and used? It doesn't need to shout; it's clearly within reach, as it whispers, "Nice to see you again. Relax. Don't worry. I'll feed your mind with unimagined pleasures." The book of Proverbs clearly states which is the better choice:

> The fear of the LORD is the beginning of knowledge;
> Fools despise wisdom and instruction (Proverbs 1:7).

> The fear of the LORD is the beginning of wisdom,

And the knowledge of the Holy One is understanding
(Proverbs 9:10).

King Solomon also states the moral consequences to the one who ignores the voice of wisdom that comes from the Word of God:

He will die for lack of instruction,
And in the greatness of his folly he will go astray
(Proverbs 5:23).

For the commandment is a lamp and the teaching
  is light;
And reproofs for discipline are the way of life,
To keep you from the evil woman,
From the smooth tongue of the adulteress
(Proverbs 6:23-24).

To protect ourselves from the seductive voice of immorality we must go back to the fundamentals of what the Bible states is necessary to stay spiritually healthy.

MY SPIRITUAL HEALTH INDICATORS

If I am to win the battle against sexual sin, I need to continually grow in:

- Fellowship — Engaging in loving, need-meeting relationships with other members of the body of Christ.
- Doctrine — Understanding and being able to defend the basic doctrines of the Christian faith taught in the Word of God.
- Worship — Responding in a variety of ways to the infinite majesty and glorious attributes of God.
- Service — Serving God and others, using the gifts and talents graciously given to me.

- Evangelism — Understanding the true gospel of grace alone through faith alone and sharing with others the good news of my hope in Christ.
- Discipleship — Helping others become loving, faithful, and obedient followers of Jesus Christ.
- Prayer — Communicating with my heavenly Father in sincere praise, repentance, and petition.

In order to do this, I must:

1. Meditate on God's Word daily. (Joshua 1:8; Psalm 1:2; 119:9-11; 2 Timothy 3:15-17)
2. Admit, confess and turn from my sin honestly. (1 John 1:9; Psalm 103:3, 8-14).
3. Take my spiritual pulse regularly.[3] (Proverbs 4:23).
4. Deal with my spiritual dryness openly.[4] (Psalm 42:1-11; 51:10-13)

DO YOU HAVE SOMETHING SPECIAL GOING ON WITH JESUS TODAY?

I no longer ask my adult children, "Did you read your Bible and pray today?" I assume they did. More often, they will hear me ask, "Did you tell Jesus you love Him today?" This is my gentle way of asking, "Do you have something special going on with Jesus today?" If not, my counsel to them and to you is to admit it to yourself, someone close to you, and, of course, to God.

It has been well said that today's spiritual neglect is the stuff of which tomorrow's immorality is made. To ignore our intimacy with God is to invite disaster. Quoting what I once heard were the last written words of an African pastor who was martyred for his faith, let's stop "meandering in the pool of mediocrity." May the heartfelt confessional of King David be the song of our hearts, as well:

Create in me a clean heart, O God,
And renew a steadfast spirit within me.
Do not cast me away from Your presence
And do not take Your Holy Spirit from me.
Restore to me the joy of Your salvation
And sustain me with a willing spirit.
Then I will teach transgressors Your ways,
And sinners will be converted to You
(Psalm 51:10-13).

chapter 21

STEP #2
FAILING IN THE DEVELOPMENT OF A HEALTHY MARRIAGE

THE MASTER GARDENER

I am a city boy through and through. While attending seminary and living in cement-ridden North Hollywood, California, I tried to grow carrots in my apartment planter box. I couldn't understand why they wouldn't grow. A farmer friend of mine, after hearing my answers to his series of questions, pointed out that it would be prudent if I stopped my daily routine of pulling the carrots out of the soil to check them. He also explained why I shouldn't be wiping off the tiny hairs. (I certainly didn't want hairy carrots.) I learned a valuable lesson from this seasoned farmer:

Things grow best when allowed to grow in good soil.

How odd of God to send someone like me to pastor a local church in the city of Fresno, located in the region of California that many consider to be the agricultural "Bread Basket of America." When I moved into our new home, I decided not to ruin my chances of having a healthy and good-looking yard. I hired a landscaper who was a master gardener. After many months and great expense, the yard was absolutely beautiful, the envy of the neighborhood. It was now my turn to take over the duties of caring for the lawns, bushes, trees, and flowerbeds. With a city boy's fervor, I cut them too short, fertilized them too much, and watered them too little. I pulled out healthy plants and left weeds behind. I even plucked the flowers off the peach tree, thinking it would help the real fruit to grow. (After all, I planted a *peach* tree, not a *flower* tree!)

Needless to say, the money I now spend on gardeners is well worth it. We often hear that the grass is always greener on the other side. That's not true:

The grass is greener where it has been taken care of properly.

This is obviously not a book about farming. However, both of these basic farming principles apply to marriage as well. Marriages grow best when allowed to grow in good soil. They also grow best when we take proper care of them.

It is in the soil of a growing, well-maintained marriage (or a healthy view of marriage on the part of singles) that we find a great deal of protection for our moral safety. It is one of the Master Gardener's best safeguards against immorality. Unfortunately, too many married partners have not taken proper care of their marriages. Many have forgotten to make sure the soil is well fed with the proper nutrients that help a marriage stay healthy and bear fruit. Too many singles have become cynical and disinterested, choosing cohabitation instead.

I admit that I have very little chance of ever becoming a great landscaper. However, I do think I am getting a handle on growing a marriage. Although my heavenly Father planted my marriage in heaven, I also know that the maintenance work has to be done one day at a time here on Earth. Thankfully, my wife and I are reaping today what we have nurtured and watered day after day, for almost forty years.

Again, through the pen of King Solomon, the Master Gardner speaks to every married couple. He also provides a mindset for singles:

Drink water from your own cistern
And fresh water from your own well.
Should your springs be dispersed abroad,
Streams of water in the streets?
Let them be yours alone
And not for strangers with you.
Let your fountain be blessed,
And rejoice in the wife of your youth.
As a loving hind and a graceful doe,
Let her breasts satisfy you at all times;
Be exhilarated always with her love.
For why should you, my son, be exhilarated with an
    adulteress
And embrace the bosom of a foreigner?
For the ways of a man are before the eyes of the LORD,
And He watches all his paths.
His own iniquities will capture the wicked,
And he will be held with the cords of his sin.
He will die for lack of instruction,
And in the greatness of his folly he will go astray
(Proverbs 5:15-23).

GETTING THINGS RIGHT WITH OUR SPOUSE

If we are going to avoid falling into the trap of immorality, we who are married must continually evaluate and improve our relationship with our spouse. Ten, twenty or thirty years from now, we can expect to live off the investment we make in our marriage today. Besides, if *we* don't spend time talking to our spouse about building a healthy relationship, *someone else* may.

What is the true condition of your marriage? Singles, what is the condition of your attitude toward marriage? Perhaps, it's time to do a little soil testing.[1]

chapter 22

STEP #3
FANTASIZING IN THE ARENA OF THE MIND

HARMLESS FANTASIES?

"A mind is a terrible thing to waste." The phrase comes from an advertisement for a college fund that helps people fill their minds with a quality education. I believe, however, the principle can also be applied to minds filled with another kind of waste: illicit sexual fantasies. If we are disregarding our relationship to God and ignoring our relationship to our spouse, it is only a short step down to the next level in the death trap of immorality: fantasizing in the arena of the mind.

Let me be direct. Men fantasize primarily about bodies—the perfect 10, with just the right amount of this, and not too much of that. In my opinion, this is certainly a part of what the apostle John refers to as "the lust of the eyes" (1 John 2:15-17). Women, on the other hand, most often fantasize about relationships—the perfect romance, the ideal mate, a man who is stronger in areas where her husband (or father) is weak, and someone sensitive and willing to pay attention to what she is saying. I refer to this as "the lust of the ears."

We are faced with a world of sex-educators who teach that sexual fantasies of any kind are merely the normal and harmless responses of an active libido. Adding to the problem is the world of media that fills our minds with its cyber-visions of perfection, offering its twisted view that fantasy sex is better, easier, and far more exciting. It is certainly less hassle.

God has a different agenda for our minds. Later, we will deal with the specifics of how to guard our minds by protecting, provisioning, purifying, and preparing them to deal with lustful thoughts and immoral behaviors. First, we need to understand the biblical relationship between the heart and the mind.

The *heart* in Scripture is really referring to the *mind*, the place where we make the decisions. With that in *mind*—or should I say, taking it to *heart*—consider the following admonitions:

> Do not desire her beauty in your heart (i.e. *your mind*),
> Nor let her capture you with her eyelids (Proverbs 6:25).

> Do not let your heart (i.e. *your mind*) turn aside to her ways (Proverbs 7:25).

> But the things that proceed out of the mouth come from the heart (i.e. *the mind*), and those defile the man. For out of the heart (i.e. *the mind*) come evil thoughts, murders, adulteries, fornications, thefts, false witness, slanders. These are the things which defile the man . . . (Matthew 15:18-20).

> You have heard that it was said, 'You shall not commit adultery'; but I say to you, that every one who looks at a woman with lust for her has already committed adultery with her in his heart (i.e. *his mind*) (Matthew 5:27-28).

Using some different words but teaching the same concept, the apostle Paul writes:

Finally, brethren, whatever is true, whatever is honorable, whatever is right, whatever is pure, whatever is lovely, whatever is of good repute, if there is any excellence and if anything worthy of praise, dwell ("calculate," Greek: *logizomai*) on these things (Philippians 4:8).

But put on the Lord Jesus Christ, and make no provision ("forethought," Greek: *pronoia*) for the flesh in regard to its lusts (Romans 13:14).

LUST LOOKING FOR AN OPPORTUNITY

When we allow our minds to continually dwell on immorality (i.e. things that fall short of God's design for sexual oneness), it is only a matter of time before we will become "lust looking for an opportunity." Our mental state will become such that if we knew for certain we couldn't get caught, we would commit the act. Unfortunately, many do, even knowing they will be discovered. In fact, some come to the point of wanting to get caught. In their minds, it seems the only real way of escape.

When the timing and atmosphere is right, I will often invite men who know they are "on the verge" of fornication or adultery to come forward for prayer. Prompted by their convicted hearts and surrounded by their fellow strugglers, many have! One of my great joys is to have witnessed them humbly asking God to transform their lives and renew their minds before the mental fantasies became behavioral reality. However, one of my heartfelt discouragements is to have also witnessed too many who have allowed those fantasies to bear even more devastating fruit. Lust looking for an opportunity easily finds one!

chapter 23

STEP #4
FLIRTING WITH THE FORBIDDEN
WORLD OF SEDUCTION

Show me someone not walking in authentic intimacy with God, whose marital attitude is suffering the pangs of indifference, and whose mind is freely engaged in illicit sexual fantasy, and I will present you with someone about to take the next step toward a covenant-breaking, immoral encounter. That person is entering into *relational limbo*. When this happens, two things commonly follow.

1. We develop a wandering eye.

Immoral people attract immoral people. People on the lookout find people on the lookout. Eye contact is made and the rest is history. The apostle Peter spoke of those who have "eyes full of adultery that never cease from sin" (2 Peter 2:14). King Solomon rightly warned his son about that deadly look: "Do not desire her beauty in your heart, / *Nor let her capture you with her eyelids*" (Proverbs 6:25, emphasis added). That certainly drives a wooden stake in the oft-quoted statement: "I can look but I just can't touch." We best not even look!

2. We develop a careless lifestyle.

We throw caution to the wind. We take risks, often thinking nothing will happen because we would never let it go too far. But it does go too far—way too far—farther than ever imagined. Our wandering eyes and careless lifestyles make us highly susceptible to the enticements of the immoral woman or man. We become unsuspecting prey for the fornicator or adulterer who is on the lookout for just the person we have become. As if writing a theatrical script, King Solomon describes the deadly scenario in dramatic detail:

> For at the window of my house
> I looked out through my lattice,
> And I saw among the naive,
> And discerned among the youths
> A young man lacking sense,
> Passing through the street near her corner;
> And he takes the way to her house,
> In the twilight, in the evening,
> In the middle of the night and in the darkness.
> And behold, a woman comes to meet him,
> Dressed as a harlot and cunning of heart.
> She is boisterous and rebellious,
> Her feet do not remain at home;
> She is now in the streets, now in the squares,
> And lurks by every corner.
> So she seizes him and kisses him
> And with a brazen face she says to him:
> 'I was due to offer peace offerings;
> Today I have paid my vows.
> Therefore I have come out to meet you,
> To seek your presence earnestly, and I have found you.
> I have spread my couch with coverings,

With colored linens of Egypt.
I have sprinkled my bed
With myrrh, aloes and cinnamon.
Come, let us drink our fill of love until morning;
Let us delight ourselves with caresses.
For my husband is not at home.
He has gone on a long journey.
He has taken a bag of money with him.
At the full moon he will come home.'
With her many persuasions she entices him;
With her flattering lips she seduces him (Proverbs 7:6-21).

THE NATURE OF ILLICIT SEDUCTION: A FATHER'S INSTRUCTIONS

As you most likely have gathered, the book of Proverbs is primarily written as a father's instruction to a son (i.e. King Solomon to his son, Rehoboam). He is understandably concerned, knowing that one of the greatest moral temptations facing his son would be a harlot or an adulteress. Given the amount he writes concerning the subject, it might just be Solomon's *greatest* concern.

The *harlot* or *adulteress* mentioned in the book of Proverbs is not always a paid prostitute. The word can refer to any woman who is trying to seduce someone other than her husband, such as a neighbor, a fellow worker, a friend's spouse, or anybody else. Whoever it is, she certainly does not have his best interest in mind: "An adulteress hunts for the precious life" (Proverbs 6:26). Solomon wants his son to understand how an immoral woman could easily seduce him to sin, especially if his fantasy life is already pre-disposing him to compromise.

The book of Proverbs is purposely fragmented, a collection of a wide assortment of wisdom statements.[1] However, this concerned father chooses to write lengthy sections concerning immorality, in hopes of protecting his son from the ravages of a seductress.

HOW DOES AN IMMORAL WOMAN ATTRACT A MAN?

I once presented this material from Proverbs to a woman who, before her conversion to Christ, had been a prostitute. She was amazed at how accurate this ancient wisdom literature was in describing her former professional methods for trapping a man. Although written some 3,000 years ago, she insisted that these same techniques are still widely used in our day, and not just by the sex-industry pros. I encourage us to take to heart Solomon's clear warnings to every man. (With a bit of adjustment, these are certainly principles that can be applied to women, as well.)

1. She appeals to him with her physical charms.

The adulteress knows most men are visually stimulated, so she dresses and looks at him seductively (Proverbs 6:25; 7:10). The old saying, related to anger, applies here, "If looks could kill, how many would kill with a look." Let's face it, sexually-speaking, there is certainly that killer look.

2. She appeals to him with her personality.

The harlot has figured out that most men are not used to being pursued sexually, so she is cunning and devises ways of seducing him (Proverbs 7:10). She is sexually boisterous and seductively rebellious (Proverbs 7:11; 9:13). She is also aggressive towards him (Proverbs 7:12-13). For men especially, who are used to being the sexual initiators, this sort of sexual aggression, can really throw off his moral compass.

3. She appeals to him with her words.

The immoral woman knows one of her main tools for seducing a man is flattery (Proverbs 6:24; 7:5, 14-15, 21; 2:16). Additionally, Solomon warns of her ability to be persuasive (Proverbs 7:21), to speak seductively (Proverbs 7:18; 5:3), and to reassure him of no danger (Proverbs 7:18-20). Flattery. Seductive words. Reassurance that everything is going to be great. A deadly combination.

4. She appeals to him by setting a seductive atmosphere.

The adulteress understands what a man fears and what pleases him. To alleviate his fear, she assures him that she and her husband are separated, both physically and emotionally (Proverbs 7:11, 19). To further entice him, she prepares a sensually pleasing atmosphere of sight and smell (Proverbs 7:16-17). Given a state of mind that is filled with illicit fantasy, there are few men who can resist this kind of seduction without direct intervention from God and others.

THANK GOD, I GOT CAUGHT BEFORE . . .

I was teaching at a leadership conference in Fremont, California. During a mini-seminar on "Safeguarding My Moral Purity," I noticed an older man fidgeting uncontrollably. He reminded me of my yet-to-be-potty-trained grandchildren, just prior to another "accident." He was obviously very uncomfortable and the crowded conditions made it impossible for him to leave unnoticed.

After the session, instead of rushing out, he shuffled forward. He pulled me aside, obviously embarrassed and said, "I cannot believe what just happened. I have always struggled with dyslexia and I ended up in Room 201, instead of Room 102. I was certainly not expecting to attend a class on purity, especially not today!" He then cried, as he confessed that he had arranged for his first extramarital affair, "right after this conference!" In fact, the woman was waiting for him in the hotel around the corner from the church.

I spent some time counseling, praying and sharing Scripture. Finally I said to him, "Call that woman right now and tell her that you have a change of heart." I watched with joy as he did. Even this dyslexic man clearly saw the words of the apostle Paul: "Now flee from youthful lusts" (2 Timothy 2:22) and "abstain from every form of evil" (1 Thessalonians 5:22).

Perhaps, unnoticed by the crowds of your fellow Christians, you are on the verge of an accident far more devastating than incontinence.

Consider yourself caught. Make that call. Better yet, run baby . . . run!

> Do not let your heart turn aside to her ways.
> Do not stray into her paths (Proverbs 7:25).

> Keep your way far from her,
> And do not go near the door of her house (Proverbs 5:8).

chapter 24

STEP #5
FALLING INTO THE TRAP OF IMMORALITY

THAT WAS FUN . . . WASN'T IT?

Believing original Playboy Hugh Hefner and Hollywood is accepting the view that sex with as many people as possible has few negative consequences. Or whatever the price is, it's negligible. After all, adultery might be fun for a season. Fornication might feel great for a moment. Then reality hits and hits hard: "'Stolen water is sweet; and bread eaten in secret is pleasant.' But he does not know that the dead are there, that her guests are in the depths of Sheol" (Proverbs 9:17-18). The New Testament concurs when it speaks of "the *passing* pleasures of sin" (Hebrews 11:25, emphasis added).

SUDDENLY . . . IT WAS NOT SO SUDDEN

If we are ignoring the counsel of God's Word, allowing our marriage to slip into nothingness, permitting fantasies to consume us, and flirting with temptation in its many seductive forms, then face the facts. We are on the brink of taking the life-threatening plunge!

> *Suddenly* he follows her
> As an ox goes to the slaughter,

Or as one in fetters to the discipline of a fool,
Until an arrow pierces through his liver;
As a bird hastens to the snare,
So he does not know that it will cost him his life
(Proverbs 7:22-23, emphasis added).

King Solomon's choice of words initially seems surprising. Given the steps to immorality he has described in other portions of Proverbs, how could he speak of this foolish young man's *sudden* moral demise. Well, *suddenly* he followed her. *Suddenly*, he made the decision to have sexual relations with her. Just as *suddenly*, he experienced the consequences. However, what preceded these *sudden* events were the many bad choices that got him there. Now it's too late. The die has been cast. It's time to pay what is due.

OH, GOD . . . OH, GOD . . . WHAT HAVE I DONE?

I was speaking at a Promise Keepers rally for men in Visalia, California. After preaching on the consequences of moral failure, I gave an invitation to those men who desired to come forward for personal prayer. Before I could finish, I heard a dramatic groan from somewhere in that large gathering. I couldn't tell exactly where it came from. I stopped speaking nonetheless.

From the middle of the crowd, a young man in his thirties suddenly stood. He rushed into the center aisle and down towards the front. He immediately fell at my feet, with outstretched arms and face buried in the carpet. All of us could hear his muffled cries: "Oh, God . . . Oh, God, what have I done?" Three or four men left their seats and gently laid their bodies on top of him, consoling him.

I was not expecting this kind of response to the simple invitation. However, what happened next really amazed and humbled me. The rest of the men in that crowded auditorium stood in absolute silence. Was it out of respect for what God was doing? Perhaps. However, talking with the men later, I learned that most of the men stood that day because they knew that what happened to this poor man could happen to them. That sober reality should make all of us stand, or perhaps, fall on our faces even now.

A few years later, I was teaching a purity seminar in Seattle, Washington. I was telling the story of this precious Visalia man. Once again I got interrupted. Once again I was surprised, as a man in the back shouted, "I am that man from Visalia!" He came forward and hugged me. We both wept. He stood before that crowd of men and shared that, although God forgave him, he experienced a pile of consequences. He went on to exhort the men as only one who had felt his pain could: "Guys, it just wasn't worth it!"

GRAVITY STINKS, MR. NEWTON

Isaac Newton ruined my life. He discovered gravity. Actually, gravity has always been around, but I still blame him. It is my awareness of the law of gravity that makes me panic a bit when I look over the sides of cliffs or when an airplane hits an air pocket and drops a few hundred feet. It is also my wife's knowledge of the law of gravity that makes her think I am crazy to climb on my two-story roof in order to impress my sons-in-law. (Apparently, competitive testosterone tops my fear of heights.)

We can choose to ignore the law of gravity or learn some creative way to attempt to refute the law. However, six decades of life experience tells me that if I hang over the edge too far, the law of gravity will still take effect and I will suffer the consequences.

There is an equally irrefutable spiritual law that many call, "The Law of Sowing and Reaping." Whatever seed we sow, we can expect to reap its fruit. You can try to refute it or minimize it, but you can never ignore it. The apostle Paul states the time-honored principle: "Do not be deceived, God is not mocked; for whatever a man sows, this he will also reap" (Galatians 6:7).

Other Scriptures reinforce Paul's words:

> According to what I have seen those who plow iniquity
> And those who sow trouble harvest it (Job 4:8).

But he who sows righteousness gets a true reward
(Proverbs 11:18).

For they sow the wind
And they reap the whirlwind (Hosea 8:7).

A wise and mature person is one who heeds the consequences of his action before he acts. An immature person is one who ignores consequences and lives for the moment. It's another of the great themes of the book of Proverbs. In the proverbs of our own day, a wise man looks before he leaps. In fact, after he looks, he most often decides not to leap.

THE PRICE WE PAY

The Bible is filled with loving but stern warnings about the dangers of immorality. They are the irrefutable laws, given as our heavenly Father's guide to protect us from the many consequences of sin:

For her house sinks down to death (Proverbs 2:18).

My son, give attention to my wisdom,
Incline your ear to my understanding;
That you may observe discretion
And your lips may reserve knowledge.
For the lips of an adulteress drip honey
And smoother than oil is her speech,
But in the end she is bitter as wormwood,
Sharp as a two-edged sword.
Her feet go down to death,
Her steps lay hold of Sheol.
She does not ponder the path of life;
Her ways are unstable, she does not know it.
Now then, my sons, listen to me

And do not depart from the words of my mouth.
Keep your way far from her
And do not go near the door of her house,
Or give your vigor to others
And your years to the cruel one;
And strangers be filled with your strength
And your hard-earned goods will go to the house of an
    alien;
And you groan at your final end,
When your flesh and your body are consumed;
And you say, 'How I have hated instruction!
And my heart spurned reproof!
I have not listened to the voice of my teachers,
Nor inclined my ear to my instructors!
I was almost in utter ruin
In the midst of the assembly and congregation'
(Proverbs 5:1-14).

Can a man take fire in his bosom
And his clothes not be burned?
Or can a man walk on hot coals
And his feet not be scorched?
So is the one who goes in to his neighbor's wife;
Whoever touches her will not go unpunished
(Proverbs 6:27-29).

The Lord is the avenger in all these things, just as we also told you before and solemnly warned you (1 Thessalonians 4:6).

So, he who rejects this is not rejecting man but the God who gives His Holy Spirit to you (1 Thessalonians 4:8).

Marriage is to be held in honor among all and the marriage bed is to be undefiled; for fornicators and adulterers God will judge (Hebrews 13:4).

chapter 25

IT BETTER BE WORTH IT

THE SPECIFIC CONSEQUENCES OF IMMORALITY

Hopefully you are familiar with Martin Luther's sixteenth-century posting of his warnings against ecclesiastical abuse, nailed to the door of the Castle Church in Wittenberg, Germany. I have often thought of posting Solomon's warnings against sexual abuse to the doors of nightclubs and bars. They also belong on the doors of every local church. God certainly wants them nailed on the doorpost of every heart.

ANCIENT WARNINGS; CURRENT RISKS

Before we decide to have sexual relations with someone other than our spouse, consider the risks we are taking. Before we choose to sin against God, ourselves, our spouse, and our loved ones, count the real cost. Then ask, "Is it worth it?"

RISK #1
SEVERE PHYSICAL CONSEQUENCES

Solomon warns about giving "your vigor to others and your years to the cruel one" (Proverbs 5:9). Immorality is painfully cruel. In Psalm 38, one of the penitential psalms, King David acknowledges the serious consequences of his sin. Consider how many of them were physical:

O LORD, rebuke me not in Your wrath,
And chasten me not in Your burning anger.
For Your arrows have sunk deep into me,
And Your hand has pressed down on me.
There is no soundness in my flesh because of Your
    indignation;
There is no health in my bones because of my sin.
For my iniquities are gone over my head;
As a heavy burden they weigh too much for me.
My wounds grow foul and fester
Because of my folly.
I am bent over and greatly bowed down;
I go mourning all day long.
For my loins are filled with burning,
And there is no soundness in my flesh.
I am benumbed and badly crushed;
I groan because of the agitation of my heart.
Lord, all my desire is before You;
And my sighing is not hidden from You.
My heart throbs, my strength fails me;
And the light of my eyes, even that has gone from me.
My loved ones and my friends stand aloof from my
    plague;
And my kinsmen stand afar off (Psalm 38:1-11).

Besides Bathsheba's unexpected pregnancy, David experienced a number of unspecified physical problems in his own body. As troubling as it may seem to some of my fellow Bible expositors, I have often wondered if Psalm 38 might be describing more than his spiritual and emotional pain. Could it not also be describing his physical suffering; even the results of his sexual sin? Imagine David visiting a modern day physician and presenting the following symptoms:

- "There is no soundness (i.e. wholeness) in my flesh."
- "My wounds grow foul and fester because of my folly."
- "I am bent over and greatly bowed down."
- "For my loins are filled with burning."
- "I am benumbed (i.e. feeble and numb) and badly crushed."
- "My heart throbs (i.e. palpitates)."
- "My strength fails me."
- "The light of my eyes, even that has gone from me."
- "My loved ones and my friends stand aloof from my plague (i.e. disease, sores)."

Perhaps some or all of these are just figures of speech, the symptoms of David's broken spirit. Perhaps they are more and David is experiencing some dramatic physical illness. Perhaps it's a mix of both. What I do know for certain is that Psalm 38:3 can rightly be translated, "There is no *shalom* in my bones." His body was in torment because of his sin.

Sexual sin can result in some very severe physical consequences. In our world of advanced medicine, we have become aware of some pretty terrifying initials:

- S.T.D. (Sexually Transmitted Diseases, such as syphilis, gonorrhea, herpes, Chlamydia)
- V.D. (Venereal Disease)
- H.P.V. (Human Papilloma Virus)
- P.I.D. (Pelvic Inflammatory Disease)
- N.S.U. (Non-Specific Urethritis)
- H.I.V. (Human Immunodeficiency Virus)
- A.I.D.S. (Acquired Immune Deficiency Syndrome)

I was grieved at the sad news of one young man who, after one short-lived extramarital affair, contracted H.I.V. He transmitted the virus to his wife and, eventually, their unborn child was infected. All three of them died of A.I.D.S. His sin left another son, born before the affair, an orphan. Don't be fooled into thinking that God will protect you from such severe physical consequences.

RISK #2
LOSS OF HONOR AND PUBLIC DISGRACE

When I was in seminary, a renowned Bible teacher stood before our student body, holding up two thick black books. One was a Bible; the other a book he said contained the names of Christian leaders who fell into immorality and left the ministry. I remember praying quietly,

> *Lord, thank you that my name is written in the Lamb's Book of Life. May my name never be written in this man's "Book of the Fallen."*

Speaking as if from the heart of one of his fellow worshipers who fell into immorality, King Solomon writes, "I was almost in utter ruin. / In the midst of the assembly and congregation" (Proverbs 5:14). He goes on to present the life-long consequences, not just in the assembly of God's people, but in the entire community: "Wounds and disgrace he will find, / And his reproach will not be blotted out" (Proverbs 6:33).

RISK #3
LOSS OF MONEY AND POSSIBLE POVERTY

Be warned. Commit adultery and "your hard-earned goods will go to the house of an alien" (Proverbs 5:10). Why? "For on account of a harlot one is reduced to a loaf of bread" (Proverbs 6:26).

Immorality is expensive. Just ask those who have suffered through medical bills for pregnancy or diseases, legal fees, alimony, and child-support payments. Many have even agreed to pay "hush money" or for an abortion they wished never happened.

I heard a report about a husband in the San Francisco Bay Area who called his wife to announce he was leaving her for a younger woman. Attempting to come off as a nice guy, he asked his wife to sell his new sports car and he would immediately give her *half* the money. In quiet revenge, she published an advertisement in the newspaper. She sold the expensive car and sent him half the proceeds—fifty cents!

RISK #4
ENTRAPMENT INTO HABITUAL SIN

Immorality leads to more immorality. Perhaps one is foolish enough to think he or she can just be involved "this one time, and that's it." The Bible presents the truth about the bondage that can follow just one immoral act: "He will be held with the cords of his sin ... in the greatness of his folly he will go astray" (Proverbs 5:22-23). Hebrews 3:13 speaks of the danger of being "hardened by the deceitfulness of sin." Jeremiah, the Old Testament prophet, wrote about those who committed adultery and "trooped" (i.e. "cut a path," Hebrew: *gadad*) to the harlot's house" (Jeremiah 5:7). Too many who thought their affair would end with one encounter have cut a well-worn path to the many open doors of infidelity. I counseled one man who had seventeen different affairs in fifteen years of marriage!

Immorality also leads to other sins. The apostle Paul reminded the Romans how their impurity resulted in "further lawlessness" (Romans 6:19). King David's immorality led to lying, deception and even the murder of Uriah, the husband of Bathsheba. His immorality also opened the doors to sin in the lives of others in his family. King David's son, Absalom, murdered his brother, Amnon, for raping his sister (2 Samuel 13:1-39). In this case the sins of the father truly did transmit to the next generation.

RISK #5
REVENGE BY OFFENDED PEOPLE

You may think you are safe from retaliation from a jilted partner, a jealous lover, or an angry parent. You may think your infidelity won't come back to haunt you. However, King Solomon presents a clear warning:

Wounds and disgrace he will find,
And his reproach will not be blotted out.
For jealousy enrages a man,
And he will not spare in the day of vengeance.
He will not accept any ransom,
Nor will he be satisfied though you give many gifts
(Proverbs 6:33-35).

Most of us have read accounts of "crimes of passion" when an angry spouse injures or kills a spouse or a spouse's lover. Early in my ministry, I officiated at a funeral for a young woman who was shot to death by a jealous boyfriend. He then turned the gun on himself.

Besides the physical revenge, consider the shameful revenge of King David's son, Absalom, who had sexual relations on the roof top with all of the King's concubines, so that all might witness his hatred of his father, as prophesied in 2 Samuel 12:12 and carried out in 2 Samuel 16:21-22.

RISK #6
PHYSICAL DEATH

The book of Proverbs gives the general caution: "The one who commits adultery with a woman is lacking sense; / He who would destroy himself does it" (Proverbs 6:32). Although there are many ways immorality can destroy a life, there is also clear biblical evidence of those who, as a consequence of their sexual sin, bring about physical death for themselves or others. As shocking as it may seem, such holy judgment of God is not to be ruled out:

- God threatened King Abimelech with death if he had relations with Sarah, Abraham's wife (Genesis 20:3).
- Under Old Testament law, adultery was punishable by death (Leviticus 20:10; Deuteronomy 22:22).

Concerning the unrepentant and immoral man in the Church of

Corinth, the apostle Paul writes some shocking words, showing the seriousness of the offense in the eyes of God: "I have decided to deliver such a one to Satan for *the destruction of his flesh*, so that his spirit may be saved in the day of the Lord Jesus" (1 Corinthians 5:5, emphasis added). Reflect also on the dramatic story of Phinehas the Priest, as he confronted the Israelites who were committing blatant immorality with the Moabite women:

> While Israel remained at Shittin, the people began to play the harlot with the daughters of Moab. . . . Then behold, one of the sons of Israel came and brought to his relatives a Midianite woman, in the sight of Moses and in the sight of all the congregation of the sons of Israel, while they were weeping at the doorway of the tent of meeting. When Phinehas the son of Eleazar, the son of Aaron the priest, saw it, he arose from the midst of the congregation and took a spear in his hand, and he went after the man of Israel into the tent and pierced both of them through, the man of Israel and the woman, through the body. So the plague on the sons of Israel was checked (Numbers 25:1, 6-8).

I have often wondered what kind of response I would get if I read this passage to a crowd, with a spear in hand! No follow up comments would be necessary.

I really do not believe God calls us to re-institute capital punishment for adultery today. However, I do believe He would have us see just how deadly an offense immorality is. Certainly, there are other risks, such as death from a sexually transmitted disease or the wrath of a jealous partner. Of course, we also must consider the saddest and most common of deadly consequences—millions of innocent babies killed in abortions!

> Her house is the way to Sheol (i.e. the place of the dead),
> Descending to the chambers of death (Proverbs 7:27).

RISK #7
DEVASTATING SPIRITUAL EFFECTS

There are substantial *spiritual* consequences to immorality, such as the loss of fellowship with our Creator, the hardening of our heart toward God, the loss of credibility in our local church, and the loss of effectiveness in prayer. Beyond these, consider the reduction of our reputation in the eyes of unbelievers. Heed the sobering words of Nathan the prophet to adulterous King David: "You have given occasion to the enemies of the LORD to blaspheme" (2 Samuel 12:14). An immoral world will hardly listen to an immoral church. In fact, it loves to mock our hypocrisy!

Consider also the devastation *within* the church. From my doctoral research and many years of counseling and consulting, I have observed that it takes most churches and parachurch ministries about five to seven years to begin to substantially heal when a key leader in their midst falls morally. In the meantime, a number of short-term consequences unfold, which have unexpected, long-term impacts on the ministry. Denial, mistrust, false accusations, power-plays and foolish decisions abound. Many hope that bringing in a godly replacement and "moving on" will help them heal quickly. Healing can and does occur. Rarely does it happen quickly. (I refer you to my materials on *Immorality in the Ministry: The Pitfalls of Pastoral Power,* available through JARON Ministries International.)

RISK #8
OTHER SOCIAL EFFECTS

Remember the story of the man who called me from a gas station. He asked me why he could not have sexual relations with a woman since he already lusted after her in his heart. I pointed out the vast difference between adultery in thought and adultery in deed, especially related to the number of people it affects. I concluded with the exhortation that lustful thoughts are just between him and God; his immoral actions are not.

Illicit sex is not a private affair. It affects the man himself, the woman herself, the man's parents, the woman's parents, the man's immediate family, the woman's immediate family, the man's future mate, the woman's future mate, the man's future in-laws, the woman's future in-laws, the man's future children, the woman's future children, the man's church family, and the woman's church family. By very conservative estimates we are talking about hundreds of people, possibly even thousands. I often say to pastors, missionaries, and others in vocational ministry, "If you want to become famous, just commit adultery. Your name will spread throughout the world. The better choice is to be faithful."

Take to heart the words of Solomon as he describes what happens when the sin is discovered and publicly exposed: "I was almost in utter ruin in the midst of the assembly and congregation" (Proverbs 5:14). Nathan, the prophet who confronted King David's sin, put it succinctly: "Indeed you did it secretly, but I will do this thing before all Israel, and under the sun" (2 Samuel 12:12). Perhaps David's lament in Psalm 38:11 reflects that severe consequence coming true: "My loved ones and my friends stand aloof from my plague; / And my kinsmen stand afar off" (Psalm 38:11). The apostle Paul even calls believers not to associate (i.e. "keep company/have intimate fellowship," Greek: *sunanamignumi*) with immoral people who claim to be believers but refuse to repent of their sexual sin (1 Corinthians 5:9-10).

RISK #9
REJECTION

Read the sad story of Tamar who was violated by one who professed to be in love with her. After taking advantage of her sexually, Amnon tossed her aside. Although this is a tragic story of incest and rape, Amnon's response is sadly common, even when the illicit sexual encounter is consensual:

> Then Amnon hated her with a very great hatred; for the hatred with which he hated her was greater than the love with which he had loved her. And Amnon said to her, "Get up, go away!" But she said to him, "No, because this wrong in sending me away is greater than the other that

you have done to me!" Yet he would not listen to her. Then he called his young man who attended him and said, "Now throw this woman out of my presence, and lock the door behind her." Now she had on a long-sleeved garment; for in this manner the virgin daughters of the king dressed themselves in robes. Then his attendant took her out and locked the door behind her. Tamar put ashes on her head and tore her long-sleeved garment which was on her; and she put her hand on her head and went away, crying aloud as she went (2 Samuel 13:15-18).

Once a person has "had his way," he (or she) can easily become disinterested. The thrill of sexual conquest is gone. There are other victims to conquer. Many have learned the folly of such hollow words as, "If you love me, you will have sex with me" or "Sex will only make our love stronger." Don't count on it.

RISK #10
A REFUSAL TO CHANGE

As hard as it is to believe, even after suffering many of the above results, some become even more stiff-necked. Solomon understood this, too: "And you say, 'How I have hated instruction! And my heart spurned reproof! I have not listened to the voice of my teachers, nor inclined my ear to my instructors!'" (Proverbs 5:12-13). The writer to the Hebrews also understood this: "But encourage one another day after day, as long as it is still called 'Today,' so that none of you will be hardened by the deceitfulness of sin" (Hebrews 3:13). How like Esau we are, willing to sell all that we have for "a single meal" (Hebrews 12:16; Genesis 25:30-34). However, if we are to hold fast to the whole counsel of God, then we must consider carefully the possibility that, unless God's mercy prevails, we could experience many, if not all, of these disturbing results of immorality.

My friend, is any sexual encounter really worth all of this? If so, then all I can say is that it better be the best sex you've ever had; it certainly will be the costliest! As one man at our purity seminar so aptly put it, "I think you are trying to scare the pants on us." So be it.

In order to drive the point home to those of you who still think the pleasures outweigh the risks, let's walk through a scenario.

HOW DO YOU FEEL?

- You have just finished an adulterous encounter with another woman. That "stolen water" really wasn't as sweet as you expected, but what's done is done.
  How do you feel?

- You leave the room and head for your car alone, very alone. There, in the back seat, is your Bible. Lying on top is the bulletin from last weekend's church service. Your mind flashes to songs about the holiness of God and the clearly-presented message from God's Word.
  How do you feel?

- You arrive home to your wife and children, who greet you at the door with unusually long hugs. She asks, "How was your day? You're late. Did something happen?" You sputter out an unrehearsed excuse for your tardiness.
  How do you feel?

- Dinner is ready and your wife asks you to pray for the evening meal. You fumble through some rote dinner blessing, trying hard not to think too much about His blessing you with a home, a wife, and a family.
  How do you feel?

- You put the kids to bed, but your wife notices that you are a little indifferent. "What's wrong?" she asks. She comes to your side and touches your arm, as if to say, "The kids are asleep. Do you want to . . . ?" You brush her off with, "I am just too tired tonight."
  How do you feel?

- The weeks go on, and one day you receive an unexpected call on your cell phone from that "other" woman. You feel the pit in your stomach as she informs you that she is pregnant. She demands financial help or she will tell your wife and family.
  How do you feel?

- She decides to tell your wife anyway and calls her one evening while you are there. Your wife confronts you with a look and words that you never before imagined. With the wailing sounds of deep anger and shock, she cries out, "How could you do this? Am I not good enough for you?"
  How do you feel?

- The children hear the commotion and come into the room. Your wife gives them the news. Their initial silence and tears precede their response, "Dad, how could you do this to Mom and to us?" You beg for forgiveness from your family, but your words are treated with disdain.
  How do you feel?

- You call your pastor and tell him just a bit of the horrific story and plead for his immediate help. He comes within the hour and you greet him at the door. Your wife and children are still in the other room, crying. After sharing the sad details and

hearing his counsel, you announce that you will be stepping down from your ministry at the church. Your pastor doesn't try to talk you out of the decision.
How do you feel?

- Over the weeks, you receive marriage counseling and, by God's grace and mercy, your wife decides to forgive you. In fact, rather than divorce you, she renews her vows and even allows you to engage in sexual intimacy with her.
How do you feel?

- Days later you are noticing some disturbing physical signs. Could it be a sexually transmitted disease? Tests reveal it is. You tell your wife that she, too, must now be tested.
How do you feel?

- Soon, you receive a letter from the other woman, itemizing what she anticipates will be the money that she needs. It is thousands. On the list is the cost of an abortion. By the way, her angry father has also decided to "tell the world," if you do not come up with the cash quickly.
How do you feel?

- As much as your family tries to keep this painful secret, word somehow gets out, not only at church but at work. That spiritually receptive man at work, with whom you have been sharing the gospel, now confronts you as the newest hypocrite in his life and another reason he doesn't need "your kind of Christianity."
How do you feel?

- Your teenage daughter is caught in an inappropriate sexual

relationship with her boyfriend. You and your wife try to talk to her. Her response is painfully direct, "Why shouldn't I, Dad? You did!"
How do you feel?

- Years later, you are driving down the road and notice something wrong. Your wife is wiping the tears from her eyes. You know what she is remembering. She whispers to herself, not concerned whether you hear or not, "How could you?"
How do you feel?

- Your world has crumbled for a few minutes of illicit sexual pleasure.
How do you feel?

- Though you know that God has forgiven your sin, you also expect there will be life-long consequences.
How do you feel?

King Solomon's ancient words have become your up-to-the-minute reality:

> The one who commits adultery with a woman is lacking
> sense; He who would destroy himself does it.
> Wounds and disgrace he will find,
> And his reproach will not be blotted out
> (Proverbs 6:32-33).

How do you feel?

PART FOUR:

THE WAY OF ESCAPE

chapter 26

IT IS A WINNABLE WAR

During the Vietnam War, I served on board the USS Kitty Hawk, an aircraft carrier. Even though our ship was highly recognized for its effectiveness in the war effort, I still remember the feelings of frustration I and many of my fellow crew members felt. We were being asked to participate in a war many believe was "half-fought" and lost.

We are at war with immorality every day of our lives. It is an unrelenting enemy with deadly missiles aimed and ready to strike. Though the conflict rages over a lifetime, these are battles we can win daily, if we fight them God's way. Half measures will never work. His "rules of engagement" are clearly defined.

History reveals some strange battle tactics men have used in their personal war with sinful lust. The third-century theologian, Origen, took the text of Matthew 19:12 literally and allowed himself to be castrated. I suspect the struggle continued in his mind. In the middle ages, monks and clerics, in the spirit of 1 Corinthians 9:27, tried to win the fight by inflicting cruel acts of penance on themselves. I have no doubt that the battle still raged in their minds and bodies. I cannot even begin to enumerate all the bizarre tactics being used in our own day.

We have not been left alone to fight against this life-long enemy. We can be assured this truly is a winnable war, if we follow the clearly defined battle methods given by the One who enlisted us and called us to active service. Consider them our marching orders:

> You need not fight in this battle; station yourselves, stand and see the salvation of the LORD on your behalf. . . . Do not fear or be dismayed . . . for the Lord is with you (2 Chronicles 20:17).

> No temptation has overtaken you but such as is common to man; and God is faithful, who will not allow you to be tempted beyond what you are able, but with the temptation will provide the way of escape also, so that you will be able to endure it (1 Corinthians 10:13).

> Finally, be strong in the Lord, and in the strength of His might. Put on the full armor of God, that you will be able to stand firm against the schemes of the devil (Ephesians 6:10).

> Therefore, take up the full armor of God, so that you may be able to resist in the evil day, and having done everything, to stand firm (Ephesians 6:13).

> Suffer hardship with me, as a good soldier of Christ Jesus. No soldier in active service entangles himself in the affairs of everyday life, so that he may please the one who enlisted him as a soldier (2 Timothy 2:3-4).

> Be of sober spirit, be on the alert. Your adversary, the devil, prowls about like a roaring lion, seeking someone to devour. But resist him, firm in your faith, knowing that the same experiences of suffering are being accomplished by your brethren who are in the world (1 Peter 5:8-9).

We are fully equipped with the power of God and fully-reinforced by the presence of God. Now, we get ready for battle by setting up three lines of defense: guarding our minds, guarding our bodies and guarding our companions.

chapter 27

LINE OF DEFENSE #1
GUARDING MY MIND

A Sunday school teacher announced to a group of teenagers, "Next week I am going to bring a sex organ to class." Word spread rapidly. Parents and pastors confronted her. She quickly showed them a bottle containing a human brain.

Sexual sin begins in the mind. Jesus said:

> For from within, out of the heart of men, proceed the evil thoughts, fornications, thefts, murders, adulteries, deeds of coveting and wickedness, as well as deceit, sensuality, envy, slander, pride and foolishness. All these evil things proceed from within and defile the man (Mark 7:21-23).

I enjoy the story of the boy who was told by his father to sit down. Twice the boy refused. The exasperated father grabbed his son by the shoulder and forced him to sit. The rebellious son retorted, "Daddy, I may be sitting down on the outside, but I'm standing up on the inside." There was a change of behavior but certainly not a change of heart.

Some of us may look morally victorious on the outside, but we can certainly be losing the battle on the inside. Our bodies may be running from immorality, but our minds are still there. Thus, no permanent change happens.

THE DEVIL REALLY DIDN'T MAKE ME DO IT

Suppose I were to ask you to stop reading and tap your head. What was it that truly made you do it? Me? No, I just "tempted" you. Your mind told your hand to touch your head. Your mind could have just as easily refused and instructed your hand not to move.

The Devil, the world, and the flesh do not make us fall into immorality. They certainly tempt us, but we choose to follow. Temptation, in itself, is not the sin. However, yielding to it is. Yielding begins in the mind. My *body* will only do what my *mind* tells it to do. Godly conduct is the product of godly thinking. Solomon's words are so very instructive: "Watch over your heart (i.e. "mind, values," Hebrew: *leb*) with all diligence (i.e. "like a guard post," Hebrew: *mishmar*), / For from it flow the springs (i.e. "the outflowings," Hebrew: *towtsa'ah*) of life" (Proverbs 4:23).

Guarding my mind, as God's first line of defense against the daily war with lust and immorality, involves protecting, provisioning, purifying, and preparing my mind. In the following chapters we will examine these in detail.

chapter 28

PROTECTING MY MIND

I have counseled many who, after a moral failure, have said, "I just don't know how it happened." I often answer, "Yes, you do. Your body did exactly what your mind wanted it to do." Sometimes they still don't make the connection and I continue with a question, "What were you feeding your mind before you made the regrettable choice?" As they tell their stories of years of immoral input from such things as television, the internet, books, and magazines, in my heart I want to shout, "What did you expect?"

Even this city-boy knows that if we plant carrot seeds we can expect carrots to grow. Plant the mental seeds of impure thoughts and we will eventually reap the bitter fruit of immoral behavior. Every frustrated computer owner should also know the principle. Keep adding corrupted data into the hard drive of our mind and we can expect a moral crash of monumental proportions. We reap what we sow! Garbage in; garbage out!

In *Part Two: God's Design*, we addressed how our Creator designed sexual union within the covenant of marriage as a means by which we humans demonstrate His oneness. We also learned in *Part Three: Man's Abuses*, that any thought, word or deed contrary to God's plan for marital oneness is, by definition, immorality. We must, therefore, guard our minds from anything that distorts our thinking regarding that divinely ordained purpose. These are the bad seeds, the garbage that pollutes our minds.

THERE IS NO SUCH THING AS CASUAL VIEWING

I am grateful for advanced technology and many of the new electronic tools available. With them I can communicate faster and farther. I can study and learn with greater ease and speed. I can even enjoy some moments of recreation with my technologically savvy grandchildren. I didn't write this book using a quill pen and parchment paper. I am so grateful for word processing and spell-check.

However, I am also well aware that we live in a day when we can no longer use these tools in a mindless way. Randy Alcorn asks a probing question: "How does something shocking and shameful somehow become acceptable because we watch it through a television instead of a window?" He goes on to state, "Parents who wouldn't dream of letting a dirty-minded adult baby-sit their children do it every time they let their children surf the channels. I cannot imagine allowing somebody to fornicate in my living room, right in front of me. Why would I allow video images of the same sinful activity?"[1]

Just as it would be foolish to think of relaxing at a pistol range, we can no longer let our guard down in front of anything that shoots out words and images. For anyone who is concerned about their moral purity, there can be no casual television or movie-watching, no indiscriminate internet or web-site use, no mindless reading of books or magazines. In this world of "telegarbage"[2] we must be on guard at all times, protecting our minds from anything that distorts God's perfect design for our sexuality.

Many years ago a dear friend was one of the first I knew to get a satellite feed for his television. I expressed concern about the ease with which he could now be faced with great visual temptation from hundreds of channels. I encouraged him to tape some words of warning on the remote control. Perhaps you might want to do the same on all your equipment and whatever else you allow to input your mind. Consider some suggestions:

- "As for me and my *mouse*, we will serve the Lord."
- "Lord, don't let me drown my life channel surfing."

Perhaps you would prefer to write some key passage from the Word of God, written not only on your electronic equipment but on your submissive and obedient heart. Here's a few to consider:

- You shall be holy for I am holy (1 Peter 1:16)
- I will set before my eyes no vile thing (Psalm 101:3, New International Version).
- Glorify God in your body (1 Corinthians 6:20).

I hasten to add one more reminder. No matter what brand of media equipment we use, they all have the same thing in common—an off switch! Use it often and may "the peace of God . . . guard your hearts and your minds in Christ Jesus" (Philippians 4:7).

chapter 29

PROVISIONING MY MIND

I became a born-again Christian at the age of twenty-one when I trusted Jesus Christ alone for the salvation my sinful life desperately needed. It was by pure grace apart from anything I could earn or deserve (Ephesians 2:8-9; Titus 3:5; John 6:44).

This is not to say those first years were easy. As a new believer, I struggled with the pornographic memories of a former life in bondage to sin. I thank God for the counsel I received, challenging me to memorize and meditate on large amounts of Scripture. Little did I know just how much that would change my life from the inside out and help me win "the war within"—even the battle in my dreams (2 Corinthians 3:18; Romans 12:2).

I recently read, "We are no more responsible for the evil thoughts that pass through our minds than a scarecrow for the birds which fly over the seed plot he has to guard. The sole responsibility in each case is to prevent them from settling."[1] True enough. However, I believe we must take some responsibility for what goes in and comes out of our minds. I believe we can influence our minds, even our *subconscious* minds, by infusing them with Scripture. The apostle Paul said it this way:

> For though we walk in the flesh, we do not war according
> to the flesh, for the weapons of our warfare are not of

the flesh, but divinely powerful for the destruction of fortresses. We are destroying speculations and every lofty thing raised up against the knowledge of God, and we are taking *every thought captive to the obedience of Christ* (2 Corinthians 10:3-5, emphasis added).

One night I experienced a horribly graphic dream that is much too profane to describe. In the middle of that dream, however, I began to quote the third chapter of Colossians my family and I committed to memory that week:

> *If then you have been raised up with Christ, keep seeking the things above, where Christ is, seated at the right hand of God. Set your mind on the things above, not on the things that are on earth. For you have died and your life is hidden with Christ in God. When Christ, who is our life, is revealed, then you also will be revealed with Him in glory.*

Without pause, my dream continued from the fifth verse:

> *Therefore consider the members of your earthly body as dead to immorality, impurity, passion, evil desire, and greed, which amounts to idolatry. For it is on account of these things that the wrath of God will come, and in them you also once walked, when you were living in them. But now you also, put them all aside: anger, wrath, malice, slander, and abusive speech from your mouth. Do not lie to one another, since you laid aside the old self with its evil practices, and have put on the new self who is being renewed to a true knowledge according to the image of the One who created him — a renewal in which there is no distinction between Greek and Jew, circumcised and uncircumcised, barbarian, Scythian, slave and freeman, but Christ is all, and in all.*

I wasn't done. It was almost as if I was driving a stake in the heart of the evil thoughts as I continued on from the twelfth verse:

And so, as those who have been chosen of God, holy and beloved, put on a heart of compassion, kindness, humility, gentleness and patience; bearing with one another, and forgiving each other, whoever has a complaint against any one; just as the Lord forgave you, so also should you. And beyond all these things put on love, which is the perfect bond of unity. And let the peace of Christ rule in your hearts, to which indeed you were called in one body; and be thankful. Let the word of Christ richly dwell within you, with all wisdom teaching and admonishing one another with psalms and hymns and spiritual songs, singing with thankfulness in your hearts to God.

To my amazement, I woke up reciting the seventeenth verse:

Whatever you do in word or deed, do all in the name of the Lord Jesus, giving thanks through Him to God the Father.

Instead of feeling defeated, as I often did when these dreams occurred, I arose from my bed claiming an amazing victory. I also learned a lesson I have never forgotten. God's Word truly can become deeply hidden in *the inner recesses of my heart*, exactly where I need it most. The promise of Psalm 119:9-11 had never been more real:

How can a young man keep his way pure (i.e. "clean,"
   Hebrew: *zakah*)?
By keeping it according to Your word.
With all my heart I have sought You
Do not let me wander from Your commandments.

Your word I have treasured (i.e. "hidden," Hebrew: *tsaphan*)
    in my heart (i.e. "mind," Hebrew: *leb*),
That I may not sin against You (Psalm 119:9-11).

HOW DO WE GET RID OF THOSE IMPURE THOUGHTS FOREVER?

What is the best way to get the air out of a glass? A vacuum? No, it might break the glass and render the vessel useless. The best way to remove the air is to fill the glass with something. So it is with the immorality that has filled our minds with its muck.

The apostle Paul wrote: "But I say, walk by the Spirit, and you will not carry out the desire of the flesh" (Galatians 5:16). Notice that as we walk in the power of the Holy Spirit, our sinful passions are dealt with—such fleshly desires as immorality, impurity and sensuality, to name just a few on the list (Galatians 5:19-21).

It is not enough to just rid our minds of the garbage of immoral thoughts. To do so just creates a vacuum for other sins of the mind. We must fill our minds with the truth, especially concerning what God says about immorality. Yes, I am talking about memorizing Scripture.

BUT I CAN'T MEMORIZE

I can imagine some of your thoughts, "I can't memorize Scripture." You most certainly can. Almighty God has given us the capacity to memorize large amounts of data, beyond the capability of any known computer. Most of us have memorized the information needed to drive a car, cook a meal, play a sport, and solve a math problem, all with very little effort. Watch a teenager texting, watching television, and doing homework, all at the same time!

There are two basic principles that come from the study of mnemonics, techniques for improving memory. They are especially worth bearing in mind as we discuss Scripture memorization.

MNEMONIC PRINCIPLE #1
WE MEMORIZE THAT WHICH IS VALUABLE TO US

I am amazed at the number of men who can recite the earned run averages of numerous baseball pitchers, the size of engines and maximum horsepower in scores of vintage automobiles, or the average increase in interest rates over the past five years. These same men tell me they can't memorize Scripture. Oh, really? I am impressed with most women's ability to remember exactly what someone said years ago. These same women try to convince me they could never hide Scripture in their hearts. I don't buy it!

Examine the following numbers: 20 - 57 - 12 - 35. If I were to tell you that this is the combination to a safe that contains a million dollars for anyone who can open it, how quickly do you think your mind would memorize these? That combination is no longer just a bunch of random numbers; it now has life-changing value.

What the Bible says regarding our moral purity is far more precious "than thousands of gold and silver pieces" (Psalm 119:72), especially if it saves us from the painful consequences of sexual sin. Scripture memory is valuable. Morally-speaking, it becomes a matter of life and death.

MNEMONIC PRINCIPLE #2
WE MEMORIZE THAT WHICH WE REPEAT NUMEROUS TIMES

Memory experts say that if we repeat something forty times, it becomes imprinted for life. Wise teachers and coaches know this; advertisers count on it. Bombard an audience forty times with the same message and they will never forget the product. Who among us doesn't recognize the uniquely-shaped Coca Cola bottle or the golden arches of McDonalds? How did that happen? Repetition!

To illustrate this principle in our seminars, I often recite from memory the words of an advertisement from a particular brand of toothpaste, which "has been shown to be an effective decay-preventive dentifrice that can be of significant value when used in a conscientiously applied program of oral hygiene and regular professional care." It usually brings applause. Some think I need to get a life.

I can assure you that I didn't intend to memorize this. This is hardly information that has value to me. So, how did it happen? Most every time I stooped over the sink to brush my teeth, those words shot from the back of the toothpaste tube and into my sponge-like brain. If my rapidly aging brain can memorize such trivia with so little effort, imagine what all of our minds can do with a little bit of work as we memorize the life-changing Word of God.

You might want to begin with 1 Thessalonians 4:3-8. Read over this passage at least forty times. It will be yours for life. Then move on to other Bible verses.[2] Our moral safety depends on this deeply ingrained lifeline of Scripture.

chapter 30

PURIFYING MY MIND

X-CELLENT!

One of the practices we have done in my home, at conferences, and in churches, is to engage people in what I call "Alphabetical Worship." Beginning with the first letter of the alphabet, I encourage folks to recite some names and characteristics of God. You try it:

> "Thank you, God, for being A _____."
> "I praise you, heavenly Father, for B _____."
> "Thank you, Jesus, for showing me your C _____."

As I was leading this exercise at a youth camp, one young lady responded to the letter X with a profound word of praise, "Thank you, God, for your X-ray vision in my life." Her high school boyfriend quickly added his simple insight, "Thank you, Lord, for being so X-cellent." That wasn't the time to correct his spelling; his heart was right!

How do we stop looking at the world through "porn-tinted spectacles?"[1] Besides protecting and provisioning our minds, we must also purify our minds. The Bible declares that this is accomplished by moving beyond simple memorization to substantial meditation and reflecting deeply on who God is and what He has said in His Word:

How blessed is the man who does not walk in the counsel
    of the wicked,
Nor stand in the path of sinners,
Nor sit in the seat of scoffers!
But his delight is in the law of the LORD,
And in His law he meditates ("muses," Hebrew: *hagah*)
    day and night (Psalm 1:1-2).

This book of the law shall not depart from your mouth,
but you shall meditate ("muse," Hebrew: *hagah*) on it day
and night, so that you may be careful to do according to
all that is written in it; for then you will make your way
prosperous, and then you will have success (Joshua 1:8).

And do not be conformed (Greek: *suschematizo*) to this
world, but be transformed (Greek: *metamorphoo*) by the
renewing (Greek: *anakainosis*) of your mind, so that you
may prove what the will of God is, that which is good and
acceptable and perfect (Romans 12:2).

The apostle Paul reminds his fellow Christians that we have "the mind
of Christ" (1 Corinthians 2:16) and therefore we are to make sure we are
"taking every thought captive to the obedience of Christ" (2 Corinthians
10:5). He also writes one of the clearest statements of what is to be the
central focus of our minds:

Finally, brethren, whatever is true, whatever is honorable,
whatever is right, whatever is pure, whatever is lovely,
whatever is of good repute, if there is any excellence and
if anything worthy of praise, dwell on ("weigh heavily,
ponder," Greek: *logizomai*) these things" (Philippians 4:8).

How do we meditate on the Word of God? How do we renew minds that have accumulated years of filth and garbage? How do we think like those who have the mind of Christ? How do we take every illicit and vile thought captive to the obedience of Christ? It isn't enough to be able to recite the communicable and incommunicable attributes of God. That's what we Bible teachers sometimes call Theology Proper. It isn't even sufficient to do endless word studies on the names of God, as wonderful as that may be. If we are to purify our minds from the filth, we must also engage our minds in Practical Theology, in what I like to call, "*So What Theology.*" For example:

GOD IS . . .	SO WHAT?
• God is all-powerful.	*Therefore, He can empower me to deal with my struggles.*
• God is holy.	*Therefore, He calls me to a walk of personal holiness.*
• God is everywhere.	*Therefore, He sees what I am doing, even when others don't.*
• God is patient.	*Therefore, He won't give up on me.*
• God is merciful.	*Therefore, He doesn't punish me like I deserve.*
• God is my creator.	*Therefore, He didn't make a mistake designing me to be holy.*
• God is gracious.	*Therefore, He gives me everything I need to be godly.*
• God is love.	*Therefore, He gave His Son to bear my sin on the cross.*

Now, it's your turn.

- God is _____.   *Therefore, He _____.*

    I will meditate on all Your work,
    And muse on Your deeds (Psalm 77:12).

    I remember the days of old;
    I meditate on all Your doings;
    I muse on the work of Your hands (Psalm 143:5).

chapter 31

PREPARING MY MIND

Like most pastors, I have walked with people through some of life's most horrific circumstances. I've looked upon the bloodied faces of accident victims. I've witnessed the distorted faces of parents gasping for that first breath after hearing the news that their child has been killed. I have held tightly to a young mother as she caressed the lifeless body of her three-month-old baby. Yet, in all my ministry years, I have never seen a face so stricken with horror than on one particular morning in my church office.

Sitting across the desk from me was a couple married for seventeen years. He had called the meeting. "Pastor Jim, I want to tell my wife something in your presence." His voice shook as he turned to her and confessed, "Honey, I have been unfaithful to you—again!"

There was complete silence as she crossed her arms, cradling herself like a little baby. She then wagged her head and moaned. It was the tragic voice I heard scores of times in funeral homes and hospitals, "Oh God! No!" She then looked at him and shouted, "I'd rather hear that you were dead!" I wish I had a picture of that grieving wife's face for you to look at each time you are tempted to mess around. Better yet, I wish you could see a stack of pictures of the shocked faces of your own loved ones.

BUILDING YOUR OWN ALBUM OF HORROR

In Part Three, *Man's Abuses*, I presented an imaginary scenario of the consequences of one man's infidelity, entitled, *How Does It Feel?* It was, of course, a fictional account even though it was based on many years of observation and counseling. An even more effective safeguard is for each of us to build an album full of mental pictures of the potential effects of our own immorality.[1] Each of us can then carry that album of horror in our heart and mind.

Many years ago, I was asked to lead a purity seminar for a group of Christian bankers, lawyers, and businessmen in the financial district of San Francisco. It was held in a beautiful office towering over "The City by the Bay." Every man there was dressed for success.

Well into the seminar, I gave the men about twenty minutes to write out what they thought would happen if they were caught in the act of adultery. I left the room and returned to find what I would have never expected in such a professional context.

Complete silence. Men with heads buried in their hands. One man lying on the carpet, crying. They weren't discussing cost-benefit ratios or some probability index. There, in that elaborately decorated high rise office, these powerful men of finance came to grips with the high cost of sin.

chapter 32

LINE OF DEFENSE #2
GUARDING MY BODY

HOUSES OF IMMORALITY?

I have a fundraising idea that would make a great deal of money for your church. Set aside a room, purchase some old army cots, hire a few prostitutes, and collect their earnings. Would it make money? Absolutely. Would anyone in his right mind turn a local church building into a house of prostitution? Of course not! We are shocked at even the suggestion. Then, why is it that we are less disturbed about turning our bodies, the temples of the Holy Spirit, into houses of immorality? It seems a little inconsistent, doesn't it? Read carefully the apostle Paul's words, observing all he says about our bodies:

> All things are lawful for me, but not all things are profitable. All things are lawful for me, but I will not be mastered by anything. Food is for the stomach and the stomach is for food, but God will do away with both of them. Yet the *body* is not for immorality, but for the Lord, and the Lord is for the *body*. Now God has not only raised the Lord, but will also raise us up through His power. Do you not know

that your *bodies* are members of Christ? Shall I then take away the members of Christ and make them members of a prostitute? May it never be! Or do you not know that the one who joins himself to a prostitute is one *body* with her? For He says, "The two shall be called one flesh." But the one who joins himself to the Lord is one spirit with Him. Flee immorality. Every other sin that a man commits is outside the *body*, but the immoral man sins against his own *body*. Or do you not know that your *body* is a temple of the Holy Spirit who is in you, whom you have from God, and that you are not your own? For you have been bought with a price: therefore glorify God in your *body* (1 Corinthians 6:12-20, emphasis added).

As we saw in the last few chapters, our first line of defense against lust and immorality is to guard our minds. We do this by protecting, provisioning, purifying, and preparing our minds. Our second line of defense involves guarding our bodies. This is accomplished by presenting, promising, and protecting our bodies. As followers of Christ, our bodies were designed to be vessels of honor:

Now in a large house there are not only gold and silver vessels, but also vessels of wood and earthenware, and some to honor and some to dishonor. Therefore, if anyone cleanses himself from these things, he will be a vessel for honor, sanctified, useful to the Master, prepared for every good work. Now flee from youthful lusts and pursue righteousness, faith, love and peace, with those who call on the Lord from a pure heart (2 Timothy 2:20-22).

chapter 33

PRESENTING MY BODY

WHO REALLY OWNS ME?
GOD OWNS THE HEAVENLY TITLE DEED TO MY BODY

If I lease a car, I have no right to do with it as I wish. If I rent a home, I do not get to change its design without permission from the owner. So it is with the Creator who owns me (1 Corinthians 6:19-20). I do not have the right to use this body for anything other than that which the Owner would permit. This body that houses my spirit and the Holy Spirit is a rental. God holds the heavenly title deed. The next time I consider doing something immoral, I best ask the Owner. Of course, if I already know His answer, why even ask?

REVIEWING THE CONTRACT

As a safeguard to our moral safety and the protection of our bodies, it would do us well if we daily reminded ourselves that we are not our own. In fact, this is exactly what God calls us to do.

The apostle Paul's epistle to the Romans commands us repeatedly to present our bodies as an offering to God Himself. In fact, the Greek verb he uses throughout Chapter 6 and at the beginning of Chapter 12 (*paristemi*) is the same word used when placing a sacrificial offering on an altar. It is also used metaphorically to speak of something being brought into intimate fellowship. Whereas we used to offer ourselves as slaves to godless immorality, because of our new relation to God in Christ, we can now offer our bodies to the one true, holy, and merciful God. Reflect on his words carefully:

> Even so consider yourselves to be dead to sin, but alive to God in Christ Jesus. Therefore do not let sin reign in your mortal body so that you obey its lusts, and do not go on presenting the members of your body to sin as instruments of unrighteousness; but *present yourselves* to God as those alive from the dead, and your members as instruments of righteousness to God. For sin shall not be master over you, for you are not under law but under grace.... Do you not know that when you *present yourselves* to someone as slaves for obedience, you are slaves of the one whom you obey, either of sin resulting in death, or of obedience resulting in righteousness? ... For just as you *presented your members* as slaves to impurity and to lawlessness, resulting in further lawlessness, so now *present your members* as slaves to righteousness, resulting in sanctification. (Romans 6:11-14, 16, 19, emphasis added).

> Therefore I urge you, brethren, by the mercies of God, to *present your bodies* a living and holy sacrifice, acceptable to God, which is your spiritual service of worship (Romans 12:1, emphasis added).

When was the last time you presented your entire body as a formal and intimate offering as well as a living and holy sacrifice to the God who purchased you with the blood of His Son? This is not to be merely a one-time event, but a daily practice. Perhaps you should take the time to do this now:

A PRAYER OF DEDICATION TO THE GOD WHO OWNS ME

> *"Lord God Almighty, I present the heavenly title deed of my body to You. I present myself as a living and holy sacrifice, acceptable to You. Here I am, Lord. All that I am, I give to You at this moment. Help me to use this body today as You would use it. In Jesus' Name. Amen."*

We held a private Purity Ring Ceremony for each of our teenaged daughters. After explaining (once again) the value of remaining sexually pure before marriage, we placed a ring on the finger of each girl and prayed a dedication prayer. When my oldest daughter hugged me afterwards, she noticed the small (very small!) diamond and exclaimed, "Oh, I get it. Every time I hug a boy, I will see this ring and be reminded to stay pure." Yes, indeed!

MY SPOUSE HAS THE EARTHLY RIGHTS TO MY BODY

Although God owns the heavenly title deed, my wife owns the earthly rights to my body. If I were unmarried, the earthly rights would belong to my future spouse or to God, if I remained unmarried:

> The husband must fulfill his duty to his wife, and likewise also the wife to her husband. The wife does not have authority over her own body, but the husband does; and likewise also the husband does not have authority over his own body, but the wife does (1 Corinthians 7:3-4).

Another moral safeguard is to seriously consider the authority our spouse has over our body. To make the point, I regularly challenge married couples to look in each other's eyes and ask, "Honey, may I commit adultery?" You can well imagine the response. One woman said to her husband, "Go ahead, but then I'll have you killed!" I think she was joking.

Beyond knowing our spouse's (or future spouse's) authority over our body, guarding our body also involves regularly expressing our dedication to that understanding. If you are married, take this to your spouse so that both of you can prayerfully complete this assignment:

A WORD OF DEDICATION TO THE SPOUSE WHO OWNS ME

> *"I present the heavenly title deed of my body to My Lord. I grant to you, my spouse, the earthly rights to my body. I renew my commitment to be faithful to God and to you."*

Since God owns the heavenly title deed and my spouse has the earthly rights to my body, then I'm just a manager of that which belongs to them. Both the owners expect me to be a faithful steward or manager of their property. In the simple and timeless words of the apostle Paul, "In this case, moreover, it is required of stewards that one be found trustworthy" (1 Corinthians 4:2).

chapter 34

PROMISING MY BODY

Job, the patriarch of old, is known throughout Scripture for his patience and endurance especially in the midst of suffering. However, he also struggled with lust. Not surprising, given his spiritual fortitude, he dealt with it forthrightly like the deadly enemy it is. In particular, Job was committed to the practice of making covenants with the specific parts of his body that tempted him to stumble. It is obvious that he saw this as a requirement for his moral safety, as well as the protection of his spouse:

> I have made a covenant with my eyes;
> How then could I gaze at a virgin? . . .
> If my heart has been enticed by a woman,
> Or I have lurked at my neighbor's doorway,
> May my wife grind for another,
> And let others kneel down over her.
> For that would be a lustful crime;
> Moreover, it would be an iniquity punishable by judges.
> For it would be fire that consumes to Abaddon,
> And would uproot all my increase
> (Job 31:1, 9-12).

God is not only concerned about our whole body, but also each of the individual parts. Isaiah the prophet, spoke of one who "shakes his *hands* so that they hold no bribe . . . stops his *ears* from hearing about bloodshed and shuts his *eyes* from looking upon evil" (Isaiah 33:15). In Proverbs 4:20-27 Solomon addressed the importance of watching over our *ears, eyes, heart* (i.e. *mind*), *mouth, lips,* as well as our *feet.* Jesus, speaking metaphorically, cautioned us that if our *hand* or *foot* or *eye* causes us to stumble, cut it off or pluck it out. (Matthew 18:8-9). The apostle Paul wrote concerning the need to continually present the *parts* of our bodies to God:

> Do not go on presenting the *members* of your body to sin as instruments of unrighteousness; but present yourselves to God as those alive from the dead, and your *members* as instruments of righteousness to God (Romans 6:13, emphasis added).

> For just as you presented your *members* as slaves to impurity and to lawlessness, resulting in further lawlessness, so now present your *members* as slaves to righteousness, resulting in sanctification (Romans 6:19, emphasis added).

One of the ways to safeguard our moral purity is by making covenant agreements with God concerning every part of our bodies. Personally, I have followed this practice for a number of years and I can attest to its usefulness.

NECKABOVE!

Many years ago, I made a formal covenant with my eyes not to stare at women inappropriately. It's a contract with myself I call *Neckabove.*[1] That's the only place I will allow my eyes to focus on a woman other than my wife—neck and above! The way some women dress can really put that covenant to the test.

A young woman and her husband came to my office seeking marriage counseling. He removed her coat and she turned to face me. Only a blind man would have failed to notice that her dress was loosely laced "from stem to stern." Only a liar would deny that first look. She was so blatant, I honestly thought this was a cruel joke. Frankly, it quickly stopped being attractive and made me angry to be placed in such a position. I was getting a stiff neck keeping my policy of *Neckabove*. In this case, I even refused to look at her face. I became instantly committed to *None-of-the-Above*.

MY OTHER COVENANTS

Following Job's example and the exhortation from the apostle Paul in Romans, I have made a host of covenants with the parts of my own body. For example:

- I have made an agreement with my feet not to walk near newsstands, especially in foreign cities, in order to avoid the temptation of looking at the blatantly displayed pornographic magazines and postcards.
- I've made a contract with my hands not to "click on" internet pornography, a covenant with my ears not to listen to foul jokes, and a contract with my mouth not to engage in coarse joking.
- I even have an agreement with my knees to pray for the moral protection of my wife and family.

I am committed to not letting my right eye, left ear, or big toe compromise my calling to bring glory to God. I encourage you to do the same.[2] Start at the top of your head and prayerfully work your way to the bottom of your right foot. The ultimate goal, remember, is to "glorify God in your *body*" (1 Corinthians 6:20, emphasis added).

chapter 35

PROTECTING MY BODY

If you are on a diet (okay, a food-management program) you don't go to a bakery and pray over the custard-filled chocolate donut. Smart dieters stay away. When in morally precarious situations, mature people don't stick around and hope things will not get too far out of control. They get out of there now.

God calls us to protect our bodies from falling into immorality by running from evil. Heed the clear instruction of Scripture:

Flee immorality (1 Corinthians 6:18).

Now flee youthful lusts (2 Timothy 2:22).

Abstain from every form of evil (1 Thessalonians 5:22).

Do not let your heart turn aside to her ways.
Do not stray into her paths (Proverbs 7:25).

SEE JOSEPH. SEE MRS. POTIPHAR. SEE JOSEPH RUN!

You are most likely familiar with the story of Joseph, the son of Jacob, whose jealous brothers sold him into slavery (Genesis 37:28). Joseph was not only blessed with a keen mind; he was also blessed with a great body and good looks. However, it wasn't always such a blessing:

> Now Joseph was well-built and handsome, and after a while his master's wife took notice of Joseph and said, "Come to bed with me!" But he refused. "With me in charge," he told her, "my master does not concern himself with anything in the house; everything he owns he has entrusted to my care. No one is greater in this house than I am. My master has withheld nothing from me except you, because you are his wife. How then could I do such a wicked thing and sin against God?" And though she spoke to Joseph day after day, he refused to go to bed with her or even be with her. One day he went into the house to attend to his duties, and none of the household servants was inside. She caught him by his cloak and said, "Come to bed with me!" But he left his cloak in her hand and ran out of the house (Genesis 39:6-12, New International Version).

Day after day, Joseph tried to reason with Mrs. Potiphar. She grew tired of waiting for him and tried to rip off his clothes. The time for talk had passed. His only protection was to run.

THE "ONE STEP BACK" PRINCIPLE

Joseph ran. King David didn't. David's son, Solomon was compelled to warn his son: "Keep your way far from her, and do not go near the *door* of her house" (Proverbs 5:8, emphasis added). Notice that he didn't caution his son to stay away from her *bed*. Wise Solomon knew that if his son made it as far as the *door* he would have no willpower to resist her *bed*. It's a principle I call "One Step Back." Whenever we are in a morally dangerous setting, we need to reflect on the real intent of Proverbs 5:8:

- Don't go near the *door*, near the *bed* in her house
- Don't go near the *street*, near the *door*, near the *bed* in her house.
- Don't go near the *town*, near the *street*, near the *door*, near the *bed* in her house.

Whatever safeguards are needed to avoid a fall, use them. Set some self-imposed rules that you can break without falling into sin. In other words, establish boundaries that give the Holy Spirit time to speak to you in that "still small voice" and well before He has to shout, "Get out of there!"

WELL, HOW FAR CAN WE GO?

I have been honored to speak on the subject of moral purity at a number of Christian colleges and universities. I have often been asked by students, "How far can we go?" (I wish they were asking about their educational goals.)

These Christian students admit their understanding of the Bible's prohibitions against fornication and adultery but are unclear about those "other" matters. They especially ask about those many other sexual activities not involving intercourse.

My *biblical* caution comes primarily from Solomon's counsel in Proverbs 5:8, "Keep your way far from her, / and do not go near the *door* of her house." My *general* caution is simple, "Do not stimulate desires that you cannot righteously fulfill." My *specific* cautions are what this book is all about.[1]

SO WHAT ABOUT "PETTING?"

"What about stimulating the sexual organs of someone other than your spouse?" That's another common question many ask, especially in light of former U.S. President Bill Clinton's statement that he did not consider such activity as "having sex." Let's consider a passage that might shed some much needed light on the subject.

In Ezekiel 23 God is speaking symbolically of Israel's idolatry as immoral behavior (i.e. her spiritual adultery). Notice His description:

> [Israel] played the harlot in Egypt. They played the harlot in their youth; there their breasts were pressed and there their virgin bosom was handled" (Ezekiel 23:3).

> She did not forsake her harlotries from the time in Egypt; for in her youth men had lain with her, and they handled her virgin bosom and poured out their lust on her (Ezekiel 23:8).

> They uncovered her nakedness (Ezekiel 23:11).

> Thus you longed for the *lewdness* (Hebrew: *zimmah*) of your youth, when the Egyptians handled your bosom because of the breasts of your youth (Ezekiel 23:21).

Israel (God's bride) let someone (Egypt, who was not her spouse) touch her inappropriately. The fact that God uses this as a symbol of lewd, immoral, and unchaste behavior (Hebrew: *zimmah*) suggests to me that fondling breasts, uncovering someone else's nakedness and other such sexually stimulating acts are not a part of God's design outside of the covenant of marriage.

JUST A BIT OBVIOUS

I couldn't believe my ears as the desperate man asked for my counsel, "Pastor, every time I go to the beach, I struggle. Please, tell me what to do!" You can well imagine what I said. I looked at him sternly and said, "Well then, don't go to the beach!" I still wonder if he ever caught the silliness of his question and the simplicity of my advice. Another expressed his daily battle, "There's this woman at work who sits at her desk with her skirt hiked high. What do

I do?" I said, "Avoid her desk." He quickly responded, "The only way to do that would be to go outside the building and come back through another door." Noticing his obvious weight problem, I whispered to him, "Listen to me carefully. You not only need to run from this situation for your moral safety; you can really use the exercise. It's a win-win solution, my brother."

What morally dangerous situations are you facing? What do you need to run from at home, at work, in the community, at church, or while traveling? You know what to do to avoid them. Like Joseph, don't stand there debating the obvious. Get out of there now!

chapter 36

LINE OF DEFENSE #3
GUARDING MY COMPANIONS

A WALL OF SHIELDS

The ancient Roman army was known for its effective battle tactics. Each soldier was equipped with a curved shield called the *scutum* that was roughly the size of a small door. As the army marched in formation into the thick of battle, the men in the front placed their shields in front of themselves, the men on the sides placed their shields to the outside, and the men in the middle placed their shields above their heads. It was called the *testudo*, or tortoise. Few things could penetrate that wall of shields marching toward the enemy.

So it is with the body of Christ. As soldiers in the Army of God, we cannot resist temptation alone. Our shield of faith does not protect our flanks against the destructive tactics and the fiery darts of the Enemy (Ephesians 6:11,16), nor was it designed to do so. For my protection, I need you with your shield of faith hoisted high. For your protection, you need me to do the same. All of us need the rest of our brothers and sisters in Christ properly positioned as a spiritual *testudo*—a fortress of faith. Only then do we have a chance of resisting the Devil's attacks (1 Peter 5:8-9) and only then will we succeed in our assault on the gates of hell (Matthew 16:18). Additionally, if we are wounded in the battle or let our individual shield of faith down, our fellow soldiers can move us to the center of the pack, where we can be protected from further harm (1 Thessalonians 5:14). I need you. You need me. We need each other.

WE NEED EACH OTHER . . . TO KEEP FROM FALLING

If God had chosen to answer Cain's question in Genesis 4:9 when he asked, "Am I my brother's keeper?" what might God have said? "Absolutely!" We are our brothers' keepers. Let me hasten to say that we are not just our *brothers'* keepers; we are also our *sisters'* keepers. Of course, this can be taken to mean our earthly family, as well as our spiritual family.

I find great encouragement from the Song of Solomon. In Chapter 8, the brothers of Solomon's bride are recalling how they protected their little sister from moral danger until she was ready to be married:

> We have a little sister,
> And she has no breasts;
> What shall we do for our sister
>   on the day when she is spoken for?
> If she is a *wall*,
> We will build on her a battlement of silver;
> But if she is a *door*,
> We will barricade her with planks of cedar
> (Song of Solomon 8:8-9, emphasis added).

These older brothers had a strategy to protect their little sister. If she, even at a young age, demonstrated a sincere desire to become an impregnable wall of moral virtue, they would continue to build into her life everything she would need to fight the battle and reward her accordingly. However, if she showed any signs that she was an open door to immorality, they were committed to barricade their little sister with all the protection she needed, even against her *own* will. I love her response as she looks back over her life:

I was a wall, and my breasts were like towers (i.e. off limits
    to others);
Then I became in his (i.e. my husband, Solomon's) eyes as one
    who finds peace (Hebrew: *shalom*) (Song of Solomon 8:10).

Here was a woman grateful for brothers who guarded her purity. Here
was a young wife now experiencing the reward of having a husband who
saw God's *shalom* in her life. I think she also knew that an eternal reward
would be given to her brothers who risked even her youthful tantrums for
the greater good. These brothers were living examples of Solomon's words:

Better is open rebuke
Than love that is concealed (Proverbs 27:5).

He who rebukes a man will afterward find more favor
Than he who flatters with the tongue (Proverbs 28:23).

A man who flatters his neighbor
Is spreading a net for his steps (Proverbs 29:5).

I received the following letter from a man who lives on a small island.
Obviously, this grateful brother is giving me more credit than I deserve.
All the thanks goes to the Lord, the One who gave us such unambiguous
instruction regarding how to win the battle.

I thank God for how your ministry has touched my life.
I was at home sick today . . . and was tempted to sin. I
popped in your video series on building moral purity and
watched it all afternoon, stopping to reflect, pray, and read
my Bible, while my wife was in town with our kids. What a
blessing to have God's guidance through a man who rightly
divides the Word of God. I thank you.

Normally, I would not share such a note, but in the midst of the personal encouragement this brother exemplified the keys to safeguarding our moral purity:

- personal reflection on the cost of immorality
- prayer for his own moral safety
- spending time in the Word of God
- openly seeking the help of others
- allowing others to be used of God to help

This man may live on an island, but he is no island himself.

We must take responsibility for the battle with immorality facing all men and women, especially our fellow members of the body of Christ. A few reminders from Scripture:

> For the body (i.e. the church) is not one member, but many . . . the members may have the same care for one another. And if one member suffers, all the members suffer with it (1 Corinthians 12:14, 25-26).

> Iron sharpens iron, so one man sharpens another (Proverbs 27:17).

> We urge you, brethren, admonish the unruly, encourage the fainthearted, help the weak (1 Thessalonians 5:14).

> But encourage one another day after day, as long as it is still called "Today" so that none of you will be hardened by the deceitfulness of sin (Hebrews 3:13).

> Let us consider how to stimulate one another to love

and good deeds, not forsaking our own assembling together, as is the habit of some, but encouraging one another; and all the more, as you see the day drawing near (Hebrews 10:24-25).

Be of sober spirit, be on the alert. Your adversary, the devil, prowls about like a roaring lion, seeking someone to devour. But resist him, firm in your faith, knowing that the same experiences of suffering are being accomplished by your brethren who are in the world (1 Peter 5:8-9).

WE NEED EACH OTHER . . . WHEN WE FALL

Later, in *Part Five*, we will examine God's specific plan for restoration. In advance of that study, I want to reinforce our responsibility to help each other, even those who fall victim to the battle with immorality:

Two are better than one, because they have a good return
  for their work.
If one falls down, his friend can help him up.
But pity the man who falls and has no one to help him up!
Also, if two lie down together, they will keep warm.
But how can one keep warm alone?
Though one may be overpowered, two can
  defend themselves.
A cord of three strands is not quickly broken
(Ecclesiastes 4:9-12, New International Version).

Brethren, even if anyone is caught in any trespass, you who are spiritual (i.e. mature), restore such a one in a spirit of gentleness; each one looking to yourself, so that you too will not be tempted (Galatians 6:1).

My brethren, if any among you strays from the truth and one turns him back, let him know that he who turns a sinner from the error of his way will save his soul from death, and will cover a multitude of sins (James 5:19-20).

chapter 37

PRAYING FOR MY COMPANIONS

A church member stood at our men's retreat and shared his deep concern: "Brothers, will you pray for me? I am going to be traveling to Europe on a business trip and there's a woman in our work group that is very attractive to me. I've been struggling with my thought life and I am really afraid of what might happen."

I was pleased that a number of our men immediately committed to call him in Europe, especially at specific times when he told them he would be most vulnerable. The rest of the group got on their knees and prayed for him on the spot. Needless to say, the trip was a big success, at least in terms of his moral purity. Here is a group of men who saw the power of prayer and accountability in helping a brother win a decisive battle.

In the very context of putting on the armor of God to do battle in our spiritual warfare, the apostle Paul reminds us of the importance of praying for each other: "With all prayer and petition pray at all times in the Spirit, and with this in view, be on the alert with all perseverance and petition for all the saints" (Ephesians 6:18). In His Sermon on the Mount, Jesus taught us to pray for each other's protection: "And do not lead *us* into temptation, but deliver *us* from evil" (Matthew 6:13, King James Version, emphasis added).

If we are going to see a revival of moral purity in our midst, we must make the solemn commitment to regularly pray for our fellow Christians. As is so aptly put, "When all is said and done, when it comes to prayer, a lot more is said than done." May this not be true of us.

I encourage you to make a list of those for whom you will pray, especially concerning this matter of personal purity. Besides your family, friends, and fellow church members, remember to pray that your church and government leaders will also live godly lives:

> First of all, then, I urge that entreaties and prayers, petitions and thanksgivings, be made on behalf of all men, for kings and *all who are in authority*, in order that we may lead a tranquil and quiet life *in all godliness and dignity* (1 Timothy 2:1-2, emphasis added).

Alan Redpath, in his book, *The Making of the Man of God*, makes this astute observation regarding the need to pray, especially for our leaders:

> Oh, from what heights of blessing it is possible for a man to fall! To what depths of sin a man can descend, even with all that spiritual background! The higher the pinnacle of blessing, authority, and publicity he has attained by grace, the deeper and more staggering can be his collapse. There is never a day in any man's life but that he is dependent upon the grace of God for power and the blood of Jesus for cleansing. If ever you pray for men in positions of Christian leadership, you are praying for those who are the special targets of the attack of the Devil.[1]

Rather than move on, why not just take a few minutes now to pray for the moral safety of the following people:

- Your spouse or future spouse
- Your children and grandchildren (and even the generation to follow)
- Your children's friends (especially those who are a great moral influence in their lives)
- Your other family members
- Your friends
- Your church and ministry leaders
- Your local, state and national leaders
- Others God puts on your heart to pray for today

chapter 38

PROTECTING MY COMPANIONS

Early in my pastoral ministry I heard someone say, "If you stick your head above a crowd, someone is going to throw a brick at it." Little did I realize how these words apply to our God-given role as our brothers' keepers. There is even more to guarding our companions than praying for each other; we must also be willing to stick our necks out and protect each other, even when to do so is most risky. This brings up the whole matter of personal accountability. Unfortunately, like prayer, the subject has resulted in far more banter than behavior.

ISN'T ACCOUNTABILITY A GAME?

I was speaking with a well-known radio Bible teacher who was lamenting what he felt was the great weakness of accountability. He said to me, "What makes you think that someone who is committing adultery wouldn't lie to his accountability partner?" At first I was taken aback, admitting he was right in some respects. However, if I had the opportunity again, I would now answer him, "To be faithful in little is to be faithful in much. If we begin maintaining the practice of honest and consistent accountability, I believe two things will happen: First, we might be quick to share the slightest hint of a struggle. Secondly, because of a regular practice of this kind of honesty, we will be less prone to lie about an even more serious compromise."

THE THREE FACETS OF ACCOUNTABILITY

Let me make my own distinction between *responsibility* and *accountability*. I often hear ministers and missionaries tell me, "I am *accountable* to my board." I am quick to say to them, "Is your board truly free to ask you probing questions about your personal life? And do they? Are you regularly honest with them about your struggles with impurity, greed, selfish ambition, anger, fear, loneliness, or jealousy? If not, you may be *professionally responsible* to them, but I doubt if you are *personally accountable*."

A fellow minister shared with me his helpful insights in what he believes to be the three facets of accountability. Knowing him as I do, these are not just outline points; they are vital life principles:

1. Consistent Accountability: "Knowing that I will be tempted, I need to meet *with somebody regularly.*"

2. Defensive Accountability: *"Before I am tempted, I want to share my particular struggles with somebody."*

3. Offensive Accountability: "I am being tempted right now. Somebody please help."[1]

THE BENEFITS OF ACCOUNTABILITY

Lust thrives on secrecy. Nothing diffuses it like exposure.[2]
   —Randy Alcorn—

In the early days of my ministry a newspaper blew up against the front door of my church office. I soon realized it was the advertising section of a pornographic tabloid. I curiously stood at the door reading the ludicrous and obscene ads. After a few minutes, my conscience and the Holy Spirit got my attention. I confessed my sin and prayed. I then asked, "Now what do I do, Lord?" I felt His prompting to take the paper home and confess to my wife what I did. I was so ashamed. Karon and I prayed together as we burned that "newspaper from hell" in our fireplace.

This still wasn't enough. I didn't have peace to get on with my day. I asked, "What now, Lord?" and I sensed God moving me to call the Chairman of the Elder Board. I confessed to him, as well. After we prayed, he spoke the simple words, "Jim, you know I love you. But never do that again!"

I thought the matter was over, until I felt God's Spirit saying, "Now, you're on the right track, but there is one more call you need to make. Your wife and board chairman know you and they are quite willing to forgive. They are your safe harbors. However, to really get your attention, I want you to call and confess what you did to Arzella."

"Arzella!" I shouted in my spirit. Here was one of those precious older saints who placed me on quite an undeserved pedestal of pastoral perfection. When she called me, "Pastor Jim" it was as if flowers flowed from her lips.

I couldn't believe the Spirit of God was asking me to confess my sin to this dear lady. After many minutes of debating in my heart and trying to dismiss this as a devilish impulse, I submitted to Him and called her. As I told Arzella the gruesome story, there were no flowers in her voice as she softly said, "Oh, Pastor Jim. How could you?" To my surprise, she was quite understanding and hearing my broken heart, she granted her forgiveness. However, I could hear the *clunk* as I fell from that pedestal.

I was humiliated, emotionally exhausted, and thoroughly disgusted at my bad choice. After that long and embarrassing ordeal, I made a life-changing observation. Reading that sin-filled material simply wasn't worth it!

What happened to that dear old woman? Did she reject me as some pastoral reprobate? On the contrary. From that day on she became one of my greatest prayer warriors until her death a few years later. In fact, on her deathbed, I held her hands and whispered in her ear, "Arzella, we have had some very precious times together. I'm going to miss you. I will especially miss knowing you are praying for my moral safety. I have one last request.

When you get to heaven, will you tell Jesus I love Him? Will you ask Him for an extra measure of power to deal with the sin in my life and to preach the Word from a pure life?" Although I'm not exactly sure what happened when she arrived in heaven a few hours later, I know God graciously received the message from my repentant heart.

THE PRACTICE OF ACCOUNTABILITY

That all happened over twenty five years ago. To this day I am deeply committed to a regular practice of personal accountability. When I am struggling with temptation or fall into compromise, no matter how small it may seem to my rationalizing heart, I share it with my *testudo*—my wife, a fellow shepherd, a friend, a board-member or a co-worker. It may be embarrassing, but it sure keeps things in check. I fully expect that if I am faithful to share the little compromises, I will have a far better chance of never having to share some huge moral blunder.

From the depths of my heart and soul, I want to make a strong suggestion; call it a command, if that works best for you. I urge you to schedule a weekly meeting with a few trusted companions of the same sex—your hand-picked *testudo*. During that time, ask each other questions designed to check your spiritual, mental, physical, marital, and integrity pulse. Here are some I use that you also might consider using:

MY PERSONAL ACCOUNTABILITY QUESTIONS

1. Have you been faithful in the Word and prayer? Are you growing in your intimacy with God?

2. Have you been sensitive to the needs of your spouse? Your family?

3. Have you been struggling with impure thoughts?

4. Have you been looking at questionable materials that would bring shame to the Lord?

5. Have you been alone with someone in any kind of situation when your feelings or actions became inappropriate or where others could have suspected something?

6. Are you experiencing any physical problems? Eating right? Getting adequate rest and sufficient exercise?

7. Are you facing challenges that are negatively affecting your physical, emotional, or spiritual well-being?

8. Have you lied or compromised your answer to any of the above questions?[3]

chapter 39

CONFRONTING MY COMPANIONS

"I KNEW IT WOULD HAPPEN!"

My Italian blood steams when I hear people say such things about a fellow Christian who has succumbed to sexual sin. Trying hard not to be too intimidating, I ask, "If you knew it was going to happen, why didn't you try to stop him?" I hold my breath waiting for the familiar answer, "Who am I to judge people?" Then I jump to respond: "Every believer is called by God to judge as long as we judge according to His standards; not our own. Does immorality violate His standards? If it does, then God has already judged it. We have every right to pass His judgment on sin."

I then remind them of what the apostle Paul said to his fellow Christians, "Do you not know that we shall judge angels? *How much more, matters of this life?*" (1 Corinthians 6:3, emphasis added). I also point them to what Jesus said about standing by and letting things happen that offend the heart of God. In His view there really is *a sin of toleration.*[1]

If we are not willing to appropriately and biblically confront our brothers and sisters in Christ then we simply do not have God's concerns in mind. We also do not love them. A couple of biblical reminders:

> Faithful are the wounds of a friend, but deceitful are the
> kisses of an enemy (Proverbs 27:6).

Brethren, even if anyone is caught in any trespass, you who are spiritual, restore such a one in a spirit of gentleness; each one looking to yourself, so that you too will not be tempted. Bear one another's burdens, and thereby fulfill the law of Christ (i.e. to *love our neighbor*) (Galatians 6:1-2).

TACKLE THEM AND SHACKLE THEM

In his first letter to the Thessalonians, the apostle Paul makes an impassioned appeal for those new believers to be involved in helping their brethren, "We urge you, brethren, admonish the unruly, encourage the fainthearted, help the weak" (1 Thessalonians 5:14). Rather than do an extended exposition of this amazing passage, let me suggest my own loose paraphrase, based on the meaning of each of these Greek words and what I believe to be the apostle Paul's intent:

I beg you to warn those who are out of step, come alongside those who are faint-hearted, little souls and cling to those who are emotional and spiritual weaklings. If you have to, tackle and shackle them to keep them from harming themselves (1 Thessalonians 5:14, personal paraphrase).

REVIEWING OUR TACTICS

Though often overlooked, our gracious God has given us an infallible plan to combat the immorality in our lives. He hasn't left us alone in our daily battle with lust.

Our first line of defense in our war against immorality is by guarding our minds. As we've seen, we do this by:

- Protecting our minds from anything that distorts our understanding of God's design for our sexuality.

- Provisioning our minds with what God says about immorality.
- Purifying our minds by meditating on what God says about Himself.
- Preparing our minds by considering the devastating results of immorality.

Our second line of defense in our battle with sexual sin is by guarding our bodies. We do this by:

- Presenting our bodies daily to God and regularly to our spouse.
- Promising our bodies by making covenants with God concerning every part.
- Protecting our bodies by running from morally dangerous situations.

Our third line of defense in this life-long conflict is by guarding our companions. We do this by:

- Praying for them.
- Holding them accountable.

We have everything we need to fight the daily battles and ultimately win the war. I find great encouragement from the words of the apostle Peter to all of his spiritual comrades in arms. He begins with *God's* provision:

> Grace and peace be multiplied to you in the knowledge of God and of Jesus our Lord; seeing that His divine power has granted to us everything pertaining to life and godliness, through the true knowledge of Him who called us by His own glory and excellence. For by these He has granted to us His precious and magnificent promises, so that by them you may become partakers of the divine nature, having escaped the corruption that is in the world by lust (2 Peter 1:2-4).

The apostle Peter continues with *our* responsibility in the process:

> Now for this very reason also, applying all diligence, in your faith supply moral excellence, and in your moral excellence, knowledge, and in your knowledge, self-control, and in your self-control, perseverance, and in your perseverance, godliness, and in your godliness, brotherly kindness, and in your brotherly kindness, love. For if these qualities are yours and are increasing, they render you neither useless nor unfruitful in the true knowledge of our Lord Jesus Christ. For he who lacks these qualities is blind or short-sighted, having forgotten his purification from his former sins (2 Peter 1:5-9).

SALUTING OUR COMMANDER

In the Fall of 2003 I was invited to South Africa to speak at the Pan-Africa Christian Police Association Conference (PACPAC). On the first evening, hundreds of participants marched into the auditorium in a wide assortment of police uniforms. To a shortened version of each country's national anthem, each squad saluted their country's flag. About a dozen countries were represented that night, mostly from Africa. I was impressed with the many multi-colored flags and unique national anthems. I had never seen so many different styles of salute. I was struck by the beauty of their diversity. I was also deeply impacted by the words of Mike Harris, chairman of the PACPAC board: "We have to be revived before we can be a part of revival; we have to be changed before we can make change."[2] I spent the next days speaking about a revival of personal purity among evangelical leaders as a major part of God's answer to the many problems in Africa.

On my last day of teaching, I shared how impressed I was with the first night's ceremony. "However," I continued, "I am even more impressed with the Christian unity I have seen among you, even amidst so many cultural differences." I asked if they would be willing to stand united with me, not to salute a national flag, nor a human superior officer, but to salute the King of Kings and Lord of Lords. I will never forget that crowd of Christian police officers, now dressed in civilian clothes, joining me in saluting our Sovereign Lord and Savior, Jesus Christ.

God has a mighty army of His people, unified by His Spirit and empowered by the Word of God, who will stand with us in this battle for personal purity and holiness. Together, we salute His authority and follow His orders. Together, we guard our minds, guard our bodies, and guard each other. Together, we help each other to never get entangled in the web of impurity. Our mutual goal is to please the One who enlisted us to be a part of His army (2 Timothy 2:3-4) and to say with the apostle Paul, "I have fought the good fight, I have finished the course, I have kept the faith" (2 Timothy 4:7). Onward, Christian soldiers! March on, Ambassadors of Purity!

PART FIVE:

THE WAY BACK

chapter 40

A WORD TO THE WOUNDED AND FALLEN

Many of us have been wounded by our own bad choices. Some of us have fallen headlong in the battle with immorality. Sadly, it has been my observation that Christianity is the only army in the world that shoots its wounded and ignores the fallen. It is no wonder why some have revised the commandment to say, "Thou shalt not *admit* adultery." Too many of our wounded or fallen brothers and sisters in Christ refuse to seek help. Just as sad is the number of our fellow Christians who refuse to render aid to those who are hurting because of their sin. How contrary to the instruction of Scripture:

> Brethren, even if anyone is caught in any trespass, you who are spiritual, *restore such a one in a spirit of gentleness*; each one looking to yourself, so that you too will not be tempted (Galatians 6:1, emphasis added).

> We urge you, brethren, *admonish the unruly, encourage the fainthearted, help the weak, be patient with all men* (1 Thessalonians 5:14, emphasis added).

If your brother sins, go and show him his fault in private; if he listens to you, *you have won your brother* (Matthew 18:15, emphasis added).

My brethren, if any among you strays from the truth and one turns him back, let him know that *he who turns a sinner from the error of his way will save his soul from death*, and will cover a multitude of sins (James 5:19-20, emphasis added).

For the wounded or fallen soldiers in the army of God the healing and restoration process is clearly defined. We who are strong are called to be a part of that process as we come along side those who are weak. We must accept that mandate to "leave no soldier behind." Instead, with Bibles in hand, we must choose to tell our wounded and fallen warriors, "Help is on the way!"

SEXUAL SIN IS NOT THE "UNPARDONABLE SIN"

Rest assured, fellow sinners. If we are born-again believers who have sincerely trusted in Jesus Christ alone for our salvation, we are in a permanent covenant relationship with God. We are His sheep and no one can snatch us out of His hand (John 10:27-29). Whom the Lord calls to be His, will always be His. Our eternal life is kept secure, not by our own power, but by the power of God (1 Peter 1:5). Nothing can change that, not even our deepest sin (Romans 8:28-39). This is the great news about grace; the really good news of the gospel.

However, our security in Christ does not give us the excuse to be "grace-abusers." The apostle Paul's words are quite clear: "Are we to continue in sin so that grace might increase? May it never be! How shall we who died to sin still live in it?" (Romans 6:1-2). Although our sin is not cause for eternal rejection by God, it is cause for a temporary rift in our fellowship with Him. Most of us know how this distance feels. I still hold fast to the old saying, "If we don't feel close to God, guess who moved?"

THE STORY OF ROBERT ROBINSON

Not many know the life story of the hymn writer, Robert Robinson, who lived almost two hundred years ago. Although his life is unfamiliar, his feelings about his distance from God are not:

> It was a bright Sunday morning in 18th century London, but Robert Robinson's mood was anything but sunny. All along the street there were people hurrying to church, but in the midst of the crowd, Robinson was a lonely man. The sound of church bells reminded him of years past when his faith in God was strong and the church was an integral part of his life. It had been years since he set foot in a church—years of wandering, disillusionment, and gradual defection from the God he once loved. That love for God—once fiery and passionate—had slowly burned out within him, leaving him dark and cold inside. Robinson heard the *clip-clop, clip-clop* of a horse-drawn cab approaching behind him. Turning, he lifted his hand to hail the driver. But then he saw that the cab was occupied by a young woman dressed in finery for the Lord's Day. He waved the driver on, but the woman in the carriage ordered the carriage to be stopped. "Sir, I'd be happy to share this carriage with you," she said to Robinson. "Are you going to church?" Robinson was about to decline, then he paused. "Yes," he said at last. "I am going to church." He stepped into the carriage and sat down beside the young woman. As the carriage rolled forward Robert Robinson and the woman exchanged introductions. There was a flash of recognition in her eyes when he

stated his name. "That's an interesting coincidence," she said, reaching into her purse. She withdrew a small book of inspirational verse, opened it to a ribbon-bookmark, and handed the book to him. "I was just reading a verse by a poet named Robert Robinson. Could it be. . .?" He took the book, nodding. "Yes, I wrote these words years ago." "Oh, how wonderful!" she exclaimed. "Imagine! I'm sharing a carriage with the author of these very lines!" But Robinson barely heard her. He was absorbed in the words he was reading. They were words that would one day be set to music and become a great hymn of the faith, familiar to generations of Christians:

> Come, Thou Fount of every blessing,
> Tune my heart to sing Thy grace,
> Streams of mercy, never ceasing,
> Call for songs of loudest praise.

His eyes slipped to the bottom of the page where he read:

> Prone to wander, Lord, I feel it—
> Prone to leave the God I love;
> Here's my heart, O take and seal it,
> Seal it for Thy courts above.

He could barely read the last few lines through the tears that brimmed in his eyes. "I wrote these words—and I've lived these words, 'Prone to wander . . . prone to leave the God I love.'" The woman suddenly understood. "You also wrote, 'Here's my heart, O take and seal it.' You *can* offer your heart again to God, Mr. Robinson. It's not too late." And it wasn't too late for Robert Robinson. In that

moment he turned his heart back to God and walked with
him the rest of his days.[1]

Like Mr. Robinson, all of us are prone to wander. However, too many
of us are just as prone to think of repentance as saying a quick "I'm sorry" to
heaven and a few words of remorse to those we have hurt on earth. Though
God will never forsake us, our sin disrupts our fellowship with our heavenly
Father. It also affects our relationships with others. Only after restoring our
fellowship with Him can we ever hope to truly mend our relationship with
those we have hurt. We are foolish to think that true restoration to intimacy
can be accomplished with a simple bandage when battlefield surgery is
needed. The problem lies not so much in God's willingness to draw near to
us but our willingness to draw near to Him for more than an instant. In his
epistle, James presents the process of restoration:

> Draw near to God and He will draw near to you. Cleanse
> your hands, you sinners; and purify your hearts, you
> double-minded. Be miserable and mourn and weep; let
> your laughter be turned into mourning, and your joy to
> gloom. Humble yourselves in the presence of the Lord, and
> He will exalt you (James 4:8-10).

Like an army medic's field gear, let's unpack this portion of Scripture.
If we draw near to God, cleanse our hands of sin, and purify our hearts of
rebellion, our fellowship with God will be restored. If we are deeply grieved
to the point of being miserable and even weeping over our sin, He will heed
our cries for forgiveness. If we humble ourselves before God, then He will
draw near to us and even exalt us. In other words, He will allow people to
see us in a different light, even those our sin has hurt so deeply. I love the
words of hope the Lord speaks through the prophet Isaiah:

For thus says the high and exalted One who lives forever,

whose name is Holy, "I dwell on a high and holy place, and also with the contrite and lowly of spirit in order to revive the spirit of the lowly and to revive the heart of the contrite (Isaiah 57:15).

Did you catch that? Holy God dwells with the sincerely humble, contrite, and broken-hearted sinner. It is His desire to revive (i.e. "to bring them to life and health," Hebrew: *chayah*) those who will draw near to Him in true repentance. In the parable of the prodigal son, found in Luke 15:11-32, the rebellious young man squandered his father's wealth on prostitutes, yet he was eventually forgiven and restored to fellowship with his father. The same can happen to us.

Then why is it so hard? Because we think this all happens in an instant. We want microwave restoration for sin that has been stewing for years. Remorse can happen in that instant when we finally face the weight of our sin. However, true restoration of our relationship to God and others involves a longer process of *admitting* our sin, *confessing* our sin, *turning* from our sin and, by God's grace, *strengthening* others who have been hurt. I call these four steps, "The A.C.T.S. of Repentance."

chapter 41

THE A.C.T.S. OF REPENTANCE

STEP #1
ADMITTING MY SIN (Greek: *metanoeo*)

I love the story of the Prussian king, Frederick the Great, touring a Berlin prison. The prisoners fell on their knees before him and declared their "innocence"—all except one man who remained silent. King Frederick called to him, "Why are you here?" "Armed robbery, Your Majesty," was the reply. "And are you guilty?" asked the King. "Yes indeed, Your Majesty, I deserve my punishment." Frederick then summoned the jailer and ordered him, "Release this guilty wretch at once. I will not have him kept in this prison where he will corrupt all the fine innocent people who occupy it."[1]

We humans have mastered the art of cover up and denial. And when our sin is discovered we resort to blaming, minimizing and rationalizing. We have learned well the ways of our ancestors and contemporaries. Unfortunately, we have not learned well the ways of our Master.

The Bible is clear as to the first step to true repentance and restoration— full admission. Throughout the New Testament we find many references regarding the importance of being completely honest about our sin and its consequences. The word that is often used is *metanoeo* or in it's noun form *metanoia*. It refers to matters, once hidden, brought to the forefront of our minds, where it can be dealt with openly. Very simply stated, it is God's desire that we stop repressing and suppressing our sin.

After rebuking the Corinthian Christians for their sin, the apostle Paul writes a follow-up letter in which he expresses his joy that his confrontation did more than cause them to grieve over the *consequences* of their sin. It also brought them to a point of *admitting* who was truly to blame. In so doing, they were fulfilling the will of God:

> I now rejoice, not that you were made sorrowful, but that you were made sorrowful to the point of repentance ("a change of mind," Greek: *metanoia*); for you were made sorrowful according to the will of God . . . (2 Corinthians 7:9-10).

With God's desire in mind, let's break this *admission* step (*metanoeo*) into three components: refusing to hide my sin, stopping blaming others for my sin and grieving over my sin.

REFUSING TO HIDE MY SIN

Hiding our sin is as human as humans can be. In fact, Adam was our first human example. Discovered by God, he presents his reason for running, "I was afraid . . . so I hid myself" (Genesis 3:10). In other words, "Lord, I know what You told me would be the consequences if I disobeyed you. I did it anyway and I ran in fear of what might happen." Acknowledging this very human propensity to hide our sin in fear of the consequences, Job comments:

> Have I covered my transgressions like Adam,
> By hiding my iniquity in my bosom,
> Because I feared the great multitude,
> And contempt of families terrified me,
> And kept silent and did not go out of doors?
> (Job 31:33-34).

Dear friends, the time for playing hide and seek with God is over. It's not a game. He will always catch us. The first act of true repentance involves *admitting* our sins—all of them; the ones we know we are hiding and the secret ones that we expect God will reveal to us.

In Psalm 19:12 King David wrote, "Acquit me (Hebrew: *naqah*) of *hidden* (Hebrew: *cathar*) faults (Psalm 19:12). In essence he is saying, "Lord, sometimes I don't know what errors I have done; sometimes I do. Bring to the forefront of my mind those *hidden* sins I don't know, as well as those *secret* sins I do know, so I can deal with all of them and be cleansed by You."

That's the essence of David's prayer in Psalm 139:23-24. Rather than just read the familiar words, why not make them the prayer of your heart right now?

> Search me, O God, and know my heart;
> Try me and know my anxious thoughts;
> And see if there be any hurtful way in me,
> And lead me in the everlasting way (Psalm 139:23-24).

STOPPING BLAMING OTHERS FOR MY SIN

We live in a world of blame. "It's not really my fault," has become the mantra of many. I could write volumes on the famous excuses we sinners have given. Many in my generation remember "The Twinkie Defense" in which a change in diet from health food to sugary food was said to be the underlying cause for murder and other criminal behavior. Feeble excuses for sinful behavior is not a modern phenomenon. Once again, it all started with Adam, the first excuse-maker: "The *woman* whom *You* gave to be with me, *she* gave me from the tree, and I ate" (Genesis 3:12, emphasis added).

Did you catch his words? "Lord, I know it looks bad because I'm hiding but really, it's not my fault. It's the *woman's* fault. *She* gave me the fruit. No . . . wait a minute! God, *You* are the One that gave that woman to me. It's *Your* fault!"

Folks, we have been perfecting Adam's excuse-making ever since. It's time we put a stop to this, at least in our own lives. A part of the *admission* step is to stop the blame game. The Devil, the flesh and the world didn't make me sin. G.K. Chesterton was once asked, "What's wrong with the world?" He replied, "I am." The Bible agrees:

> But each one is tempted when he is carried away and enticed by his *own* lust. Then when lust has conceived, it gives birth to sin; and when sin is accomplished, it brings forth death. *Do not be deceived*, my beloved brethren" (James 1:14-16, emphasis added).

GRIEVING OVER MY SIN

In Ephesians 4:30, the apostle Paul presents a graphic picture, pointing out that when we sin we actually *grieve* the Holy Spirit of God. The Greek word *lupeo* means to cause deep sorrow, like the grief we may have felt at the death of a loved one. True repentance begins by acknowledging how much our sin grieves the Lord. It also requires that we stop treating our sin lightly. Instead, we join God in mourning and weeping over our bad choices (James 4:9). Anything less not only grieves Him further but causes our fellow believers to also mourn over our lack of sincere repentance (2 Corinthians 12:21).

Beloved, the God who searches and knows our hearts is calling us to tell the whole truth. The solution to hiding is full disclosure. No more pretending or hiding. No more cover-up, rationalizing, making excuses or minimizing the severity of our sin. It's time to listen to the Holy Spirit's deepest promptings. Without a guilty plea there can be no true change nor can we expect to receive God's fullest blessing. King David taught us well, "How blessed is he . . . in whose spirit there is no deceit!" (Psalm 32:1-2). So did Solomon, his son: "He who conceals his transgression will not prosper" (Proverbs 28:13).

STEP #2
CONFESSING MY SIN (Greek: *homologeo*)

Perhaps you have heard some form of the expression, "From my mouth to God's ears." That's a pretty fair description of the next step in the restoration process. After *admitting* our sin in our *mind*, we now must *confess* our sin with our *mouth*:

> I acknowledged my sin to You,
> And my iniquity I did not hide;
> I said, "I will confess my transgressions to the LORD";
> And You forgave the guilt of my sin (Psalm 32:5).

> For I confess my iniquity; I am full of anxiety because of my sin (Psalm 38:18).

> If we confess our sins, He is faithful and righteous to forgive us our sins and to cleanse us from all unrighteousness (1 John 1:9).

Here in 1 John 1:9 we find the Greek word *homologeo*. It comes from two words, *homo* and *logeo*, meaning to express the same words. Theologically speaking, to *confess* something is to express the *same words* that God would say. Thus the apostle Paul declares, "That if you *confess* (*homologeo*) with your mouth, 'Jesus is Lord'. . ." (Romans 10:9, New International Version). *Jesus is Lord*—the same words our heavenly Father would *confess* about His Son, Jesus Christ. Sincere confession is not saying:

> "I am *sorry* I got caught . . ."
> "Lord, *if* I offended you . . ."
> "*Maybe* it was wrong, *but* . . ."

True confession expresses what our Holy God might say about that sin: "That sin that you are finally admitting falls short of My character, My attributes, My glory. It is inconsistent with who you are as My child and it deeply grieves Me."

When I was nine years old I memorized a prayer that, in some traditions, is called *The Act of Contrition*. It still stirs my heart, just as it did when I first learned it over fifty years ago:

> *O my God, I am heartily sorry for having offended Thee, and I detest all my sins because of Thy just punishments, but most of all because they offend Thee, my God, Who art all-good and deserving of all my love. I firmly resolve with the help of Thy grace, to sin no more and to avoid the near occasions of sin.*

STEP #3
TURNING FROM MY SIN (Greek: *epistrepho*)

A Sunday school teacher asked her class what the word *repentance* meant. One student responded, "It is being sorry for your sins." Another spoke up, "No, it's being sorry enough to quit!" Our third step of restoration moves us from *admitting* sin in the *mind*, *confessing* sin with our *mouth*, to *turning* from sin in our *manner*—i.e. changing our actions.

In his book, *I Surrender*, Patrick Morley writes about the great misconception "that we can add Christ to our lives, but not subtract sin. It is a change in belief without a change in behavior." He goes on to say, "It is revival without reformation, without repentance."[2]

One of my favorite passages of Scripture contains the comforting words of Jesus to Simon Peter just before the arrogant apostle commits his infamous denials of Christ:

> Simon, Simon, behold, Satan has demanded permission to sift you like wheat; but I have prayed for you, that your faith may not fail; and you, when *once you have*

turned again, strengthen your brothers (Luke 22:31-32, emphasis added).

Here we find the Greek word *epistrepho*, which quite literally means to *turn around*, *return* or, in this context, *repent*. I'm told that this same word used to be printed on refillable soda bottles in Greece. If it's true, it makes sense. The word *epistrepho* can certainly mean, "Return for Filling."

Sin empties us of the fruit of the Spirit and our intimacy with God. We can easily feel like an empty soda bottle lying in the dirt. However, once we *admit* and *confess* our sin, we can *turn* from that sin and *return* to God for filling. He cleanses us, refills us with His Spirit, and re-uses us to refresh others. The word *epistrepho* also implies that when we do *return* to God for filling, we do so with the resolve to never again *return* to that sin:

> Search me, O God, and know my heart;
> Try me and know my anxious thoughts;
> And see if there be any hurtful way in me,
> And *lead me in the everlasting way*
> (Psalm 139:23-24, emphasis added).

The *everlasting way* speaks of a new pattern of life—a life of submission and obedience to the will of God in the midst of our on-going struggle. William Booth, founder of the Salvation Army, said it well, "The greatness of a man's power is the measure of his surrender."[3] That turning *to* God and *away* from sin—that complete surrendering—must be done immediately. As I have often said to my children and my congregation, "Postponed obedience is just another form of disobedience."

STEP #4
STRENGTHENING OTHER SINNERS (Greek: *sterizo*)

Confession is good for the soul. It's also good for other people's souls. One of the many results of admitting (*metanoeo*), confessing (*homologeo*), and turning (*epistrepho*) from the sin is a renewed emphasis on strengthening (*sterizo*) others. To continue the alliteration, true repentance moves from the *mind* to the *mouth* to the *manner* and, finally, to the *ministry*. In other words, the process of restoration results in being used again in the lives of others, even those our sin has wounded. It also opens the doors to reaching those who do not know the Lord. King David's famous prayer gives us hope:

> Restore to me the joy of Your salvation
> And sustain me with a willing spirit.
> *Then I will teach transgressors Your ways,*
> *And sinners will be converted to You*
> (Psalm 51:12-13, emphasis added).

Besides King David, the Scriptures are filled with examples of repentant people who went on to powerfully serve the Lord. The Bible doesn't tell of Simon Peter ever committing adultery or having someone murdered like David did. However, he did something the Bible never records even sinful David ever doing. Simon Peter denied that he even knew the Lord—three times in one night! (Luke 22:34; Matthew 26:69-75). He really could have written the words, "Prone to wander, Lord I feel it. Prone to leave the God I love." Yet, like David, God did not forsake Simon Peter. Consider again what Jesus said to him:

> Simon, Simon, behold, Satan has demanded permission to sift you like wheat; but I have prayed for you, that your faith may not fail; and you, when once you have turned again (Greek: *epistrepho*), strengthen (Greek: *sterizo*) your brothers (Luke 22:31-32).

Even before Peter sinned, Jesus promised that his faith would not completely fail ("black out or eclipse," Greek: *eclipso*). That's such good news! Once Peter admitted the sin, confessed, and repented of the sin, Jesus would open the doors for him to strengthen others. In essence, he was saying, "Simon, you are going to blow it. But once you come to your senses and deal openly and honestly with your sin, I will open the doors for you to serve Me by building up others."

I remind you of the story I told earlier about the Visalia man who is now helping men gain victory over sexual temptation. His honest admission turned to sincere confession, which led to turning from that sin and ultimately serving his brothers. He was an object of God's mercy and that mercy stimulated him to greater ministry in the life of others. It can do the same for us:

> Therefore I urge you, brethren, *by the mercies of God*, to present your bodies a living and holy sacrifice, acceptable to God, which is your *spiritual service of worship*" (Romans 12:1, emphasis added).

chapter 42

DAVID'S STORY TOPS THEM ALL

Stories abound concerning those who have suffered the consequence of sexual sin and have gone through the healing process of restoration. They are our wounded and fallen warriors who are now mended and returned to active duty. To pick one story to tell is to ignore the many others. Yet, there is one account that tops them all—the story of David's adultery, his subsequent sins, and his restoration. It is the account of a fallen soldier who once again becomes an Ambassador of Purity.

The actual *record* of David's sins and their consequences is primarily found in a number of chapters, beginning in 2 Samuel 11. However, how David *felt* about all of this is described in his own words in such penitential psalms as Psalm 32, 38, and 51. By merging these passages we clearly see the progression of his spiritual rebellion, the pattern of his spiritual renewal, and the results of his spiritual restoration. As we review David's life and consider his words, I believe we will also find our strongest illustration of the lifelong effectiveness of the A.C.T.S. of Repentance. This is more than just an historical record. Holy God presented this account for our benefit:

> Now these things happened as examples for us. . . . Nor
> let us act immorally, as some of them did. . . . Nor let us
> try the Lord, as some of them did. . . . Now these things

happened to them as an example, and they were written for our instruction. . . . Therefore let him who thinks he stands take heed that he does not fall. No temptation has overtaken you but such as is common to man; and God is faithful, who will not allow you to be tempted beyond what you are able, but with the temptation will provide the way of escape also, so that you will be able to endure it. Therefore, my beloved, flee from idolatry (1 Corinthians 10:6, 8-9, 11-14).

So that we might easily recall the steps that led up to David's sin and the path that led back to his fellowship with God, I have chosen to present the story in outline form:

THE PROGRESSION OF HIS SPIRITUAL REBELLION
1. HE LET HIS GUARD DOWN

Then it happened in the spring, at the time when kings go out to battle. . . . But David stayed at Jerusalem (2 Samuel 11:1).

There were obviously things going on in David's heart and life that brought him to a point of sinning against the Lord he loved so much. If I were the one counseling him after his adultery, I might have asked, "What were the seeds of rebellion that you planted in your mind the days before? What was that point when you became 'lust looking for an opportunity?' How was your walk with God that day?"

We just don't know the answers. What we do know is that David wasn't where he was supposed to be—at battle *physically* against the enemies of Israel and *spiritually* against the enemies of his soul. He let his guard down and it cost him dearly. Don't miss the first three words of the text, "Then it happened . . ." (2 Samuel 11:1). Perhaps he didn't really want it to but, given his failure to be on guard, it was bound to happen.

2. HE WAS TEMPTED TO SIN

> Now when evening came David arose from his bed and
> walked around on the roof of the king's house, and from
> the roof he saw a woman bathing; and the woman was
> very beautiful in appearance (2 Samuel 11:2).

If only David had made and kept that important covenant with his eyes
(Job 31:1). If only he had fled from that rooftop, like Joseph from Potiphar's
wife (Genesis 39:12). Instead, David allowed his fantasies to run amuck.
He asked his servants to identify this naked woman, later commanding
them to bring her to his royal bedroom. Her name was Bathsheba, the wife
of Uriah the Hittite, one of David's elite warriors (2 Samuel 11:3-4; 23:39).
We do not know whether David had met Bathsheba before. What we do
know is that the seeds of lust in David's sinful heart were now about to bear
the ungodly fruit of immorality.

3. HE YIELDED TO SIN

> David sent messengers and took her, and when she came to
> him, he lay with her; and when she had purified herself from
> her uncleanness, she returned to her house (2 Samuel 11:4).

One wonders whether King David's son, Solomon, had this story in
mind when he warned his own son, David's grandson, Rehoboam:

> Suddenly he follows her
> As an ox goes to the slaughter,
> Or as one in fetters to the discipline of a fool,
> Until an arrow pierces through his liver;
> As a bird hastens to the snare,
> So he does not know that it will cost him his life
> (Proverbs 7:22-23).

4. HE HID HIS SIN

A couple of months later Bathsheba sent word to King David that she was pregnant (2 Samuel 11:5). Her husband, Uriah, was away at war. There was no question. Uriah was certainly not the father. Rather than deal openly and immediately with his sin, David began a grievous process of cover-up that rivals few, if any, in history. He arranged with Joab, his General of the Army, to invite Uriah to come home from the battle. David hoped that Uriah would have sexual relations with his wife who is now about two months pregnant. Perhaps King David's strategy was for people to think Uriah's baby was born pre-maturely. The plan failed.

In honor of his fellow soldiers who were suffering in the field of battle, Uriah refused to stay with his wife. Instead, he slept at the door of the king's house (2 Samuel 11:6-12). Imagine David's shock!

The King then befriended Uriah, inviting him to dinner. Uriah must have thought he was being honored. However, David's plan was to get him drunk, thinking that a drunken soldier would certainly want to have relations with his wife. That didn't work either (2 Samuel 11:13).

In David's twisted and rebellious mind, there was only one thing left to do. He ordered Uriah back to the thick of the battle. As a part of the deception, he gave Uriah the honor of being a special emissary of the King, ordering him to carry a personal letter to General Joab. Little did Uriah know he was carrying his own death sentence:

> Now in the morning David wrote a letter to Joab, and sent it by the hand of Uriah. He had written in the letter, saying, 'Place Uriah in the front line of the fiercest battle and withdraw from him, so that he may be struck down and die' (2 Samuel 11:14-15).

This time David's plot worked. Faithful Uriah was killed in the field of battle. (I look forward to meeting this mighty man and honorable war-hero in heaven.) The report of Uriah's death was sent to David and the king faked his grief over the tragedy (2 Samuel 11:20-25). Bathsheba then entered into obligatory mourning. When that time was over, King David married her.

Oh, how the King must have been applauded by the common people for rescuing this poor, pregnant wife of a fallen war hero. However, those within the palace, especially the servants who had brought Bathsheba to David's bedroom, knew the real story. The King continued to keep the closely guarded secret for many more months. Certainly, he knew that God was not fooled: "But the thing that David had done was evil in the sight of the Lord" (2 Samuel 11:27).

5. HE SUFFERED THE CONSEQUENCES OF HIS SIN

I am certain David never imagined the full weight of his sin:

- Bathsheba bore a son (2 Samuel 11:27) that became ill and died, even after David begged God to spare the child's life His servant's feared David was suicidal (2 Samuel 12:14-23).
- David's son, Amnon, raped his half-sister, Tamar and then discarded her (2 Samuel 13:1-20).
- Absalom, David's son and Tamar's brother, retaliated and killed Amnon (2 Samuel 13:21-32).
- Absalom then rebelled against King David (2 Samuel 15-18), eventually raping and disgracing his father's concubines on a public rooftop (2 Samuel 16:21-22).
- Absalom was later killed by General Joab (2 Samuel 18:9-17) and David mourned deeply (2 Samuel 18:33).
- Violence and bloodshed followed David for the rest of his life (2 Samuel 12:10).

Other consequences followed. However, the one that I think tore at David's heart the most was God's refusal to allow him to build a permanent temple for the Lord, because he was now a man of bloodshed (1 Chronicles

17:4; 28:2-3). This may not seem much to us, but to King David this was the most devastating price he paid for his sin.

David's personal descriptions of the consequences of his sin are heart-felt and real:

> For Your arrows have sunk deep into me,
> And Your hand has pressed down on me (Psalm 38:2).

Even during the lengthy period of silence and cover-up David was fully aware of his sin. Although he seemed on the outside to be cold and calculating, David's inner life was in complete turmoil. In fact, after he repented, David wrote a number of Psalms describing how deeply his sin affected him physically, emotionally, and spiritually. Let us take some time to dwell on his own personal testimony:

THE PHYSICAL CONSEQUENCE

> When I kept silent about my sin, my body wasted away
> Through my groaning all day long.
> For day and night Your hand was heavy upon me;
> My vitality was drained away as with the fever heat of
>   summer (Psalm 32:3-4).

THE EMOTIONAL CONSEQUENCE

> I am full of anxiety because of my sin (Psalm 38:18).

THE SPIRITUAL CONSEQUENCE

> For I know my transgressions,
> And my sin is ever before me. . . .
> Do not cast me away from Your presence
> And do not take Your Holy Spirit from me.
> Restore to me the joy of Your salvation

And sustain me with a willing spirit. . . .
Deliver me from bloodguiltiness, O God, the God of my
    salvation (Psalm 51:3, 11-12, 14).

What David penned in Psalm 38 puts all the consequences together. In fact, in this Psalm of Repentance it is hard to sort out the physical results of David's sin from the emotional and the spiritual. Like a spiders web, they are inextricably linked:

O LORD, rebuke me not in Your wrath,
And chasten me not in Your burning anger.
For Your arrows have sunk deep into me,
And Your hand has pressed down on me.
There is no soundness in my flesh because of Your
    indignation;
There is no health in my bones because of my sin.
For my iniquities are gone over my head;
As a heavy burden they weigh too much for me.
My wounds grow foul and fester because of my folly.
I am bent over and greatly bowed down;
I go mourning all day long.
For my loins are filled with burning,
And there is no soundness in my flesh.
I am benumbed and badly crushed;
I groan because of the agitation of my heart.
Lord, all my desire is before You;
And my sighing is not hidden from You.
My heart throbs, my strength fails me;
And the light of my eyes, even that has gone from me.
My loved ones and my friends stand aloof from my
    plague;
And my kinsmen stand afar off.

Those who seek my life lay snares for me;
And those who seek to injure me have threatened
    destruction,
And they devise treachery all day long.
But I, like a deaf man, do not hear;
And I am like a mute man who does not open his mouth.
Yes, I am like a man who does not hear,
And in whose mouth are no arguments (Psalm 38:1-14).

The story is far from over. We move from the progression of his spiritual rebellion to the pattern for his spiritual renewal.

THE PATTERN FOR HIS SPIRITUAL RENEWAL

Even before all the consequences unfolded, the Lord sent Nathan the prophet to confront King David. He told a story about a very rich man who took a poor man's only lamb (2 Samuel 12:1-4). David responded in self-righteous fervor: "The man who did this deserves to die" (2 Samuel 12:5-6). Risking his life at the hand of an adulterous and murderous king, Nathan boldly declared, "You are the man!" (2 Samuel 12:7). David had been caught: "Behold, you have sinned against the Lord, and be sure your sin will find you out" (Numbers 32:23). Holy God then spoke His words of judgment through Nathan:

> Now therefore, the sword shall never depart from your house, because you have despised Me and have taken the wife of Uriah the Hittite to be your wife. Thus says the LORD, "Behold, I will raise up evil against you from your own household; I will even take your wives before your eyes, and give them to your companion, and he shall lie with your wives in broad daylight. Indeed you did it secretly, but I will do this thing before all Israel, and under the sun" (2 Samuel 12:10-12).

There was nothing left for David to do, but to finally acknowledge publicly what he did.

1. HE ADMITTED HIS SIN

David was tired of hiding. He was drained physically, emotionally, and spiritually. Perhaps he wanted to get caught. When confronted, he made no excuses and told no more lies. Instead, he declared to Nathan, "I have sinned against the LORD" (2 Samuel 12:13).

Later in his own testimony, David writes, "I acknowledged my sin to You, / And my iniquity I did not hide" (Psalm 32:5). Admitting his sin was the first step to legitimate confession and spiritual renewal. It was, however, just the beginning of the process of his restoration.

2. HE CONFESSED HIS SIN

For I confess my iniquity . . . (Psalm 38:18).

For I know my transgressions,
And my sin is ever before me.
Against You, You only, I have sinned
And done what is evil in Your sight,
So that You are justified when You speak
And blameless when You judge
(Psalm 51:3-4).

3. HE TURNED FROM HIS SIN

King David was completely broken. Although some might wonder, I believe he had every intention of never repeating the sin of adultery again. He returned to the honest and deep fellowship with God he once enjoyed.

Most likely, during the time of rebellion, David offered sacrifices to the Lord. It was a good show for his people. Now that he admitted, confessed, and repented, things were different. He understood how his outward signs of phony repentance fooled not only his people but his own sinful heart. It didn't fool his God:

> For You do not delight in sacrifice, otherwise I would give it;
> You are not pleased with burnt offering.
> The sacrifices of God are a broken spirit;
> A broken and a contrite heart, O God, You will not despise
> (Psalm 51:16-17).

THE RESULTS OF HIS SPIRITUAL RESTORATION

I am struck once again by how closely King David followed the pattern for true restoration expressed one thousand years later in James 4:8-10. King David had cleansed his hands and purified his heart. He was miserable and wept and mourned over his sin. His laughter turned into mourning and his joy to gloom. In other words, he sincerely humbled himself in the presence of the Lord. Now, for the first time in about a year, he drew near to God. God also drew near to him. The results were amazing.

1. HIS SIN WAS REMOVED

Sin had stained his soul, smeared his reputation and stifled his ministry. Given his understanding of the holiness of God and His hatred of sin, David also knew that his sin could cost him his life (Hebrews 10:31; Romans 6:23; Proverbs 7:23). He lived in constant fear of well-deserved judgment! Imagine how David's remorse-filled heart felt when he heard the redemptive words of the prophet Nathan that day:

> Then Nathan said to David, "The LORD also has taken away your sin; you shall not die" (2 Samuel 12:13).

What an incredible pronouncement! "David, you are an adulterer, murderer, liar, and spiritual phony, but because you have admitted it, confessed it and repented, the Merciful Lord has removed your sin. Though you certainly deserve it, you will not pay the penalty of death." Throughout the Psalms, we read David's response to this undeserved reprieve:

> How blessed is he whose transgression is forgiven,
> Whose sin is covered!
> How blessed is the man to whom the LORD does not
>   impute iniquity,
> And in whose spirit there is no deceit! . . .
> I acknowledged my sin to You,
> And my iniquity I did not hide;
> I said, "I will confess my transgressions to the LORD;
> And You forgave the guilt of my sin" (Psalm 32:1-2, 5).

> Be gracious to me, O God, according to Your lovingkindness;
> According to the greatness of Your compassion blot out
>   my transgressions. . . .
> Purify me with hyssop, and I shall be clean;
> Wash me, and I shall be whiter than snow.
> Make me to hear joy and gladness,
> Let the bones which You have broken rejoice.
> Hide Your face from my sins
> And blot out all my iniquities (Psalm 51:1, 7-9).

2. HIS SPIRIT WAS RENEWED

During that year of stubborn and unconfessed sin, David felt very alone. The inward spiritual direction upon which he always relied was gone. There was no longer even a flicker of the joy that used to come from God's presence in his life. However, after repenting of his sin, David had a renewed sensitivity to the Holy Spirit's leading in his life. With it, the inward joy returned. And with the inward joy came the outward praise and singing:

Behold, You desire truth in the innermost being,
And in the hidden part You will make me know
    wisdom....
Create in me a clean heart, O God,
And renew a steadfast spirit within me.
Do not cast me away from Your presence,
And do not take Your Holy Spirit from me.
Restore to me the joy of Your salvation
And sustain me with a willing spirit....
Deliver me from bloodguiltiness, O God, the God of my
    salvation;
Then my tongue will joyfully sing of Your righteousness.
O Lord, open my lips,
That my mouth may declare Your praise
(Psalm 51:6, 10-12, 14-15).

3. HIS SERVICE WAS RESTORED

From the time he was a child, David delighted in serving the Lord. That *passion* to serve God never left; the *power* to serve Him did! His sin removed the ability to effectively bear witness to the world concerning the majesty of God. In fact, his sin gave occasion for the enemies of the Lord to mock and blaspheme God (2 Samuel 12:14). However, after David was restored to intimate fellowship with God, he once again experienced Spirit-led *passion* and God-infused *power* to effectively serve the Lord. In Psalm 51 he described his expectation of restoration to ministry: "Then I will teach transgressors Your ways, / And sinners will be converted to You" (Psalm 51:13).

God didn't put King David on his "Unusable Believers Shelf." Certainly there would be life-long consequences to his sin but God was not finished with him.

We have no record of David ever repeating this sin. However, we do have reports of him ministering to thousands of his fellow sinners. He who began his ministry as a man after God's own heart (1 Samuel 13:14) returned to that same spiritual state and died "in a ripe old age, full of days" (1 Chronicles 29:28). He grew old and died, having "served the purpose of God in his generation" (Acts 13:36).

Such is the grace and mercy of God! David's *sins* were forgiven, his *spirit* was renewed, and his *service* was restored. It was the promised fruit of confession and repentance that was his to enjoy. Call it revival, renewal, restoration or reformation. There really is life after sin. Count on it! Repentant King David did:

> Many are the sorrows of the wicked,
> But he who trusts in the LORD, lovingkindness shall
> surround him.
> Be glad in the LORD and rejoice, you righteous ones,
> And shout for joy, all you who are upright in heart
> (Psalm 32:10-11).

Only sinners who have truly experienced the grace, mercy, and forgiveness of God can imagine how David felt when he sat down to write Psalm 103. Count me in as one of them!

> Bless the LORD, O my soul,
> And all that is within me, bless His holy name.
> Bless the LORD, O my soul,
> And forget none of His benefits;
> Who pardons all your iniquities,
> Who heals all your diseases;
> Who redeems your life from the pit,
> Who crowns you with lovingkindness and compassion;
> Who satisfies your years with good things,
> So that your youth is renewed like the eagle. . . .
> He has not dealt with us according to our sins,

Nor rewarded us according to our iniquities.

For as high as the heavens are above the earth,

So great is His lovingkindness toward those who fear Him.

As far as the east is from the west,

So far has He removed our transgressions from us.

Just as a father has compassion on his children,

So the LORD has compassion on those who fear Him.

For He Himself knows our frame;

He is mindful that we are but dust (Psalm 103:1-5, 10-14).

LESSONS FROM DAVID'S LIFE

In his book, *The Myth of the Greener Grass*, J. Allan Petersen makes some important life applications from David's sin and restoration:

1. No one, however chosen, blessed, and used of God, is immune to an extramarital affair.
2. Anyone, regardless of how many victories he has won, can fall disastrously.
3. The act of infidelity is the result of uncontrolled desires, thoughts and fantasies.
4. Your body is your servant or it becomes your master.
5. A Christian who falls will excuse, rationalize, and conceal, the same as anyone else.
6. Sin can be enjoyable but it can never be successfully covered.
7. One night of passion can spark years of family pain.
8. Failure is neither fatal nor final.[1]

PART SIX:

THE WAY FORWARD

chapter 43

FROM "WHAT?" TO "SO WHAT?" TO "NOW WHAT?"

IN SEARCH OF A REVIVAL OF PURITY

John Chrysostom was one of the early church fathers. The clarity of his preaching in the fourth century earned him the Greek surname that means "golden-mouthed." With respect to our need for a revival of personal purity in the body of Christ, we could use his golden preaching today. In his book, *Personal Holiness in Times of Temptation*, Dr. Bruce Wilkinson quotes Chrysostom:

> If only ten among us be righteous, the ten will become twenty, the twenty fifty, the fifty a hundred, the hundred a thousand, and the thousand will become the entire city. As when ten lamps are kindled, a whole house may easily be filled with light; so it is with the progress of spiritual things. If but ten among us lead a holy life, we shall kindle a fire which shall light up the entire city.[1]

The eighteenth-century revivalist preacher, John Wesley, is also known to have said, "Give me a hundred men who love nothing but God and hate nothing but sin and I will change the world."

For the decades I have been in the ministry, my fellow Christian leaders have been crying out for a reformation in our national thinking about sexual morality, personal purity, and holiness. This book is about such a revival, presenting a biblical understanding of our Creator's marvelous design for human sexuality and calling us to a passionate and daily commitment to do nothing in thought or deed that would violate that design. I so appreciate the work of my contemporaries whose hearts beat with the same desire for this kind of purity in the body of Christ. I am especially indebted to Randy Alcorn, whose many articles and books address the problem head on:

> In writing and researching the book *Restoring Sexual Sanity*, I discovered that a prominent earmark of the early church was its sexual purity. If we do not reclaim this lost ground, today's church and its leadership are destined to spiritual impotence. Why? Because an unholy world will never be won to Christ by an unholy church."[2]

British Evangelist Leonard Ravenhill, expressed a profound and related thought: "The greatest miracle that God can do today is to take an unholy man out of an unholy world, and make that man holy and put him back into the unholy world and keep him holy in it.[3]

I believe *national* revival, in any country on any continent, is possible, but not apart from *individual* commitment to personal purity and holiness. Anything else is, at best, a glitzy show of spiritual pomp and circumstance. It may even be a counterfeit movement inspired by the Father of Lies himself. The Devil is thrilled to hear a crowd of hearty "amens" and "hallelujahs" from people whose inner lives are beset with sexual sin and have no real commitment to change.

A REVIVAL OF PURITY. . . ONE PERSON AT A TIME

The president of a well-known Christian relief agency was once asked, "How do you feed a hungry world?" He replied, "One person at a time."

How do we start a revival of purity and holiness in a morally bankrupt and spiritually depraved world? One person at a time!

In the summer of 1997, I attended a Promise Keepers gathering in my home town of Fresno, California. On the first night, Dr. Bruce Wilkinson, founder of Walk Thru the Bible Ministries, challenged the assembly to honestly repent of immorality. The invitation was given for those men who were truly sincere about changing to get on their knees and pray with him. One by one, thousands of men responded. They would, in the days to follow, become known as "The Fresno Ten Thousand." The Bible reminds us that with God as our Rock one can overpower a thousand and two can "put ten thousand to flight" (Deuteronomy 32:30). Imagine the impact of ten thousand men confessing the sin of sexual immorality and living out their commitment to a life of purity and holiness.

The good news is that they are not alone. They join the ranks of countless thousands of my fellow Ambassadors of Purity around this globe, who have joined in praying that godliness would prevail in our homes, our churches, and our communities. I trust you have heard and responded to that same call. How do we change an immoral world? One heart at a time, beginning with ours.

A FINAL WORD TO MY DESCENDANTS—BOTH PHYSICAL AND SPIRITUAL

Hugh Hefner, the founder and editor-in-chief of *Playboy* magazine, is a direct descendant of the Mayflower passenger and seventeenth-century Puritan, Governor William Bradford. Bradford was known for his commitment to the lordship of Jesus Christ and his stand for personal holiness. I once heard Hugh Hefner being interviewed on CNN's *Larry King Live Show*, in which he lamented the puritanical views and values held by his famous ancestor.[4]

It is also common knowledge in my family that the infamous American gangster, Alfonse Capone, is one of my cousins. In spite of a life of well-documented bootlegging, gambling, sex trafficking, and murder, he was able to avoid being killed by his gangland enemies. However, it was his sexual sin that dealt the final blow. Even while serving a short term at Alcatraz Penitentiary, he was mentally incapacitated, suffering from the effects of the advanced stages of neurosyphilis. This sexually transmitted disease hastened his death at forty-eight years old. He may have dodged the bullet for his public crimes but he, nonetheless, paid the price for his private immorality.

I suppose Hefner's life goal is similar to mine in one respect. Neither "Hef" nor I are responsible for the moral views and practices of our ancestors, good or bad. However, we are both striving to influence our descendants.

As for me, I am committed to undo the immoral influences of people like Cousin Al and promote the holy standards of those like Hefner's godly ancestor. I, therefore, present this book to my physical and my spiritual descendants—my earthly and my heavenly family. My prayer is that each one of you will, "glorify God in your body" (1 Corinthians 6:20).

Soli Deo Gloria.

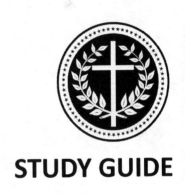

STUDY GUIDE

QUESTIONS FOR REFLECTION AND DISCUSSION

This book has been designed for both personal reflection (individually or as a married couple) and group discussion (with people of the same sex.) The first eight meetings are for discussion of the content of the book. These are followed by optional group accountability meetings, utilizing the worksheets in the *Personal Accountability Program*. Of course, I encourage you to design your discussion group any way that suits your style and need. Here is my suggestion:

WEEK #1 DISCUSSION GUIDE
INTRODUCTORY SESSION

Assignment: Read all the introductory pages up to, but not including, the first chapter. Be prepared to answer the following questions:

Due Date: _____

1. What were your expectations and apprehensions about reading this book?

2. Why do you think it is appropriate to describe the struggle for purity in military terms?

3. What does it mean to be an Ambassador of Purity?

WEEK #2 DISCUSSION GUIDE
PART ONE: THE NEED

Assignment: Read Chapters 1-4   Due Date: _____

1. What did you find most helpful in this section and why?

2. Do you believe that immorality is a greater problem in our day than in the past? Why?

3. Why is it necessary to first look at the problem of immorality among the people of God?

4. What does it mean to be proactive regarding moral purity? What proactive steps do you need to take in your life?

5. Why is 1 Thessalonians 4:1-8 such a vital passage regarding moral purity? How did it impact you? Would you be willing to make an agreement to read 1 Thessalonians 4:1-8 forty times in the next two weeks?

6. Besides holiness being the will of God, who else in your life desires you to be pure?

7. What are the "Red Light!" issues in your life?

8. Was your early education regarding human sexuality consistent with God's view?

9. In what ways have you seen God avenge immorality?

10. What does it mean to be called by God to be pure?

11. Why is it possible to maintain a walk of personal purity and holiness?

WEEK #3 DISCUSSION GUIDE
PART TWO: GOD'S DESIGN

Assignment: Read Chapters 5-15   Due Date: _____

1. What one thing did you agree or disagree with the most? Why?

2. Is the concept of "sexual unity as a reflection of God's oneness" new to you?

3. How might this understanding of the *echad* of God affect your attitude toward sex in marriage? Outside of marriage?

4. What is the importance of understanding covenantal and restorative oneness?

5. How does the concept of "sacred sex" as a form of worship affect our attitudes and actions.

6. Considering God's design for sex in marriage as developing physical, emotional and spiritual oneness, which do you feel is most often neglected in marriages? In your marriage?

7. How do you define romance? How does your spouse define it?

8. What "one another" do you need the most work on?

9. Which of God's purposes for giving a sexual drive to singles is most ignored among singles today?

WEEK #4 DISCUSSION GUIDE
PART THREE: MAN'S ABUSES

Assignment: Read Chapters 16-25   Due Date: _____

1. What principle or idea from these chapters did you find most challenging? Why?

2. What specific things that miss the target of God's oneness do you struggle with?

3. Who do we get to blame for our struggle with lust?

4. Give a personal example of the The Perishing Principle you have experienced.

5. When is the last time you went through a season of spiritual dryness? How are you doing today?

6. How do you rate the health of your marriage? How do you think your spouse would respond to this same question?

7. What is the harm in engaging in sexual fantasy?

8. In what areas are you being careless in your relationships with the opposite sex? What do you think you should do about this?

9. Are you presently in a morally dangerous situation from which you need to run?

10. Which of the consequences of immorality frightens you the most?

11. How do you view your prospects for victory?

WEEK #5 DISCUSSION GUIDE
PART FOUR: THE WAY OF ESCAPE

Assignment: Read Chapters 26-39   Due Date: _____

1. What one thing did you find most helpful? Why?

2. Do you believe your personal war with immorality is winnable?

3. From what immoral influences to you need to most protect your mind?

4. What passages of Scripture are you especially in need of memorizing?

5. What attribute of God is most meaningful to you in your battle with immorality?

6. Besides your fellowship with the Lord, what relationship would be most affected if you were to fall into sexual sin? What do you think would happen?

7. Have you presented your body to God today? Has this become a regular practice?

8. What are some of the covenants you have made regarding specific parts of your body?

9. How does the Principle of "One Step Back" apply to you? Give an example.

10. In what specific ways do we need each other as a safeguard for our sexual purity?

11. Who do you feel is most in need of prayer for their moral safety?

12. Why do so many Christians resist engaging in personal accountability with other believers?

13. Share the names of a few trusted accountability partners that you meet with regularly to ask each other the *hard* questions.

Note: In Week #8 you will be asked to come with the names of at least four accountability partners who have agreed to meet with you in subsequent weeks to complete the Personal Accountability Program.

WEEK #6 DISCUSSION GUIDE
PART FIVE: THE WAY BACK

Assignment: Read Chapters 40-42   Due Date: _____

1. What principle or idea from this chapter did you find most challenging? Why?

2. What part of admitting sin is most difficult for you? Hiding? Blaming? Grieving?

3. What is the difference between true confession and simply saying, "I'm sorry, Lord"?

4. What are some evidences that a person has truly repented?

5. What are some of the results of admitting, confessing and turning from sin?

6. What lessons from King David's process of restoration most impacted you?

WEEK #7 DISCUSSION GUIDE
PART SIX: THE WAY FORWARD

Assignment: Read Chapter 43   Due Date: _____

1. What did you find most helpful? Why?

2. Do you believe a revival of moral purity is possible in your nation? What has to happen first? What would it take to start "a generation of purity" in your family?

3. Write a single sentence describing what it means to "glorify God in your body" (1 Corinthians 6:20).

4. (Optional Assignment) Discuss the *Suggested Reading on Moral Purity and Biblical Sexuality*, found in the Appendix. Share with your group which resources in this list you would find most interesting to read. Be prepared to make your own suggestions and recommendations.

WEEK #8 DISCUSSION GUIDE
INTRODUCTION TO THE PERSONAL ACCOUNTABILITY PROGRAM

Assignment: Read through the introduction to the *Personal Accountability Program* in the following pages, including the list of all the worksheet titles. Do a quick overview of at least four of the accountability worksheets. Complete *Accountability Worksheet #1* only.

Due Date: _____

Discuss with the group your personal responses to *Accountability Worksheet #1: Taking My General Pulse.*

Be prepared to discuss your plan for the *Personal Accountability Program* in the coming weeks.

Instructions: You will begin meeting in weekly accountability groups of *no more than six people of the same sex* to participate in the rest of the *Personal Accountability Program.* You may also decide to meet for any number of weeks and then change partners. If so, I recommend at least six weeks with the same accountability group.

Using the planning schedule sheet on the next page, design the program around your accountability group's particular needs, including repeating worksheets that are particularly helpful.

My Personal Accountability Program

Week #1
Meeting Date:_____ Worksheet # _____ Partners' Initials: _____
Week #2
Meeting Date:_____ Worksheet # _____ Partners' Initials: _____
Week #3
Meeting Date:_____ Worksheet # _____ Partners' Initials: _____
Week #4
Meeting Date:_____ Worksheet # _____ Partners' Initials: _____
Week #5
Meeting Date:_____ Worksheet # _____ Partners' Initials: _____
Week #6
Meeting Date:_____ Worksheet # _____ Partners' Initials:_____
Week #7
Meeting Date:_____ Worksheet # _____ Partners' Initials: _____
Week #8
Meeting Date:_____ Worksheet # _____ Partners' Initials: _____
Week #9
Meeting Date:_____ Worksheet # _____ Partners' Initials:_____
Week #10
Meeting Date:_____ Worksheet # _____ Partners' Initials: _____
Week #11
Meeting Date:_____ Worksheet # _____ Partners' Initials: _____
Week #12
Meeting Date:_____ Worksheet # _____ Partners' Initials:_____
Week #13
Meeting Date:_____ Worksheet # _____ Partners' Initials: _____
Week #14
Meeting Date:_____ Worksheet # _____ Partners' Initials: _____
Week #15
Meeting Date:_____ Worksheet # _____ Partners' Initials: _____
Week #16
Meeting Date:_____ Worksheet # _____ Partners' Initials: _____
Week #17
Meeting Date:_____ Worksheet # _____ Partners' Initials: _____
Week #18
Meeting Date:_____ Worksheet # _____ Partners' Initials: _____

PERSONAL ACCOUNTABILITY PROGRAM

PERSONAL ACCOUNTABILITY PROGRAM

Today's neglect is the beginning of tomorrow's mistake. Therefore, we must set apart time to take a healthy look at ourselves:

> Watch your life and doctrine closely. Persevere in them (1 Timothy 4:16, New International Version).

We also need to look after others. The Scriptures are also clear about this:

> But encourage one another daily, as long as it is called Today, so that none of you may be hardened by sin's deceitfulness (Hebrews 3:13, New International Version).

> Two are better than one, because they have a good return for their work: If one falls down, his friend can help him up. But pity the man who falls and has no one to help him up! Also, if two lie down together, they will keep warm. But how can one keep warm alone? Though one may be overpowered, two can defend themselves. A cord of three strands is not quickly broken (Ecclesiastes 4:9-12, New International Version).

> And let us consider how we may spur one another on toward love and good deeds. Let us not give up meeting together, as some are in the habit of doing, but let us encourage one another — and all the more as you see the Day approaching (Hebrews 10:24-25, New International Version).

> As iron sharpens iron, / So one man sharpens another (Proverbs 27:17, New International Version).

THE THREE FACETS OF PERSONAL ACCOUNTABILITY

1. I need consistent accountability.
   Knowing I *will be* tempted, I need to meet with someone regularly.

2. I need defensive accountability.
   Before I am tempted, I need to share my particular struggles with someone.

3. I need offensive accountability.
   I am being tempted *right now*. I need help.

THE PRACTICE OF PERSONAL ACCOUNTABILITY

The following pages contain a series of different accountability worksheets specifically designed for personal reflection and sharing with a few trusted partners. Some are related to moral purity; the rest to other areas of the Christian life.

Here's how the Personal Accountability Program works:

1. Find a few partners *of the same sex* who will commit to regular meetings of at least thirty minutes of discussion time.

2. Complete each worksheet alone, prior to meeting with your accountability partners.

3. Meet to discuss your responses on the worksheet as well as for prayer and encouragement.

4. The worksheets may be done in any order. Pre-arrange the schedule with your partners.

Worksheet

_____ Personal Accountability Worksheet #1: Taking My General Pulse

_____ Personal Accountability Worksheet #2: Taking My Spiritual Pulse (Part One)

_____ Personal Accountability Worksheet #3: Taking My Spiritual Pulse (Part Two)

_____ Personal Accountability Worksheet #4: Taking My Spiritual Pulse (Part Three)

_____ Personal Accountability Worksheet #5: Taking My Marital Pulse (Part One) (For Husbands Only)

_____ Personal Accountability Worksheet #6: Taking My Marital Pulse (Part Two) (For Wives Only)

_____ Personal Accountability Worksheet #7: Taking My Marital Pulse (Part Three) (For Married Couples)

_____ Personal Accountability Worksheet #8: Taking My Ministry Pulse (For Those in Christian Service)

_____ Personal Accountability Worksheet #9: Taking My Physical Pulse

_____ Personal Accountability Worksheet #10: Taking My Mental Pulse

_____ Personal Accountability Worksheet #11: Stating My Moral Boundaries

_____ Personal Accountability Worksheet #12: Safeguarding My Travel Time

_____ Personal Accountability Worksheet #13: Rehearsing the Consequences of Moral Failure

_____ Personal Accountability Worksheet #14: Restoring Fellowship With My God

_____ Personal Accountability Worksheet #15: Worksheet for Resolving a Conflict

_____ Personal Accountability Worksheet #16: Making Covenants With the Parts of My Body

_____ Personal Accountability Worksheet #17: My Spiritual Health Indicators

_____ Personal Accountability Worksheet #18: My Prayer of Dedication

PERSONAL ACCOUNTABILITY WORKSHEET #1

TAKING MY GENERAL PULSE
FOR REVIEW: READ "THE PURITY WAR" - CHAPTER 38

1. Have I been faithful in the Word and prayer? Am I growing in my intimacy with God?

2. Have I been sensitive to the needs of my spouse? My family?

3. Have I been struggling with impure thoughts?

4. Have I been looking at questionable material that would bring shame to the Lord?

5. Have I been alone with someone in any kind of situation when my feelings or actions became inappropriate or where others could have suspected something?

6. Am I experiencing any physical problems? Eating right? Getting adequate rest and sufficient exercise?

7. Am I facing challenges that are negatively affecting my physical, emotional, or spiritual well-being?

8. Have I lied or compromised my answer to any of the above questions?

My Prayer for Today:

PERSONAL ACCOUNTABILITY WORKSHEET #2

TAKING MY SPIRITUAL PULSE (PART ONE)
(BASED ON COLOSSIANS 3:1-17, NEW AMERICAN STANDARD BIBLE)
FOR REVIEW: READ "THE PURITY WAR" - CHAPTER 20

I am:	Text	Winning	Struggling	Losing
-continually seeking and thinking about things of God	Col. 3:1-4	10 9 8	7 6 5 4	3 2 1
-living in such a manner that others see Christ in me		10 9 8	7 6 5 4	3 2 1
-putting to death immorality (fornication) *		10 9 8	7 6 5 4	3 2 1
-putting to death impurity (uncleanness) *		10 9 8	7 6 5 4	3 2 1
-putting to death sinful passion (inordinate affection) *	Col. 3:5-7	10 9 8	7 6 5 4	3 2 1
-putting to death evil desire (evil concupiscence) *		10 9 8	7 6 5 4	3 2 1
-putting to death greed (covetousness) *		10 9 8	7 6 5 4	3 2 1
-putting aside anger		10 9 8	7 6 5 4	3 2 1
-putting aside wrath		10 9 8	7 6 5 4	3 2 1
-putting aside malice	Col. 3:8	10 9 8	7 6 5 4	3 2 1
-putting aside slander (blasphemy) *		10 9 8	7 6 5 4	3 2 1
-putting aside abusive speech (filthy communication) *		10 9 8	7 6 5 4	3 2 1
-stopping lying		10 9 8	7 6 5 4	3 2 1
-acting like one who has laid aside the old self and has put on the new self	Col. 3:9-11	10 9 8	7 6 5 4	3 2 1

		10 9 8	7 6 5 4	3 2 1
-living as one who is being renewed according to the image of the One who created me		10 9 8	7 6 5 4	3 2 1
-putting on a heart of compassion (bowels of mercy) *		10 9 8	7 6 5 4	3 2 1
-putting on kindness		10 9 8	7 6 5 4	3 2 1
-putting on humility	Col. 3:12	10 9 8	7 6 5 4	3 2 1
-putting on gentleness (meekness) *		10 9 8	7 6 5 4	3 2 1
-putting on patience (longsuffering) *		10 9 8	7 6 5 4	3 2 1
-bearing with others	Col. 3:13	10 9 8	7 6 5 4	3 2 1
-forgiving others		10 9 8	7 6 5 4	3 2 1
-putting on unifying love	Col. 3:14	10 9 8	7 6 5 4	3 2 1
-letting the peace of Christ rule in me	Col. 3:15	10 9 8	7 6 5 4	3 2 1
-being continuously thankful		10 9 8	7 6 5 4	3 2 1
-letting God's Word dwell in me richly	Col. 3:16	10 9 8	7 6 5 4	3 2 1
-teaching and admonishing others		10 9 8	7 6 5 4	3 2 1
-putting Christ first in everything I think, do and say	Col. 3:17	10 9 8	7 6 5 4	3 2 1

* Words in parentheses are from the King James Version

PERSONAL ACCOUNTABILITY WORKSHEET #3

TAKING MY SPIRITUAL PULSE (PART TWO)
(BASED ON ROMANS 12:1-21, NEW AMERICAN STANDARD BIBLE)
FOR REVIEW: READ "THE PURITY WAR" - CHAPTER 20

I am:	Text	Winning	Struggling	Losing
-regularly presenting my body to God as a living sacrifice, holy and acceptable to Him	Rom. 12:1	10 9 8	7 6 5 4	3 2 1
-not being conformed to this world	Rom. 12:2	10 9 8	7 6 5 4	3 2 1
-being transformed by the renewing of my mind		10 9 8	7 6 5 4	3 2 1
-not thinking more highly of myself than I ought	Rom. 12:3	10 9 8	7 6 5 4	3 2 1
-thinking so as to have sound judgment (according to my faith)		10 9 8	7 6 5 4	3 2 1
-recognizing that there are many members of the body of Christ with different functions	Rom. 12:4	10 9 8	7 6 5 4	3 2 1
-recognizing that I am a unique member of the body of Christ	Rom. 12:5	10 9 8	7 6 5 4	3 2 1
-exercising my gifts according to the grace and faith given me	Rom. 12:6-8	10 9 8	7 6 5 4	3 2 1
-letting my love be without hypocrisy		10 9 8	7 6 5 4	3 2 1

-abhorring (hating) what is evil	Rom. 12:9	10 9 8	7 6 5 4	3 2 1
-clinging to what is good		10 9 8	7 6 5 4	3 2 1
-devoted to other members of the body of Christ in brotherly love	Rom. 12:10	10 9 8	7 6 5 4	3 2 1
-giving preference to others in honor		10 9 8	7 6 5 4	3 2 1
-not lagging behind in diligence		10 9 8	7 6 5 4	3 2 1
-being fervent in spirit	Rom. 12:11	10 9 8	7 6 5 4	3 2 1
-serving the Lord		10 9 8	7 6 5 4	3 2 1
-rejoicing in hope		10 9 8	7 6 5 4	3 2 1
-persevering in tribulation	Rom. 12:12	10 9 8	7 6 5 4	3 2 1
-devoted to prayer		10 9 8	7 6 5 4	3 2 1
-contributing to the needs of the saints	Rom. 12:13	10 9 8	7 6 5 4	3 2 1
-practicing hospitality		10 9 8	7 6 5 4	3 2 1
-blessing those who persecute me and not cursing them	Rom. 12:14	10 9 8	7 6 5 4	3 2 1
-rejoicing with those who rejoice	Rom. 12:15	10 9 8	7 6 5 4	3 2 1
-weeping with those who weep		10 9 8	7 6 5 4	3 2 1
-being of the same mind toward others in the body of Christ		10 9 8	7 6 5 4	3 2 1
-not being haughty (proud) but willing to associate with the lowly	Rom. 12:16	10 9 8	7 6 5 4	3 2 1
-not elevating my own wisdom		10 9 8	7 6 5 4	3 2 1

-not paying back evil for evil		10 9 8	7 6 5 4	3 2 1
	Rom. 12:17			
-respecting what is right in the sight of all men		10 9 8	7 6 5 4	3 2 1

-at peace with all men (to the extent that this depends on me)	Rom. 12:18	10 9 8	7 6 5 4	3 2 1

-not taking revenge into my own hands but leaving this up to God	Rom. 12:19	10 9 8	7 6 5 4	3 2 1
-caring for my enemies	Rom. 12:20	10 9 8	7 6 5 4	3 2 1
-overcoming evil with good	Rom. 12:21	10 9 8	7 6 5 4	3 2 1

PERSONAL ACCOUNTABILITY WORKSHEET #4

TAKING MY SPIRITUAL PULSE (PART THREE)
(BASED ON GALATIANS 5:16-23, NEW AMERICAN STANDARD BIBLE)
FOR REVIEW: READ "THE PURITY WAR" - CHAPTER 20

In *general* I am:	Text	Winning 10 9 8	Struggling 7 6 5 4	Losing 3 2 1
-walking by the Spirit	Gal. 5:16-18			
-not carrying out the the deeds of the flesh		10 9 8	7 6 5 4	3 2 1

Specifically, here's how I am doing in my battle with:	Text	Winning	Struggling	Losing
-immorality		10 9 8	7 6 5 4	3 2 1
-impurity	Gal. 5:19	10 9 8	7 6 5 4	3 2 1
-sensuality		10 9 8	7 6 5 4	3 2 1
-idolatry		10 9 8	7 6 5 4	3 2 1
-sorcery		10 9 8	7 6 5 4	3 2 1
-enmities		10 9 8	7 6 5 4	3 2 1
-strife		10 9 8	7 6 5 4	3 2 1
-jealousy	Gal. 5:20	10 9 8	7 6 5 4	3 2 1
-outbursts of anger		10 9 8	7 6 5 4	3 2 1
-disputes		10 9 8	7 6 5 4	3 2 1
-dissensions		10 9 8	7 6 5 4	3 2 1
-factions		10 9 8	7 6 5 4	3 2 1

	Text			
-envying		10 9 8	7 6 5 4	3 2 1
-drunkenness	Gal. 5:21	10 9 8	7 6 5 4	3 2 1
-carousing		10 9 8	7 6 5 4	3 2 1
-things like these		10 9 8	7 6 5 4	3 2 1
(List some below)				
_____		10 9 8	7 6 5 4	3 2 1
_____		10 9 8	7 6 5 4	3 2 1
_____		10 9 8	7 6 5 4	3 2 1

Specifically, here is how I am doing in manifesting the fruit of the Spirit and becoming more like Jesus Christ in my:	Text	Winning	Struggling	Losing
-love		10 9 8	7 6 5 4	3 2 1
-joy		10 9 8	7 6 5 4	3 2 1
-peace		10 9 8	7 6 5 4	3 2 1
-patience	Gal. 5:22	10 9 8	7 6 5 4	3 2 1
-kindness		10 9 8	7 6 5 4	3 2 1
-goodness		10 9 8	7 6 5 4	3 2 1
-faithfulness		10 9 8	7 6 5 4	3 2 1
-gentleness		10 9 8	7 6 5 4	3 2 1
-self-control	Gal. 5:23	10 9 8	7 6 5 4	3 2 1

PERSONAL ACCOUNTABILITY WORKSHEET #5

TAKING MY MARITAL PULSE (PART ONE)
(FOR HUSBANDS ONLY)
FOR REVIEW: READ "THE PURITY WAR" - CHAPTER 21

As a husband I am:	Text	Winning	Struggling	Losing
-doing my part to make sure we have a healthy sex life	Prov. 5:15-19	10 9 8	7 6 5 4	3 2 1
-treating my wife as a precious gift from God	Prov. 18:22; 19:13-14; 31:10	10 9 8	7 6 5 4	3 2 1
-rewarding my wife for her hard work	Prov. 31:27-28	10 9 8	7 6 5 4	3 2 1
-giving my wife the praise she deserves	Prov. 31:28-31	10 9 8	7 6 5 4	3 2 1
-loving my wife as Christ loves the church		10 9 8	7 6 5 4	3 2 1
-sacrificing for my wife	Eph. 5:25-30	10 9 8	7 6 5 4	3 2 1
-loving my wife as my own body		10 9 8	7 6 5 4	3 2 1
-nourishing and cherishing my wife		10 9 8	7 6 5 4	3 2 1
-not embittered against my wife	Col. 3:19	10 9 8	7 6 5 4	3 2 1
-living with my wife in an understanding way		10 9 8	7 6 5 4	3 2 1
-understanding my wife's physical limitations	1 Peter 3:7	10 9 8	7 6 5 4	3 2 1

-respecting her emotional differences	10 9 8	7 6 5 4	3 2 1
-honoring her as a joint heir in Christ	10 9 8	7 6 5 4	3 2 1

	Excellent	Good	Poor
1. I would rate my marriage as:	10 9 8	7 6 5 4	3 2 1
2. My wife would rate our marriage as:	10 9 8	7 6 5 4	3 2 1
3. I would rate my family life as:	10 9 8	7 6 5 4	3 2 1
4. My wife would rate our family life as:	10 9 8	7 6 5 4	3 2 1

PERSONAL ACCOUNTABILITY WORKSHEET #6

TAKING MY MARITAL PULSE (PART TWO)
(FOR WIVES ONLY)
(BASED ON 1 PETER 3:1-6, 8-9, NEW AMERICAN STANDARD BIBLE)
FOR REVIEW: READ "THE PURITY WAR" - CHAPTER 21

As a wife I am:	Text	Winning	Struggling	Losing
-following my husband's spiritual leadership	1 Peter 3:1	10 9 8	7 6 5 4	3 2 1
-winning him over without nagging (when he is disobedient to the Word)	1 Peter 3:1	10 9 8	7 6 5 4	3 2 1
-living an observable life of purity and worship	1 Peter 3:2	10 9 8	7 6 5 4	3 2 1
-not just focusing on my outward beauty (hair, jewelry, clothes)	1 Peter 3:3	10 9 8	7 6 5 4	3 2 1
-working on my inner self	1 Peter 3:4	10 9 8	7 6 5 4	3 2 1
-clothing myself with an unfading gentle and quiet spirit which has great worth in God's eyes	1 Peter 3:4	10 9 8	7 6 5 4	3 2 1
-finding my worth in my relationship to God	1 Peter 3:4	10 9 8	7 6 5 4	3 2 1
-adorning myself with the ageless beauty of hope in God	1 Peter 3:5	10 9 8	7 6 5 4	3 2 1
-doing what is right in allowing my husband to lead me	1 Peter 3:6	10 9 8	7 6 5 4	3 2 1
-not giving way to fear in my life	1 Peter 3:6	10 9 8	7 6 5 4	3 2 1

STUDY GUIDE

I would rate our marriage as:		Excellent	Good	Poor
-harmonious		10 9 8	7 6 5 4	3 2 1
-sympathetic		10 9 8	7 6 5 4	3 2 1
-brotherly		10 9 8	7 6 5 4	3 2 1
-kindhearted	1 Peter 3:8-9	10 9 8	7 6 5 4	3 2 1
-humble in spirit		10 9 8	7 6 5 4	3 2 1
-not returning evil for evil		10 9 8	7 6 5 4	3 2 1
-giving a blessing instead		10 9 8	7 6 5 4	3 2 1

	Excellent	Good	Poor
1. Overall, I would rate my marriage as:	10 9 8	7 6 5 4	3 2 1
2. My husband would rate our marriage as:	10 9 8	7 6 5 4	3 2 1
3. I would rate my family life as:	10 9 8	7 6 5 4	3 2 1
4. My husband would rate our family life as:	10 9 8	7 6 5 4	3 2 1

PERSONAL ACCOUNTABILITY WORKSHEET #7

TAKING MY MARITAL PULSE (PART THREE)
(FOR COUPLES ONLY)
FOR REVIEW: READ "THE PURITY WAR" - CHAPTER 21 - STEP #2

A Discussion Agenda For Married Couples

1. Have we been meeting each other's needs?

2. Have we been too busy to focus on each other?

3. Have we been communicating well lately?

4. Have we been holding a grudge or harboring bitterness?

5. Have we been protecting our day off?

6. Have we been playing together?

7. Have we been eating meals together?

8. Have we gone on a meaningful date recently?

9. Have we been enjoying each other?

10. Have we been praying together?

11. Have we been going to bed at the same time?

12. Have we been romancing each other?

13. Have we lost the joy of our sexual union?

14. What do we believe are the three greatest issues in our relationship?

HUSBAND'S CONCERNS: **WIFE'S CONCERNS:**

1. _____ 1. _____

2. _____ 2. _____

3. _____ 3. _____

15. What are we committed to do to build our marriage?

AS YOUR HUSBAND, I WILL: **AS YOUR WIFE, I WILL:**

1. _____ 1. _____

2. _____ 2. _____

3. _____ 3. _____

4. _____ 4. _____

Husband's Signature: _____ Date_____

Wife's Signature: _____ Date_____

PERSONAL ACCOUNTABILITY WORKSHEET #8

TAKING MY MINISTRY PULSE
(FOR THOSE IN CHRISTIAN SERVICE)

1. In regards to my overall ministry, I feel:

__ encouraged	__ frustrated	__ angry	__ disappointed
__ tired	__ abused	__ dry	__ confident
__ buried	__ indifferent	__ optimistic	__ challenge
__ hopeful	__ excited	__ misunderstood	__ falsely accused
__ joyful	__ fulfilled	__ fearful	__ burned out
__ trapped	__ stimulated	__ jealous of others	__ burdened
__ inadequate	__ appreciated	__ lonely	__ supported
__ rejected	__ unappreciated	__ motivated	__ empty

Comments:

2. In regards to my relationship to my ministry board or supervisors, I feel:

__ encouraged	__ frustrated	__ angry	__ disappointed
__ tired	__ abused	__ dry	__ confident
__ buried	__ indifferent	__ optimistic	__ challenge
__ hopeful	__ excited	__ misunderstood	__ falsely accused
__ joyful	__ fulfilled	__ fearful	__ burned out
__ trapped	__ stimulated	__ jealous of others	__ burdened
__ inadequate	__ appreciated	__ lonely	__ supported
__ rejected	__ unappreciated	__ motivated	__ empty

Comments:

3. In regards to my relationship with the people I serve, I feel:

__ encouraged   __ frustrated   __ angry   __ disappointed
__ tired   __ abused   __ dry   __ confident
__ buried   __ indifferent   __ optimistic   __ challenged
__ hopeful   __ excited   __ misunderstood   __ falsely accused
__ joyful   __ fulfilled   __ fearful   __ burned out
__ trapped   __ stimulated   __ jealous of others __ burdened
__ inadequate   __ appreciated   __ lonely   __ supported
__ rejected   __ unappreciated   __ motivated   __ empty

Comments:

4. In regards to my relationship with my fellow workers, I feel:

__ encouraged   __ frustrated   __ angry   __ disappointed
__ tired   __ abused   __ dry   __ confident
__ buried   __ indifferent   __ optimistic   __ challenged
__ hopeful   __ excited   __ misunderstood   __ falsely accused
__ joyful   __ fulfilled   __ fearful   __ burned out
__ trapped   __ stimulated   __ jealous of others __ burdened
__ inadequate   __ appreciated   __ lonely   __ supported
__ rejected   __ unappreciated   __ motivated   __ empty

Comments:

5. In regards to how I am presently using my gifts and talents, I feel:

__ encouraged	__ frustrated	__ angry	__ disappointed
__ tired	__ abused	__ dry	__ confident
__ buried	__ indifferent	__ optimistic	__ challenged
__ hopeful	__ excited	__ misunderstood	__ falsely accused
__ joyful	__ fulfilled	__ fearful	__ burned out
__ trapped	__ stimulated	__ jealous of others	__ burdened
__ inadequate	__ appreciated	__ lonely	__ supported
__ rejected	__ unappreciated	__ motivated	__ empty

Comments:

6. In regards to my outlook concerning my ministry future, I feel:

__ encouraged	__ frustrated	__ angry	__ disappointed
__ tired	__ abused	__ dry	__ confident
__ buried	__ indifferent	__ optimistic	__ challenged
__ hopeful	__ excited	__ misunderstood	__ falsely accused
__ joyful	__ fulfilled	__ fearful	__ burned out
__ trapped	__ stimulated	__ jealous of others	__ burdened
__ inadequate	__ appreciated	__ lonely	__ supported
__ rejected	__ unappreciated	__ motivated	__ empty

Comments:

7. Some encouraging things that have happened recently are:

8. My present concerns are:

9. Some fresh insights I have recently learned are:

10. My greatest need today is:

11. Other comments or things I'd like to share:

PERSONAL ACCOUNTABILITY WORKSHEET #9

TAKING MY PHYSICAL PULSE

1. I am getting plenty of rest.   Yes   No
   Comment:

2. I am getting sufficient exercise.   Yes   No
   Comment:

3. I have had a recent physical examination.   Yes   No
   Comment:

4. I am taking a regular day off.   Yes   No
   Comment:

5. I am in need of a few days off soon.   Yes   No
   Comment:

6. I am in need of a short vacation soon.   Yes   No
   Comment:

7. I am in need of an extended break.   Yes   No
   Comment:

8. I am pleased with my present body weight.   Yes   No
   Comment:

9. I am pleased with my present eating habits.   Yes   No
   Comment:

10. Overall, my health is: Excellent   Good   Fair   Poor

11. My last blood pressure reading was: High   Normal   Low
    Date of reading: _____

12. My present health problems are:

13. To improve the present condition of my health I promise to:

    1. _____ 2. _____

    3. _____ 4. _____

Signature:_____Date_____

PERSONAL ACCOUNTABILITY WORKSHEET #10

TAKING MY MENTAL PULSE
(BASED ON PHILIPPIANS 4:8, NEW AMERICAN STANDARD VERSION)
FOR REVIEW: READ "THE PURITY WAR" - CHAPTER 29-30

I am letting my mind dwell on things that are:	Text	Winning	Struggling	Losing
-true		10 9 8	7 6 5 4	3 2 1
-honorable		10 9 8	7 6 5 4	3 2 1
-right		10 9 8	7 6 5 4	3 2 1
-pure		10 9 8	7 6 5 4	3 2 1
-lovely	Phil. 4:8	10 9 8	7 6 5 4	3 2 1
-of good repute		10 9 8	7 6 5 4	3 2 1
-excellent		10 9 8	7 6 5 4	3 2 1
-worthy of praise		10 9 8	7 6 5 4	3 2 1

The garbage that has been polluting my mind lately is:

Read briefly through the following references. Mark those that you particularly need to meditate on this week. Share them with your partners.

____ Psalm 119:9-11   ____ 1 Thessalonians 4:1-8   ____ Colossians 3:1-17
____ Proverbs 5:8   ____ Romans 12:1-2   ____ Galatians 5:16-26
____ Romans 6:11-19   ____ Psalm 51:1-17   ____ Mark 7:21-23
____ James 1:14-16   ____ Philippians 4:8   ____ Matthew 5:27-28
____ 1 Peter 1:14-17   ____ Philippians 3:7-16   ____ 2 Corinthians 10:3-6
____ Psalm 103:1-14   ____ Psalm 38:1-14   ____ 1 Corinthians 6:12-20

PERSONAL ACCOUNTABILITY WORKSHEET #11

STATING MY MORAL BOUNDARIES

Realizing the impact of my past sin, the reality of my present struggles with the flesh, and the certainty of future temptations from the world and Satan, I will endeavor to keep the following specific rules or safeguards for myself:

Regarding the Abuse of Sex

        I will: I will not:

_____   _____

_____   _____

Regarding the Abuse of Money

        I will: I will not:

_____   _____

_____   _____

Regarding the Abuse of Power

        I will: I will not:

_____   _____

_____   _____

My Signature:_____

Accountability Partner's Signature:_____

PERSONAL ACCOUNTABILITY WORKSHEET #12

SAFEGUARDING MY TRAVEL TIME

MORALLY DANGEROUS COMBINATIONS FOR THOSE WHO TRAVEL

The following is a list of suggestions gathered from those who spend much of their time traveling. They recognize the key dangers to their moral safety while traveling:

- Anonymity
- Discretionary Funds
- Leisure Time
- Broken Routine
- Loneliness

They submit these traveling tips in hopes that some of their ideas will be helpful in your desire for moral victory on the road. Mark those that are most helpful, adding your own comments and ideas at the bottom. Discuss these with your accountability partners.

TRAVELING TIPS FOR BUILDING PERSONAL PURITY IN MY LIFE

- Pre-plan your trip and how you will avoid the things that tempt you (e.g. newsstands, magazines, internet, movies, flirtations, solicitations)
- Ask your friends to pray for your moral safety on the trip and then report to at least one of them after the trip. Be ready to answer the hard questions.
- Give your family and friends a specific itinerary and be prepared to explain delays.
- If possible, avoid traveling alone. Travel with your spouse or someone of the same sex.

- Walk past that newsstand with questionable material. Buy your newspaper, magazine or book before you travel.
- If possible, stay in homes of friends and acquaintances; not hotels.
- Ask the hotel to give you a room where there is no TV or have them remove it. If they won't, there are plenty of hotels that will.
- If you do have a television with easy access, put a towel over the television as a reminder to do something else. Or just unplug it.
- When you do watch television, be intentional. "Channel surfing" is out while traveling. Once that selected program is over, turn off the TV.
- When using the internet, be on guard, especially in foreign countries whose censorship standards may be different. Do not "surf the net."
- Bring photos of your spouse and family and look at them at least once a day.
- Avoid being anonymous. Introduce yourself or wear a nametag.
- Contact your spouse and children regularly. If communication is impossible, send them a note to let them (and yourself) know you were thinking of them.
- Listen to Christian music in your room and while traveling.
- Attend church, mid-week services or Christian fellowships in the area. Some hotels even hold church services.
- Set up a network of Christian friends and fellowship groups in areas where you frequently travel.
- Don't meet alone with someone of the opposite sex, publicly or privately. Arrange for an associate to come along with you. If you must meet, then be sure it is a very public place and that you stick to business.
- Don't drink alcohol. Drinking lowers your moral inhibitions and dulls your spiritual sensibilities.
- Pre-plan and hold to a daily Bible-reading schedule for the duration of the trip.
- Keep on hand a number of Scriptures for quick referral when needed throughout the day. Better yet, begin a memorization plan to "hide" these verses in your heart.

- Think and treat every person you meet as a (potential) brother or sister in Christ.
- Pray for your own moral safety throughout the trip.
- Run from any hint of moral trouble.
- If temptation is getting to you, call a friend for help. Better yet, call someone even before temptation arises.

Add your own suggestions to this list.

_____

_____

PERSONAL ACCOUNTABILITY WORKSHEET #13

REHEARSING THE CONSEQUENCES OF MORAL FAILURE
FOR REVIEW: READ "THE PURITY WAR" - CHAPTER 25

Using the following as a guideline, write out what you could expect if you were caught in the act of sexual immorality. Be specific. Use names or initials.

- Its effect on my relationship with the Lord:

- Its effect on my spouse (or future spouse):

- Its effect on my children:

- Its effect on other family members:

- Its effect on my church family:

- Its effect on my work:

- Its effect on those to whom I am witnessing:

- Its effect on my ministry:

- Its effect on me physically:

- Its effect on me emotionally:

- Its effect on me spiritually:

- Its effect on me socially:

- Its effect on me economically:

- Its effect on me sexually:

- Its effect on my future:

- Its effect on the generations that follow me:

PERSONAL ACCOUNTABILITY WORKSHEET #14

RESTORING FELLOWSHIP WITH MY GOD
FOR REVIEW: READ "THE PURITY WAR" - CHAPTER 42

This assignment is for those who have experienced moral failure and its consequences. Write your own testimony, using the following outline. Be specific.

THE PROGRESSION OF MY SPIRITUAL REBELLION

1. I let my guard down:

2. I was tempted to sin:

3. I yielded to sin:

4. I hid my sin:

5. I suffered the consequences of my sin:

   - The physical consequences:

   - The emotional consequences:

   - The spiritual consequences:

THE PATTERN OF MY SPIRITUAL RENEWAL

1. I admitted my sin:

2. I confessed my sin:

3. I turned from my sin:

    - Behavior changes:

    - Attitude changes:

THE RESULT OF MY SPIRITUAL RESTORATION

1. My sin was removed:

2. My spirit was renewed:

3. My service to the Lord was restored:

"... once you have turned again (i.e. *repented*), strengthen your brothers" (Luke 22:32).

PERSONAL ACCOUNTABILITY WORKSHEET #15

WORKSHEET FOR RESOLVING A CONFLICT
FOR REVIEW: READ "THE PURITY WAR" - CHAPTER 11-12

Briefly describe the specific nature of the conflict:

Instructions:
1. *With the details of the conflict in mind, read thoughtfully through the list of "one another" verses <u>three</u> times.*
2. *The first time through place an X next to those you feel the other person has or has not done to you. Comment on each point you mark.*
3. *The second time through put an O next to those you feel you have done or have not done to the other person. Comment on each point you mark.*
4. *The third time through put your initials next to those you believe the Spirit of God is calling you to apply right away in order to bring reconciliation to this situation. Comment on each point you mark.*

- Confess your faults to one another (James 5:16)

- Be of the same mind toward one another (Romans 12:16; Romans 15:5; cf. Philippians 2:1-5)

- Forgive one another (Colossians 3:13; Ephesians 4:32)

- Submit to one another (Ephesians 5:21; 1 Peter 5:5)

- Restore one another (Galatians 6:1)

- Bear one another's burdens (Galatians 6:2)

- Accept (receive and welcome) one another (Romans 15:7)

- Greet one another (Romans 16:16; 1 Peter 5:14; 1 Corinthians 16:20)

- Don't cause one another to stumble (to sin) (Romans 14:13; 1 Corinthians 12:25)

- Edify (build up) one another (Romans 14:19)

- Love (self-sacrifice for) one another (Romans 12:9-10; 1 Peter 4:8; John 13:34; 15:12-17)

- Teach and exhort one another (Colossians 3:13,16; Hebrews 3:13)

- Admonish (warn) one another (Romans 15:14; Colossians 3:16)

- Rebuke one another (Luke 17:3)

- Contribute to the (financial) needs of one another (Romans 12:13)

- Encourage one another (1 Thessalonians 5:11; Hebrews 10:25)

- Pray for one another (James 5:16)

- Comfort one another (1 Thessalonians 4:18)

- Stimulate one another to love and good deeds (Hebrews 10:24)

- Use your gifts to serve one another (1 Peter 4:10; Galatians 5:13)

- Wash one another's feet (i.e. be a Christlike servant toward the other) (John 13:14)

- Be hospitable to one another (1 Peter 4:9; Romans 12:13)

- Be kind to one another (Ephesians 4:32)

- Give preference to one another (Romans 12:10)

- Be tenderhearted toward one another (Ephesians 4:32)

- Don't bite and devour one another (Galatians 5:15)

- Don't provoke one another (Galatians 5:26)

- Don't lie to one another (Colossians 3:9)

- Don't envy one another (Galatians 5:26)

- Don't hate one another (Titus 3:3)

- Don't speak evil against one another (James 4:11)

- Don't complain against one another (James 5:9)

- Don't judge one another (by personal standards, rather than God's) (Matthew 7:1; Romans 14:13)

Now go to that person TODAY and do what you know God wants you to do:

> In your anger do not sin: Do not let the sun go down while you are still angry, and do not give the devil a foothold (Ephesians 4:26-27).

> Do not let any unwholesome talk come out of your mouths, but only what is helpful for building others up according to their needs, that it may benefit those who listen. And do not grieve the Holy Spirit of God, with whom you were

sealed for the day of redemption. Get rid of all bitterness, rage and anger, brawling and slander, along with every form of malice. Be kind and compassionate to one another, forgiving each other, just as in Christ God forgave you (Ephesians 4:29-32).

My dear brothers, take note of this: Everyone should be quick to listen, slow to speak and slow to become angry, for man's anger does not bring about the righteous life that God desires . . . Do not merely listen to the word, and so deceive yourselves. Do what it says (James 1:19-22).

What causes fights and quarrels among you? Don't they come from your desires that battle within you? You want something but don't get it. You kill and covet, but you cannot have what you want. You quarrel and fight. You do not have, because you do not ask God (James 4:1-3).

PERSONAL ACCOUNTABILITY WORKSHEET #16

MAKING A COVENANT WITH THE PARTS OF MY BODY
FOR REVIEW: READ "THE PURITY WAR" - CHAPTER 34

> I made a covenant with my eyes not to look lustfully at a girl (Job 31:1).

> Offer the parts of your body to him as instruments of righteousness (Romans 6:13).

In preparation for this assignment you might want to review Chapter 34, *Promising My Body*. Then prayerfully complete the following:

I, _____ make a covenant agreement with God concerning:

- my eyes not to look at:

- my ears not to listen to:

- my mouth not to speak about:

- my hands not to touch:

- my feet not to run toward:

- my mind not to dwell on:

- my knees not to neglect praying for:

- my whole body not to compromise my calling to bring glory to God!

> "Glorify God in your body" (1 Corinthians 6:20).

PERSONAL ACCOUNTABILITY WORKSHEET #17

MY SPIRITUAL HEALTH INDICATORS
FOR REVIEW: READ "THE PURITY WAR" - CHAPTER 20

As a child of God, I need to grow in:

- Fellowship — Engaging in loving, need-meeting relationships with other members of the body of Christ.
- Doctrine — Understanding and being able to defend the basic doctrines of the Christian faith taught in the Word of God.
- Worship — Responding in a variety of ways to the infinite majesty and glorious attributes of God.
- Service — Serving God and others, using the gifts and talents graciously given to me.
- Evangelism — Understanding the true gospel of grace alone through faith alone and sharing with others the good news of my hope in Christ.
- Discipleship — Helping others become loving, faithful, and obedient followers of Jesus Christ.
- Prayer — Communicating with my heavenly Father in sincere praise, repentance, and petition.

Keeping in mind the above definitions, here's how I am doing in the following areas:

• Fellowship	Winning	Struggling	Losing
	10 9 8	7 6 5 4	3 2 1

I am enjoying regular fellowship with the following people:

_____

- Doctrine   Winning   Struggling   Losing

                          10 9 8   7 6 5 4   3 2 1

I am presently studying the following biblical subjects:

_____

- Worship   Winning   Struggling   Losing

                          10 9 8   7 6 5 4   3 2 1

I would describe the present condition of my intimacy with God as follows:

_____

- Service   Winning   Struggling   Losing

                          10 9 8   7 6 5 4   3 2 1

I am presently involved in the following specific ministries:

_____

- Evangelism   Winning   Struggling   Losing

                          10 9 8   7 6 5 4   3 2 1

The following are the specifics regarding my present involvement in sharing the gospel with:

         My Family:
         My Neighborhood:
         My Workplace/School:
         My City:
         My State/Province/Region:
         My Country:
         The World:

• Discipleship	Winning	Struggling	Losing
	10 9 8	7 6 5 4	3 2 1

I am actively discipling the following people:

The following people are the spiritual mentors in my life:

• Prayer	Winning	Struggling	Losing
Concerning maintaining a consistent prayer-life, I am:	10 9 8	7 6 5 4	3 2 1

As it relates to the specifics of P.R.A.Y.E.R. I am:	Winning	Struggling	Losing
• Praising	10 9 8	7 6 5 4	3 2 1
• Repenting	10 9 8	7 6 5 4	3 2 1
• Asking	10 9 8	7 6 5 4	3 2 1
• Yielding (my heart)	10 9 8	7 6 5 4	3 2 1
• Entreating (for others)	10 9 8	7 6 5 4	3 2 1
• Rejoicing (in God)	10 9 8	7 6 5 4	3 2 1

PERSONAL ACCOUNTABILITY WORKSHEET #18

MY PRAYER OF DEDICATION

The mandate for my personal purity is clear.

> In a large house there are articles not only of gold and silver, but also of wood and clay; some are for noble purposes and some for ignoble. If a man cleanses himself from the latter, he will be an instrument for noble purposes, made holy, useful to the Master and prepared to do any good work. Flee the evil desires of youth, and pursue righteousness, faith, love and peace, along with those who call on the Lord out of a pure heart (2 Timothy 2:20-22, New International Version).

God's provision for my personal purity is assured.

> Now to him who is able to keep you from stumbling, and to present you faultless before the presence of His glory with exceeding joy, to God our Savior, be glory and majesty, dominion and power, both now and forever. Amen (Jude 24-25, New King James Version).

My prayer for personal purity will be heard.

Write out your Prayer of Dedication regarding your commitment to walk in holiness and personal purity. Use a separate sheet, if needed.

Dear heavenly Father,

Sincerely,
Signature:_____Date_____

APPENDICES

MASTURBATION: CHIEF OF SINS OR GIFT OF GOD?

Look in a concordance or do a word search in any Bible program. Nowhere will we find any form of the word *masturbation* used in the Scriptures. I once heard, "When the Word of God is silent, we have two choices—to opinionate or shut up." Frankly, it is tempting for me to say nothing. However, too many have opinionated and therefore, I suppose I should speak up.

The debate, at least among Christians, has to do with whether followers of Christ can engage in self-stimulation and still please God. Opinions abound. Far too many to address here.[1] Let me do my best to summarize them.

THERE ARE THOSE WHO TEACH THAT MASTURBATION IS ALWAYS WRONG.

Some who hold this view quote the story of Onan, who was punished by God for "spilling his seed" on the ground (Genesis 38:8-10). Thus, the old word for masturbation was onanism.[2] Few today would use this argument. However, throughout church history there has been a wide range of prohibitions against wasting semen in any sexual activity, such as masturbation, and in some cases, birth control, and non-procreative sexual activities. These, of course, are the extreme views.

Others teach that masturbation is the physical expression of sinful lust and a counterfeit replacement for genuine intimacy. In his book, *The Ethics of Sex,* German theologian, Helmut Thielicke, expressed his belief that "in masturbation sex is separated from the I-Thou relationship and thus loses its meaning as being the expression of this fellowship." He goes on to express the concern that "sexual fantasy . . . roves about vagrantly." His rejection of masturbation as a practice was not so much about the offensive nature of the physical function, but more so about the spiritual effects. He referred to it as "invertedness"—a state of mind that Martin Luther called "man's being turned into himself."[3] Lewis Smedes provides an appropriate summary when he writes, "masturbation is sexual solitaire."[4] Because of God's design for sexual union between a man and woman in the covenant of marriage and the virtual impossibility of keeping one's thoughts pure, many of my fellow pastors and biblical counselors teach that masturbation is out of the question.

THERE ARE OTHERS WHO TEACH THAT MASTURBATION IS A NORMAL AND ACCEPTABLE PRACTICE.

I once heard a pastor speak of masturbation as a gift from God, an acceptable and natural release for sexual tension, as long as there is no sinful lust involved. Others in this camp would not go so far as to treat masturbation as a divine gift but would certainly argue for us to not make such a big deal out of it. The greater issue, they would say, is what is going on in our heart (i.e. our mind) and whether masturbation has become a self-absorbing habit. They also express concern that the subsequent guilt and shame have done more damage than the activity.

A widower once asked for my counsel, quite concerned that he had, in his words, "committed the sin of onanism." He explained that he was thinking about the many wonderful years of sexual relations he experienced with his wife and he masturbated. He was deeply troubled. What would you have told him? There are some who believe that, in times of separation, fantasizing about one's spouse (some even say *future* spouse) would be acceptable. Others would argue that because the man was troubled it was wrong, regardless.

THERE ARE THOSE WHO TEACH THAT MASTURBATION IS NEITHER RIGHT NOR WRONG; GOOD NOR BAD.

To these folks, masturbation is not the issue. Uncontrolled habits, sinful lust, and distorted views of intimacy become the factors to be considered. In their book, *Every Young Man's Battle: Strategies for Victory in the Real*

World of Sexual Temptation, Stephen Arterburn and Fred Stoeker simplify what might be considered the moderate view:

> If there's a "clear-minded" and "clean" form of masturbation . . . the keep-it-to-a-minimum advice would be decent counsel. But clearly, "knock it off" is the only advice for nearly all men because of the pornography and sinful lust involved. Sin binds, and such bondage is devastating."[5]

So, where do I stand on the issue? Some would say I stand with feet "firmly planted in mid-air." I believe masturbation is neither the chief of sins nor the gift of God. I am well aware of the many men and women who are sinfully addicted to the behavior, and even carry the uncontrolled habit into their marriages as a counterfeit replacement for sexual union. I also know of many whose occasional activity has crippled them with shame, making them feel like spiritual lepers. Then, there are those who, because the Bible seems silent and theologians can't agree, do whatever pleases them, whenever and wherever, without regard for whether it is right or wrong. None of these conditions are healthy.

I am often asked why I do not address the subject of masturbation directly in our purity seminars. Why? Because, the issue is really not the issue. Instead of masturbation, the greater issue is sanctification—living holy lives as vessels of honor whose main desire is to bring glory to God (1 Thessalonians 4:3; 2 Timothy 2:20-23; 1 Corinthians 10:31). Like the Galatians two millennia ago, we would much rather have external rules imposed by a religious system than to live and walk in and by the power of the indwelling Holy Spirit (Galatians 5:16-22).

Imagine how big the Bible would be if it gave specific prohibitions against every imaginable sin. Instead, the Bible calls us not to be foolish, but to attempt to understand the will of God in every area of life, based on clearly stated biblical principles (Ephesians 5:17). This is as true for masturbation as it is for any other unspecified action.

Instead of wading through the endless opinions of men, each of us must face this issue ourselves—privately, prayerfully, with Bible and heart open. I suggest we ask ourselves the following questions, most of which are the same questions we should ask of anything we are about to do that is not expressly allowed or forbidden in Scripture. Once we have honestly answered these, we should be able to decide what almighty God would have us do, regardless of what others may think or say. After all, it's *His* opinion that matters most:

- Does it enslave me? Is it profitable? Has it become an uncontrollable habit? (1 Corinthians 6:12-13; 10:23)
- Does it harm me in any way? (1 Corinthians 6:19-20)
- Does it reflect God's values or the world's—i.e. "the lust of the flesh and the lust of the eyes and the boastful pride of life"? (1 John 2:15-17)
- Does it demonstrate Christ's attributes and character? Would Jesus do this? (Colossians 3:17)
- Does it express my desire to please God? (Colossians 3:23)
- Does it produce peace in my heart? (Philippians 4:4-7)
- Does it give evidence of the fruit of the Spirit in my life, especially self-control? (Galatians 5:22-23)
- Does it prove that I am yielded to God, desiring to do His will above my own? (Roman 12:1-2)
- Does it express my understanding of God's design for my sexuality? (1 Thessalonians 4:3-8)
- Does it help my mind dwell on that which is pure and lovely? (Philippians 4:8)
- Does it reflect a life of immorality, impurity and sensuality? (Galatians 5:19)
- Does it draw me closer to or farther from the Lord? (James 4:8)
- Does it affect my sexual intimacy with my spouse (future spouse)? (1 Corinthians 7:5)

- Does it present a good example to my spouse (future spouse)? (Ephesians 5:25-33)
- Does it cause substantial doubt? (Romans 14:22-23; James 1:6-8; 4:8)
- Does it spring from my commitment to the Word and to prayer? (1 Timothy 4:4-5)
- Does it violate my conscience? Do I believe it's the right thing to do? (James 4:17)

Beloved of God, we are not alone in this struggle to do what is right. Regardless of the conflicting views of men, we can have the clear assurance of guidance from our heavenly Father and His indwelling Holy Spirit. His promises form the basis of our confidence in making the decision to do the right thing:

> Trust in the LORD and do good;
> Dwell in the Land and cultivate faithfulness.
> Delight yourself in the LORD;
> And He will give you the desires of your heart.
> Commit your way to the LORD,
> Trust also in Him, and He will do it (Psalm 37:3-5).

> I will instruct you and teach you in the way which you
>   should go;
> I will counsel you with My eye upon you (Psalm 32:8).

> Trust in the Lord with all your heart
> And do not lean on your own understanding.
> In all your ways acknowledge Him,
> And He will make your paths straight
> (Proverbs 3:5-6).

The plans of the heart belong to man,
But the answer of the tongue is from the LORD.
All the ways of a man are clean in his own sight,
But the LORD weighs the motives.
Commit your works to the LORD
And your plans will be established. . . .
The mind of man plans his way,
But the LORD directs his steps (Proverbs 16:1-3, 9).

For such is God,
Our God forever and ever;
He will guide us until death (Psalm 48:14).

But I say, walk by the Spirit, and you will not carry out the desire of the flesh. For the flesh sets its desire against the Spirit, and the Spirit against the flesh; for these are in opposition to one another, so that you may not do the things that you please. But if you are led by the Spirit, you are not under the Law (Galatians 5:16-18).

SUGGESTED READING ON MORAL PURITY AND BIBLICAL SEXUALITY

I am committed to the fact that there are only two categories of books—*The Holy Bible* and *Everything Else*. Only the Word of God is inspired and completely trustworthy as the source of our faith and practice (2 Timothy 3:16). Consider the timely words of the ancient Preacher found in the book of Ecclesiastes. I have added some clarifying comments:

> "Vanity of vanities," says the Preacher (Hebrew: *Qoheleth*), "all is vanity!" In addition to being a wise man, the Preacher also taught the people knowledge; and he pondered, searched out and arranged many proverbs. The Preacher sought to find delightful words and to write words of truth correctly. The words of wise men are like goads, and masters of these collections (i.e. *the Scriptures*) are like well-driven nails; they are given by one Shepherd. But beyond this, my son, be warned: the writing of many books is endless, and excessive devotion to books (i.e. *all other non-inspired works*) is wearying to the body. The conclusion, when all has been heard, is: fear God and keep His commandments, because this applies to every person (Ecclesiastes 12:8-13).

Having presented many of the hundreds of Scriptures on the subject of sexual purity, I am now taking the risk of suggesting resources outside of the Bible—i.e. the *other* books. My first concern is that my short list excludes many other helpful resources, old and new. Secondly, I fear that my recommendation implies an endorsement of everything these materials present or the full knowledge of the credibility and integrity of the authors. I encourage you to be a discerning reader, like the Bereans in Paul's day, examining the Scriptures to see if what you are hearing (or reading) is biblically sound (Acts 17:11) and comes from a reliable source.

With these conditions and concerns in mind, the following is my attempt at bringing a wide range of recommendations:

Alcorn, Randy. *Christians in the Wake of the Sexual Revolution*. Portland, Oregon: Multnomah Press, 1985.

Alcorn, Randy. *Guidelines for Sexual Purity*. Gresham, Oregon: Eternal Perspectives Ministries, 2005.

Alcorn, Randy. *Sexual Temptation: How Christian Workers Can Win the Battle.*
2nd Edition, Gresham, Oregon: Eternal Perspectives Ministries, 2007. *(1st Edition by InterVarsity Press, 1989).*

Alcorn, Randy. *The Purity Principle: God's Safeguards for Life's Dangerous Trails*. Sisters, Oregon: Multnomah Press, 2003.

Anderson, Nancy C. *Avoiding the Greener Grass Syndrome: How to Grow Affair Proof Hedges Around Your Marriage*. Grand Rapids, Michigan: Kregel, 2004.

Andrews, Gini. *Your Half of the Apple: God and the Single Girl*. Grand Rapids, Michigan: Zondervan, 1972.

Arterburn, Steve and Stoeker, Fred. *Everyman's Battle: Winning the War on Sexual Temptation One Victory at Time*. Colorado Springs, Colorado: Waterbrook, 2000.

Arterburn, Steve and Stoeker, Fred and Yorkey, Mike. *Every Young Man's Battle: Strategies for Victory in the Real World of Sexual Temptation*. Colorado Springs, Colorado: Waterbrook, 2002.

Arvin, Kay K. *1 + 1 = 1: How To Have a Successful and Happy Christian Marriage*. Nashville, Tennessee: Broadman, 1969.

Bridges, Jerry. *The Practice of Godliness: Godliness Has a Value for All Things*. Colorado Springs, Colorado: NavPress, 1983.

Carder, Dave. *Torn Asunder: Recovering from Extramarital Affairs*. Chicago, Illinois: Moody Press, 1992.

Cecy, James M. "Answers to Your Questions about Sexual Immorality", CONTACT Quarterly, Vol. 53 No. 2, (Summer, 1994), 7-9.

Collins, Gary R. (Editor). *The Secrets of Our Sexuality: Role Liberation for the Christian.* Waco, Texas: Word, 1976.

Cox, Dr. Paul M. *Clear Thinking on Sexuality Outside & Inside Marriage.* San Bernardino, California: Perspective Ministries & Paul Cox, 1991.

Edell, Ron. *How to Save Your Marriage From an Affair.* Indianapolis/New York: Bobbs-Merrill, 1983.

Ethridge, Shannon. *Every Woman's Battle: Discovering God's Plan for Sexual and Emotional Fulfillment.* Colorado Springs, Colorado: Waterbrook, 2003.

Feinberg, John S. and Feinberg, Paul D. *Ethics for a Brave New World.* Wheaton, Illinois: Crossway, 1993.

Foster, Richard J. *Celebration of Discipline: The Path to Spiritual Growth.* New York: Harper Collins, 2002.

Gardner, Tim Alan. *Sacred Sex: A Spiritual Celebration of Oneness in Marriage.* Colorado Springs, Colorado: Waterbrook, 2002.

Haley, Mike. *101 Frequently Asked Questions About Homosexuality.* Eugene, Oregon: Harvest House, 2004.

Harris, Joshua. *I Kissed Dating Goodbye: A New Attitude Towards Relationships and Romance.* Portland, Oregon: Multnomah, 1997.

Harris, Joshua. *Sex Is Not the Problem (Lust Is): Sexual Purity in a Lust-Saturated World.* Portland, Oregon: Multnomah, 2005.

Hart, Dr. Archibald D. *The Sexual Man.* Dallas/London/Vancouver/Melbourne: Word, 1994.

Hayford, Jack. *Fatal Attractions: Why Sex Sins Are Worse Than Others.* Ventura, California: Regal, 2005.

Heimbach, Daniel R. *True Sexual Morality: Recovering Biblical Standards for a Culture in Crisis.* Wheaton, Illinois: Crossway, 2004.

Hugenberger, Gordon P. *Marriage as a Covenant: A Study of Biblical Law and Ethics Governing Marriage, Developed from the Perspective of Malachi.* Grand Rapids, Michigan: Baker, 1998.

Jenkins, Jerry B. *Loving Your Marriage Enough to Protect It.* Brentwood, Tennessee: Wolgemuth & Hyatt, 1989.

Johnson, Rex. *At Home With Sex.* Wheaton, Illinois: Victor, 1979.

LaHaye, Tim F. *Sex Education Is For The Family.* Grand Rapids, Michigan: Zondervan, 1985.

LaHaye, Tim F. *The Act of Marriage: The Beauty of Sexual Love.* Grand Rapids, Michigan: Zondervan, 1976.

Lewis, Gregg. *Telegarbage: What You Can Do About Sex and Violence on TV.* Nashville/New York: Thomas Nelson, 1977.

MacArthur, John, Jr. *Different By Design: Discovering God's Will for Today's Man and Woman.* Wheaton, Illinois: Victor, 1994.

Mahaney, C.J. and Carolyn. *Sex, Romance, and the Glory of God: What Every Christian Husband Needs to Know.* Wheaton, Illinois: Crossway, 2004.

Mayo, Mary Ann. *A Christian Guide To Sexual Counseling: Recovering the Mystery And Reality of "One Flesh."* Grand Rapids, Michigan: Zondervan, 1987.

McDowell, Josh. *How to Help Your Child Say "No" to Sexual Pressure.* Waco, Texas: Word, 1987.

Miles, Herbert J. *Sexual Happiness In Marriage: A Christian Interpretation of Sexual Adjustment In Marriage.* Grand Rapids, Michigan: Zondervan, 1967.

Miles, Herbert J. *Sexual Understanding Before Marriage.* Grand Rapids, Michigan: Zondervan, 1971.

Mowday, Lois C. *The Snare: Avoiding Emotional and Sexual Entanglements.* Colorado Springs, Colorado: NavPress, 1988.

Muck, Terry (Editor). *Sins Of The Body: Ministry In A Sexual Society.* Carol Stream, Illinois: Word, 1989.

Penner, Clifford. *Sex 101: A Guide to Intimacy for Newlywed Couples*, Nashville, Tennessee: Thomas Nelson, 2004.

Penner, Clifford and Joyce. *The Gift of Sex: A Guide to Sexual Fulfillment.* Carol Stream, Illinois: Word, 2003.

Petersen, J. Allan (Editor). *The Marriage Affair.* Wheaton, Illinois: Tyndale House, 1971.

Petersen, J. Allan. *The Myth of the Greener Grass.* Wheaton, Illinois: Tyndale House, 1983.

Radmacher, Earl D. *You and Your Thoughts: The Power of Right Thinking.* Palm Springs, California: Ronald N. Haynes, 1977.

Redpath, Alan. *The Making of the Man of God: Studies in the Life of David,* Grand Rapids, Michigan: Fleming Revell, 1962.

Piper, John and Justin Taylor. *Sex and the Supremacy of Christ.* Wheaton: Illinois: Crossway, 2005.

Rosenau, Douglas. *A Celebration of Sex: A Guide to Enjoying God's Gift of Sexual Intimacy,* Nashville, Tennessee: Thomas Nelson, 2002 (Revised and updated edition).

Schaumburg, Harry W. *False Intimacy: Understanding the Struggle of Sexual Addiction.* Colorado Springs, Colorado: Navpress, 1992.

Shedd, Charlie & Martha. *Celebration in the Bedroom.* Waco, Texas: Word, 1979.

Small, Dwight H. *Christian: Celebrate Your Sexuality.* Old Tappan, New Jersey: Fleming H. Revell, 1974.

Small, Dwight H. *Design For Christian Marriage.* Old Tappan, New Jersey: Fleming H. Revell, 1959.

Smedes, Lewis B. *Sex For Christians: The Limits And Liberties of Sexual Living.* Grand Rapids, Michigan: Eerdmans, 1976.

Stafford, Tim. *The Sexual Christian.* Wheaton, Illinois: Victor, 1989.

Stenzel, Pam. *Discussions About Sexuality, Spirituality and Self Respect.* Grand Rapids, Michigan: Zondervan/Youth Specialties, 2003.

Struthers, William H. *Wired for Intimacy: How Pornography Hijacks the Male Brain.* Downers Grove, Illinois: InterVarsity Press, 2009.

Thielicke, Helmut. *The Ethics of Sex.* Trans. John W. Doberstein. New York, Evanston and London: Harper & Row, 1964.

Trobisch, Ingrid. *The Joy of Being A Woman . . . And What a Man Can Do*. San Francisco, California: Harper & Row, 1975.

Wheat, Ed and Wheat, Gaye. *Intended for Pleasure: Sex Technique and Sexual Fulfillment in Christian Marriage,* Fourth Edition. New Jersey: Old Tappan, New Jersey: Fleming H. Revell, 2010.

Wheat, Ed. *Love Life For Every Married Couple*. Grand Rapids, Michigan: Zondervan, 1980.

White, Jerry. *Honesty, Morality & Conscience.* Colorado Springs, Colorado: NavPress, 1978.

White, John. *Eros Defiled*. Downers Grove, Illinois: InterVarsity Press, 1977.

White, John. *Eros Redeemed: Breaking the Stranglehold of Sexual Sin*. Downers Grove, Illinois: InterVarsity Press, 1993.

Wilkinson, Bruce. *Personal Holiness in Times of Temptation*. Eugene, Oregon: Harvest House, 1998.

Willard, Dallas. *The Spirit of the Disciplines: Understanding How God Changes Lives*. New York: Harper One, 1990.

RELATED MATERIALS BY DR. JAMES M. CECY

Available through JARON Ministries International, Inc.,

4710 N. Maple, Fresno, CA. 93726 (559) 227-7997 www.jaron.org

- *Authentic Holiness* (audio series)
- *A Biblical Examination of Homosexuality:* (audio series)
- *A Revival of Purity* (audio series)
- *Ambassadors of Purity Accountability Workbook*

Note: This is a counseling manual developed by Pastor Eugene Beck using the materials developed by Dr. James Cecy. Also called *Building Personal Purity: Christian Living in an Immoral World Accountability Manual.*

- *Ambassadors of Purity* (audio series with companion workbook)
- *Building Personal Accountability* (audio recording)

- *Combating Spiritual Dryness* (audio series)
- *Communication in Marriage* (audio series with companion workbook)
- *David: The Repentant King* (audio message)
- *Immorality in the Ministry: The Pitfalls of Pastoral Power* (audio or video series with companion workbook)
- *The A.C.T. of Repentance* (audio series)
- *Life-Management 101: An Introduction to Life Skill Transformation* (audio series)
- *Lord, I Want to Grow Up* (audio or video series)
- *Mastering My Hang-ups & Habits* (audio series)
- *Profile of a Godly Family* (audio series)
- *Profile of a Pure Vessel* (audio series)
- *Wise Living in a Foolish Age: Studies in the Book of Proverbs* (workbook)

A detailed catalog of these and other materials is available upon request or can be viewed on the JARON Ministries International web site: www.jaron.org.

SPECIAL THANKS

To my precious wife, Karon, whose name means "pure one." As your name is, so you are. Thank you for being my constant encouragement for almost four decades of marriage. I truly believe that God is honoring your godly life and blessing mine because of it.

To my own "Mother Theresa." Her commitment to pray for her "preacher-son" sustained me in ministry. Even from my first fragile weeks in an incubator, she believed that God had a plan for my life. Although heaven is a far better place, a part of me wishes she was still here.

To my older brothers, Brian and David. Thanks for believing in me and giving me that final push to leave my comfort zone and start JARON Ministries International.

To my three daughters, Kimberly, DeAnna and Jamie. May you always walk in purity and faithfulness, just like your mother.

To Angie and Lisa. Of the many foster-children and friends who lived with us over the years, you especially allowed your hearts to bond with ours.

To Kyle, Rob, Josh and Brad, who married the young women we raised. You are the sons I never had and the men I most hope to influence.

To my many grandchildren. I pass the "purity baton" to you and yours. I pray you will be used of God to start a new generation of faithfulness.

To the elders, staff, and precious congregation at Campus Bible Church of Fresno and to the JARON Ministries International team of missionaries, staff, board members, volunteers and supporters. I am so honored to have spent these years serving the Lord with you, locally and globally.

To Pastor Gene Beck, the Executive Director of JARON Ministries and Pastor Matt Cook, the Executive Pastor of Campus Bible Church. Without you men standing in the gap, there is no way I would have finished this book.

To a host of pastors, teachers, counselors, readers and reviewers who made such valuable corrections and suggestions. More than your scholarship and skill, I was blessed with all of your hearts' desire to see this book influence the generations.

To My Lord, in whose Holy Name I offer this book and my life. May You be pleased with both. You alone will determine how far-reaching this work of my hands and heart will extend. To You I give all the honor and glory.

ABOUT THE AUTHOR

James Michael Cecy was born in Toronto, Canada and moved to California when he was eleven years old. He entered the U.S. Navy in 1969 and served on the aircraft carrier, the *USS Kitty Hawk*, during the Vietnam War. On November 17, 1971, the day he was discharged from active naval duty, God stirred his heart and Jim trusted in Christ alone for his salvation. He quickly became an avid student of the Bible.

Jim was called to pastoral ministry in 1975, serving churches in California for almost forty years. He has served as the Senior Pastor-Teacher at Campus Bible Church of Fresno (formerly Campus Baptist Church) since 1995. He is known for his commitment to Scripture, his enthusiastic expositional teaching, and his passion to equip God's people locally and globally.

Pastor Jim has a Bachelor of Arts degree in Speech-Communication from San Jose State University (1975). He earned his Master of Divinity degree in Bible Exposition from Talbot Theological Seminary in 1978. In 1992, Jim received his Doctor of Ministry degree from Western Seminary (San Jose Campus). His doctoral studies on why Christian leaders fall morally became the basis for a series of seminars. That research, plus years of counseling and teaching globally on this subject, forms the basis for this book.

Dr. Cecy is the founder and president of JARON Ministries International, a training ministry that equips pastors, missionaries, law enforcement officers and Christian leaders around the world. That ministry is based in Fresno, California.

In addition to his domestic ministry in North America, Jim has traveled extensively in numerous countries in Asia, Africa and Europe. His training seminars, taught by a team of skilled shepherds and missionaries, have reached hundreds of thousands of people on five continents. In addition to his studies on moral purity, Jim has produced a number of written, audio and video materials on a wide variety of subjects, which are available through JARON Ministries (www.jaron.org) or Campus Bible Church (www.campusbiblechurch.com).

Jim and his wife Karon were married in 1973. They raised three daughters and, since 1987, have cared for twenty-three foster-children. Two, even as adults, remain a part of the family. Jim and Karon are blessed with a number of grandchildren.

NOTES

CHAPTER 1: THE LAND IS FULL OF ADULTERERS

1. We could also add:

   - Shechem the Hivite, who raped Dinah, Jacob's daughter (Genesis 34:1-2)
   - Tamar, guilty of seducing her father-in-law, Judah (Genesis 38:14-18)
   - Zimri, who mocked God by taking the Midianite woman as his harlot (Numbers 25:6-14)
   - The male prostitutes engaging in cultic sexual practices in the Temple (2 Kings 23:7)
   - The harlot, Gomer, whose immoral life was a symbol of Israel's idolatry (Hosea 1-2)
   - The parable of the prodigal son who was accused by his brother of squandering his father's wealth on prostitutes (Luke 15:30)
   - The woman caught in adultery (John 8:1-11)
   - The member in the Church of Corinth who was committing fornication with either his step-mother or mother (1 Corinthians 5:1)
   - Jezebel, a symbolic name for the immoral false prophetess of the Church of Thyatira (Revelation 2:20-21)

2. It certainly can be argued that Jeremiah was speaking primarily of the spiritual adultery of Israel chasing after other gods. However, as we will see throughout this book, there is a direct correlation between spiritual adultery (*idolatry*) and sexual immorality (*adultery*). Consider the words of the apostle Paul: "Therefore consider the members of your earthly body as dead to immorality, impurity, passion, evil desire, and greed, which amounts to *idolatry*" (Colossians 3:5, emphasis added) as well as the words of James: "You *adulteresses*, do you not know that friendship with the world is hostility toward God? Therefore whoever wishes to be a friend of the world makes himself an enemy of God (James 4:4, emphasis added). It should also be noted that much of the idolatrous practices involved sexual immorality, thus the mandate of the Jerusalem Council for all true followers of Christ to abstain from idolatry and fornication (Acts 15:29).

3. William Barclay, *The Letters to the Philippians, Colossians, and Thessalonians. Revised Edition*. Philadelphia: Westminster, 1975, 199.

4. "Sexes: Attacking the Last Taboo." *Time Magazine*. (14 April 1980). The article can be found on-line at *http://www.time.com/time/magazine/article/0,9171,92366,00.html*.

5. "Sexes: Attacking the Last Taboo."

6. "Sexes: Attacking the Last Taboo."

7. Adapted from a seminar, *Sense and Sexuality: The Search for Sexual Sanity in a Confusing Culture*, taught at the European Leadership Forum in Eger, Hungary in May 2010 by Dr. Richard Winters, Professor of Practical Theology and Director of Covenant Seminary's counseling program. This information was also verified by a December 30, 2010 phone conversation with Dr. Winter.

8. Dr. Richard Winters, *Sense and Sexuality*. Seminar notes.

9. Letter to the author. Used by permission.

10. Randy Alcorn, *Sexual Temptation: How Christian Workers Can Win the Battle*. 2nd Edition, 2007, Gresham, Oregon: Eternal Perspective Ministries, *(1ˢᵗ Edition by InterVarsity Press, 1989)*, 5.

11. For further study I refer you to my audio and written materials entitled, "Immorality in the Ministry: The Pitfalls of Pastoral Power" available through JARON Ministries International, Inc. www.jaron.org.

CHAPTER 2: KILLING SPIDERS. PREVENTING FIRES.

1. Bruce Wilkinson, *Personal Holiness in Times of Temptation*. Eugene, Oregon: Harvest House, 1998, 137.

CHAPTER 3: COMMANDS, NOT SUGGESTIONS

1. I am indebted to Dr. Gary Tuck, Professor of Biblical Literature and Academic Coordinator at Western Seminary, San Jose, California, for his helpful insight on this passage. In a personal email, dated January 4, 2011, he confirmed an earlier discussion:

> All these infinitives are the expressions of 'the will of God' (v. 3) . . .
> they are functional imperatives because the will of God is by definition
> imperative. In terms of translation, these infinitives might be rendered

with English subjunctives: 'that you should abstain . . .' In both Greek and Hebrew, as in English, the indicative future can function as imperative ('You shall love the Lord your God . . .').

2. James M. Cecy, "Answers to Your Questions about Sexual Immorality." *CONTACT Quarterly*, Summer, 1994, Vol. 53 No. 2, 7-9.

3. Wilkinson, *Personal Holiness,* 131.

4. The New International Version translates this phrase as, "each of you should learn to control his own body." (See the New Revised Standard Version, the New Century Version, the English Standard Version and the New English Translation for similar uses.) However, this is not exclusively the case. The Revised Standard and the New American Bible versions favors the view that the word *vessel* refers to a wife. Consider also Kenneth Wuest's Expanded Translation: "that each one of you should know that he is to procure his own vessel [wife] in [personal] holiness and honor, not in the passion of an inordinate desire even as also the Gentiles do who do not know God." Kenneth S. Wuest, *The New Testament: An Expanded Translation*, 1 Th 4:1, Grand Rapids, MI: Eerdmans, 1997, c1961. I also found many foreign translations favoring the view that *skeuos* (i.e. vessel) refers to one's wife (e.g. Bible translations in Norwegian, Hungarian, etc.). This position is also held by other trusted commentators (e.g. Robert Jamieson, A. R. Fausset, A. R. Fausset et al., *A Commentary, Critical and Explanatory, on the Old and New Testaments*, 1 Th 4:4, Oak Harbor, WA: Logos Research Systems, Inc., 1997).

5. The word *ktaomai* is most often used to speak of *possessing, acquiring or procuring* things for oneself, such as gold (Matthew 10:9), a field (Acts 1:18), or citizenship (Acts 22:28). Although I respect the views of others, I can find no clear use in the New Testament where the word is best translated as *controlling* rather than the more common idea of *possessing*.

6. Although there are others with more extensive discussions, I appreciate Dr. Paul Cox's brief assessment, "The strongest argument for translating 'vessel' as 'wife' is that in the Septuagint (the Greek translation of the Old Testament dated 200 BC), whenever the noun 'vessel' is combined with the verb 'acquire' it means 'to marry.'" Dr. Paul M. Cox, *Clear Thinking on Sexuality Outside & Inside Marriage*. San Bernardino, California: Perspective Ministries & Paul Cox, 1991, 9.

CHAPTER 5: SEX REALLY IS GOD'S IDEA

1. Mary Ann Mayo, *A Christian Guide To Sexual Counseling: Recovering the Mystery And Reality of "One Flesh."* Grand Rapids, Michigan: Bondservant, 1987, 15.

2. Some of my fellow Bible teachers have tried to correct me, suggesting that the better illustration would be 1x1x1=1. However, the mathematicians to whom I have spoken would disagree. In their thinking, multiplication implies replication, thus the three in one would become the one times three. However, the Father, Son, and Holy Spirit are not replicas of one another, nor do we marry ourselves, nor are we cloned members of Christ's church. Mathematically speaking, 1x1x1=1 or 1x1=1 (as in the case of marriage) provides no mystery whatsoever (Ephesians 5:32). What it does provide is an unnecessary and needless redundancy. On the other hand, 1+1+1=1 brings mystery, awe, and quandary. Thus the illustration using addition rather than multiplication serves its intended purpose—distinct persons are mysteriously one in the Godhead, marriage, and the church.

3. Dr. Richard Winters, *Sense and Sexuality*. Seminar notes.

4. Lewis B. Smedes, *Sex For Christians: The Limits And Liberties of Sexual Living*. Grand Rapids, Michigan: Eerdmans, 1976, 32.

5. In his 1991 biography, *A View From Above*, basketball star, Wilt Chamberlain, claimed to have had sexual relations with approximately 20,000 women. That is equal to about 1.2 women a day since he was fifteen.

CHAPTER 7: COVENANTAL ONENESS

1. I refer you to the extensive study of this passage in Malachi presented by Dr. Gordon P. Hugenberger, in his book, *Marriage as a Covenant: A Study of Biblical Law and Ethics Governing Marriage, Developed from the Perspective of Malachi*. Grand Rapids, Michigan: Baker, *1998*. Dr. Hugenberger is a professor of Old Testament at Gordon-Conwell Theological Seminary. If you have the mind to really dig into the subject, this is the way to go.

2. Tim Alan Gardner, *Sacred Sex: A Spiritual Celebration of Oneness in Marriage*. Colorado Springs, Colorado: Waterbrook, 2002, 195.

3. Though Dr. Hugenberger takes a more literal view of an actual covering, he does refer to W.H Brownlee's translation as, "I *opened* my robe to her" (Hugenberger, 304). I

have also benefited from my past and present conversations with my ministry colleague, Dr. David Eckman. Dr. Eckman has authored the commentary, *Discovering Micah through Malachi,* and was a contributor to the New King James Study Bible. His six years of Ph.D. studies at Oxford University were in Ugaritic, the Semitic language often used by scholars to clarify obscure Hebrew terms and cultural practices. He holds to the more symbolic view, as do I, that the phrase, "I spread My skirt over you, and covered your nakedness" is a Semitic language euphemism for sexual intercourse. In her proposal to Boaz, Ruth uses a similar expression: "So spread your covering ("wing, skirt," Hebrew: *kanaph*) over your maid" (Ruth 3:9). Whereas, Ezekiel 16:8 speaks of the *past* consummation of the relationship between God and Israel (i.e. "you *became* Mine"), Ruth 3:9 pictures a *future* consummation which would seal the marriage covenant between her and her kinsman-redeemer. Dr. Gary Tuck, Professor of Biblical Literature and Academic Coordinator at Western Seminary, San Jose, California, also noted that Ezekiel 16 refers to God "covering nakedness," while Leviticus refers to sinful sexual relations as "uncovering nakedness"—the one must be honorable, the other sinful (e.g. Leviticus 18:7-17).

4.   In Deuteronomy 22:13-17 we find reference to the *evidence* for virginity. This is understood to be the bloody sheet resulting from the female hymen being "pierced" or "cut" in the first experience of intercourse. Of course, we acknowledge that the hymen can be broken in other ways and I would be quick to caution against false accusations. However, the point must still be made that the ratification of the marriage covenant, like the Abrahamic, Mosaic and new covenant, has both piercing and blood involved.

5.   Gardner, *Sacred Sex,* 196.

6.   Gardner, *Sacred Sex*, 196.

CHAPTER 8: RESTORATIVE ONENESS

1.   I suggest a study of the lovingkindness (Hebrew: *khesed*) of God. His steadfast love and His enduring loyalty to His covenants serves as an example to all who have entered into a marriage covenant.

2.   For those couples who need assistance working through the aftermath of an affair, I highly recommend Dave Carder's book, *Torn Asunder: Recovering from Extramarital Affairs*. Chicago, Illinois: Moody Press, 1992.

CHAPTER 9: SACRED ONENESS

1. Dr. Richard Winters, *Sense and Sexuality*. Seminar notes. Also verified by a December 30, 2010 phone conversation.
2. Smedes, Sex for Christians, 21.

CHAPTER 10: PROCREATIONAL ONENESS

1. Smedes, Sex for Christians, 5.
2. Dr. Richard Winters, *Sense and Sexuality*. Seminar notes. Also verified by a December 30, 2010 phone conversation.

CHAPTER 11: PHYSICAL AND EMOTIONAL ONENESS

1. The Greek word *agape* is rooted in the verb *agapao*, which in its classical sense speaks of valuing, placing worth on something or someone, based on the price paid. We have been loved by God (John 3:16), bought with a price (1 Corinthians 6:20; 7:23), and purchased with the precious blood of Jesus Christ (1 Peter 1:18). Therefore, we love (place worth on others) because He first did the same for us (1 John 4:19).
2. Smedes, *Sex for Christians,* 33.

CHAPTER 12: SPIRITUAL ONENESS

1. I refer you to the *Worksheet for Resolving a Conflict* in the Personal Accountability Program in the Study Guide.

CHAPTER 13: RECREATIONAL ONENESS

1. The word translated "ashamed" in Genesis 2:25 is the Hebrew word *buwsh* which speaks of being restrained or delaying because of shame. In other words, Adam and Eve felt complete freedom to immediately enjoy each other's nakedness.

CHAPTER 14: RULES FOR THE MARRIAGE BED

1. I encourage couples to read well-researched materials written by those who have a high view of God's design for sexual oneness within marriage. See the *Suggested Reading on Moral Purity and Biblical Sexuality* in the Appendix. For example, I recommend Ed and Gaye Wheat's book, *Intended for Pleasure: Sex Technique and Sexual Fulfillment in*

Christian Marriage, Fourth Edition. Old Tappan, New Jersey: Fleming H. Revell, 2010.

2.   Smedes, *Sex for Christians*, 31.

CHAPTER 15: SEX AND THE SINGLE PERSON

1.   Smedes, *Sex for Christians,* 34.

2.   Terry Muck, Editor, *Sins Of The Body: Ministry In A Sexual Society*. Carol Stream, Illinois: Word, 1989, 22.

3.   The word *content* (Greek: *autarkes)* gives the idea of being strong enough to stand alone.

4.   John MacArthur Jr., *Different By Design: Discovering God's Will for Today's Man and Woman*. Wheaton, Illinois: Victor, 1994, 106.

5.   I refer you to Josh Harris' book, *I Kissed Dating Goodbye: A New Attitude Towards Relationships and Romance*. Portland, Oregon: Multnomah, 1997.

6.   Randy Alcorn, *The Purity Principle: God's Safeguards for Life's Dangerous Trails*. Sisters, Oregon: Multnomah, 2003, 71.

CHAPTER 17: LUSTFUL THOUGHTS AND IMMORAL BEHAVIORS

1.   Alcorn, *The Purity Principle*, 48.

CHAPTER 18: FILLING THE BUCKET ONE GRAIN AT A TIME

1.   *The Didache: The Lord's Teaching Through the Twelve Apostles to the Nations.* Translation by Roberts-Donaldsen. *Chapter 3. Other Sins Forbidden. http://www. earlychristianwritings.com/text/didache-roberts.html.*

2.   Muck, *Sins of the Body,* 24.

3.   Ben Shapiro, *Porn Generation: How Social Liberalism is Corrupting Our Future.* Houston, Texas: Regency, 2005, 160.

CHAPTER 19: WALK INTO MY PARLOR

1.   Rather than choose from a number of modern versions, I chose to present the poem as it was first published in 1829 by Mary Howitt (1799-1888).

CHAPTER 20: *STEP #1* FALTERING IN THE SEARCH FOR BIBLICAL WISDOM

1. Alcorn, *The Purity Principle,* 56.

2. Alan Redpath, *The Making of the Man of God: Studies in the Life of David.* Grand Rapids, Michigan: Fleming Revell, 1962, 5.

3. I refer you to the Personal Accountability Program, found in the Study Guide. Accountability Worksheets #2, #3, and #4 will assist you in *Taking Your Spiritual Pulse,* an honest inventory of your life, in light of such passages as Colossians 3:1-7, Romans 12:1-21 and Galatians 5:19-22. I recommend you also complete Accountability Worksheet #17: *My Spiritual Health Indicators.*

4. I refer you to my audio series, *Combating Spiritual Dryness,* available from JARON Ministries International. I also encourage you to read works on the spiritual disciplines, such as Dallas Willard's, *The Spirit of the Disciplines: Understanding How God Changes Lives.* New York: Harper One: 1990 and Richard J. Foster's, *Celebration of Discipline: The Path to Spiritual Growth.* New York: Harper Collins, 2002.

CHAPTER 21: *STEP #2* FAILING IN THE DEVELOPMENT OF THE MARRIAGE RELATIONSHIP

1. Consult your pastor or biblical counselor regarding recommendations for effective books and materials on marriage. You may also find it beneficial to listen to my series on *Communication in Marriage* or other materials related to marriage and family available through JARON Ministries International, Inc. www.jaron.org.

CHAPTER 23: *STEP #4* FLIRTING WITH THE FORBIDDEN WORLD OF SEDUCTION

1. See my workbook, *Wise Living in a Foolish Age: Studies in the Book of Proverbs* available through JARON Ministries International, Inc. www.jaron.org.

CHAPTER 28: PROTECTING MY MIND

1. Alcorn, *Purity Principle,* 61-62.

2. Gregg Lewis, *Telegarbage: What You Can Do About Sex and Violence on TV.* Nashville/New York: Thomas Nelson, 1977.

CHAPTER 29: PROVISIONING MY MIND

1. John Churton Collins, as quoted by Bruce Wilkinson in *Personal Holiness,* 141.
2. In the Personal Accountability Program in the Study Guide you will find an account-ability worksheet entitled, *Taking My Mental Pulse*, listing a number of passages relat-ed to moral purity. You can also choose from the many other verses used throughout this book, found in the *Scripture Index*.

CHAPTER 30: PURIFYING MY MIND

1. Richard Winters, *Sense and Sexuality*. Seminar notes.

CHAPTER 31: PREPARING MY MIND

1. In the Personal Accountability Program in the Study Guide is a worksheet entitled, *Rehearsing the Consequences of My Moral Failure*. It could rightly be called, *Building Your Own Album of Horror*. The assignment invites you to write out what you think would be the specific responses of your loved ones and others, if you were to fall into sexual sin. It also asks you to consider what you might expect to happen physically, emotionally, spiritually, socially, economically and sexually.

CHAPTER 34: PROMISING MY BODY

1. Missionary and pastoral counselor, Dr. Ken Royer, rightly comments that the specif-ics of these personal covenants differ in various cultures. For example, in many places in the world the men have no problem with females displaying their breasts. In places like the Tzeltal Indian cultures of Southern Mexico, the armpits and the back of thigh are considered to be the sexiest parts of a woman's body. In those cul-tures one would expect to hear, "I made a covenant with my eyes not to look at her armpits."
2. In the Personal Accountability Program in the Study Guide is a specific worksheet entitled, *Making a Covenant with the Parts of My Body*. I encourage you to make your own specific covenants.

CHAPTER 35: PROTECTING MY BODY

1. I refer you to Part Two: *Appreciating God's Design* and especially the chapter, *Sex and the Single Person*.

CHAPTER 37: PRAYING FOR MY COMPANIONS

1. Redpath, *The Making of the Man of God*, 197.

CHAPTER 38: PROTECTING FOR MY COMPANIONS

1. Adapted and used by permission from notes and conversation with Ron McLain, Executive Director of Healthy Marriage Coalition, P.O. Box 25221, Fresno, CA 93729. fresnomarriage@gmail.com.
2. Alcorn, *The Purity Principle, 80.*
3. In the Study Guide you will find an extensive Personal Accountability Program with eighteen worksheets designed for personal reflection or discussion with accountability partners or a small group.

CHAPTER 39: CONFRONTING MY COMPANIONS

1. I encourage a study of Revelation 2:20 where Jesus confronts the Church of Thyatira for tolerating (i.e. "neglecting, leaving alone," Greek: *aphiemi*) the immorality of Jezebel.
2. Notes taken from a lecture by Mike Harris at the 2003 Pan-Africa Christian Police Association Conference (PACPAC) held in Weesgerus, Limpopo Province, South Africa, October 13-16, 2003.

CHAPTER 40: A WORD TO THE WOUNDED AND FALLEN

1. Ron Lee Davis, *Courage to Begin Again*, Harvest House, Eugene, Oregon; 1978, 145-147.

CHAPTER 41: THE A.C.T.S. OF REPENTANCE

1. Illustration originally from Today in the Word, December 4, 1992 and taken from *eSermons.com. http://www.sermonillustrations.com/a-z/c/confession.html.*
2. Patrick Morley, as quoted by Charles R. Swindoll, *John The Baptizer,* Bible Study Guide. Insight for Living, 1984, 16.
3. Bruce Wilkinson, *Personal Holiness,* 57.

CHAPTER 42: DAVID'S STORY TOPS THEM ALL

1. J. Allan Petersen, *The Myth of the Greener Grass.* Wheaton, Illinois: Tyndale House,

1983, 32.

CHAPTER 43: FROM "WHAT?" TO "SO WHAT?" TO "NOW WHAT?"

1. Bruce Wilkinson, *Personal Holiness,* 245.

2. Randy Alcorn, *Sexual Temptation,* 5-6.

3. Leonard Ravenhill, as quoted by Bruce Wilkinson in *Personal Holiness in Times of Temptation, 217.*

4. This Larry King Live interview with Hugh Hefner was aired on November 29, 2005. The actual transcript can be viewed at *http://transcripts.cnn.com/TRAN-SCRIPTS/0511/29/lkl.01.html.*

APPENDICES: "MASTURBATION: CHIEF OF SINS OR ULTIMATE GIFT OF GOD?"

1. I appreciate the overview of the issue presented in a web article by Lambert Dolphin, *Masturbation and the Bible,* found at *http://ldolphin.org/Mast.shtml.*

2. Actually, Onan did not masturbate. He engaged in what we refer to as *coitus interruptus*—i.e. withdrawal. He was being asked to father a child for his dead brother but he interrupted the process.

3. Helmut Thielicke, *The Ethics of Sex.* Trans. John W. Doberstein, New York, Evanston and London: Harper & Row, 1964, 256.

4. Smedes, *Sex for Christians,* 244.

5. Stephen Arterburn and Fred Stoeker, *Every Young Man's Battle: Strategies for Victory in the Real World of Sexual Temptation.* Colorado Springs, Colorado: Waterbrook, 2002, 112. Although a bit disturbing, you might want to read the frank discussion with women about masturbation in Shannon Ethridge's book, *Every Woman's Battle: Discovering God's Plan for Sexual and Emotional Fulfillment.* Colorado Springs, Colorado: Waterbrook, 2003, 39-45.

SCRIPTURE INDEX

SUBJECT INDEX

FOREIGN WORD INDEX

diabolos	39, 40	*rea'*	89, 90
Didache	108, 339n1	*scutum*	197
echad	37, 38, 39, 40, 41, 51, 56, 98, 101, 261	*shagah*	76
		shakach	51
eclipso	234	*shalom*	145, 199
eidololatreia	39	*Shema*	37
Elohenu	37	*Sheol*	137, 140, 149
epistrepho	232, 233, 234	*skeuos*	21, 22, 335n4
epithumeo	100	*Soli Deo Gloria*	256
epithumia	110	*stereos*	40
eutrapelia	110	*sterizo*	233, 234
gadad	147	*suschematizo*	176
Gloria	256	*suzeugnumi*	40, 45
hagah	176	*testudo*	197, 210
hagiosmos	17	*timios*	79
hamartia	98	*towtsa'ah*	164
heis	39	*tsaphan*	172
homo	231	*yada*	55, 56
homologeo	231, 233	*Yishrael*	37
kakos epithumia	110	*zakah*	171
kanaph	337n3	*zanah*	110
karath bariyth	47	*zimmah*	110, 194
khesed	337n1		
koinonia	69		
koinos	17		
ktaomai	21, 22, 335n5		
leb	164, 172		
logeo	231		
logizomai	129, 176		
malakos	110		
metamorphoo	176		
metanoeo	227, 228, 233		
metanoia	227, 228		
mishmar	164		
moicheia	110		
na'aph	110		
naqah	229		
pathos	110		
porne	110		
porneia	4, 51, 110		
pronoia	129		
Qoheleth	321		
ra'a	89		

NOTES

NOTES

NOTES

NOTES

NOTES

NOTES

For information regarding other
materials by Dr. Jim Cecy or
hosting a purity seminar
please contact:

JARON MINISTRIES
INTERNATIONAL, INC.

4710 N. Maple, Fresno, CA 93726
(559)227-7997 www.jaron.org